# Teaching English in a Foreign Land

By Barry O'Leary

Text copyright © Barry O'Leary 2012

All Rights Reserved

ISBN 978-1-291-03745-6

The right of Barry O'Leary to be identified as the author of this work has been asserted by him in accordance with the Copyright, Designs, and Patent Act 1988

Acknowledgements

My thanks need to go out to two sets of people: those involved in my TEFL adventure, and those who've helped me write *Teaching English in a Foreign Land*. I'll start with those involved in my adventure.

Firstly I'd like to thank Nish, otherwise known as the Baahaa Tuna Boy. I was fortunate enough to bump into Nish in a hostel in Rio. We lived together in Salvador, Bahia and met up in Sydney and Bangkok. Nish is a first class traveller, mate, and all round lovely bloke. I'd like to thank him for his company and advice throughout my trip, dragging me away from trouble in the Carnival, holding my hand when England lost to Portugal on penalties, and motivating me to finish this book. You go to Baahaa?

Next is King Murphy, a fellow English teacher, who befriended me in Salvador. Without Murphy's help I would never have come across the mad house that I lived in for four months, and become a tougher nut.

Another special mate is Anderson. He was a student, but mainly a friend, of mine in Bahia and is an example of how well you can learn English if you really put your mind to it. I'd like to thank him for being a good friend and teaching me essential Portuguese swear words; Beleza (not a swear word).

I'm not sure if he'll get a chance to read this because I fell out of touch with him, but I'd like to thank The Lord, a fellow teacher in Ecuador. He is also an inspiration to the world of teaching. He showed me the ropes while I worked at Harvard Institute and made working there an absolute blast. Thanks also to the Ecuadorian family who took me in for three months and treated me like a son.

Mae and Will were great bosses while working in Sydney. Thanks also to Fiona, Rob and the crew there for the crack. While travelling up the East Coast of Australia Helen, Em, and Pete made my trip special, anyone up for a game of Mallet's Mallet? Cheese.

Of all the places I lived, Bangkok will always be the most memorable. Not just because it was fun working with Miss Liz, Mr Kevin, and Mr Geoff, but also the Thai teachers, mainly Mr Sirichild and Miss Nittaya. I will always have a place in my heart for the class that I taught for seven months too. Thanks also to the crazy bunch I hung around with while in Bangkok, mainly Den, Natalia, Andy, Neil, also Chris from back home while at Patpongs. I'd like to thank Sister Leonora, my boss while in Bangkok. She was a hard woman to work for, but, as you'll see when you read my story, she became an inspiration.

Travelling overland from Bangkok wouldn't have been the same without meeting Richy Rich, Joe and Emma. Sami, the legend G-String hunter, deserves a special mention. Sami is a top lad and made my ten days in China a great laugh, without him I probably would have pulled. My last travel mention goes to Steve, the Duck. I met Steve on the Trans-Mongolian and as we were the only lager louts we stuck together for six days and hunted down the Babushkas, we did it though. See you in the Duck mate. Oh, I almost forgot, a huge thank you to the Monk on the front cover. I doubt he'll ever read this book, but if he does then thanks for the chat we had.

Now the people who helped me write this book. First I'd like to thank my parents. Not only for letting me write about their adventure in Bangkok, but also for their motivational words and support over the last seven years I've spent writing this book. My sisters, Kelly and Sarah have been equally as inspiring. Kelly helped me by reading a few chapters of my first draft, and Sarah for being a good crack in Koh Chang and helping me with the front cover. Love to all you guys.

Thanks to the rest of my family, grandparents and mates back home who have all been great. My Aunties deserve a special thank you. Col and Carrie have been supportive and encouraging and Marg kick started me into writing. It was while chatting with her on the phone when I was in Thailand that I first thought about writing. She's been great reading a few drafts and the perfect motivator.

A huge thanks goes out to my editor and agent. She's been amazing over the last few years reading my book over and over again, helping me with corrections, guidance, and ideas. She even came up with the book name. It's been a long time coming, but we did it. Thanks Auntie Den.

I'd also like to thank Marium for her advice over the years, Katie at i-to-i for her enthusiasm with my articles and blog, and Richard, director of ELI, Seville, for his editing skills.

My Spanish family deserves a mention too. They constantly ask me to write for them in Spanish; maybe that can be my next project. Gracias a Manuel, Aurelia, Nando, Miguel y todos por su apoyo durante estos años, os quiero.

My last thanks goes to a very special person indeed. Before I met her I wasn't a writer, but telling her about my travels and experiences made me realize I had a story to tell. It was while showing her pictures of my journey that we fell in love. It's thanks to her patience, encouragement, and support that I've been able to devote so many hours producing this book. If it wasn't for her, I may have given up three years ago after the first draft, but her confidence in me has been an inspiration. Maybe now she'll actuaelly read it. Thanks wifey.

## Contents

| | |
|---|---|
| 1 Ecuador: The Fear of Returning | 1 |
| 2 The Secrets of Teaching | 9 |
| 3 The Buzz of Teaching Overrules | 14 |
| 4 The Highs and Lows of Being a Teacher | 18 |
| 5 *Feliz Navidad, Año Nuevo, y Adiós* | 27 |
| 6 Peru: Tension on the way to Machu Picchu | 35 |
| 7 Bolivia: A Mere One Night Stand | 47 |
| 8 Brazil: Rio de Janeiro – From High to Low | 58 |
| 9 Salvador: The Hectic Build Up to Carnival | 66 |
| 10 The Carnival in Bahia | 76 |
| 11 Settling In | 84 |
| 12 Falling in Love with Teaching and Salvador | 91 |
| 13 USA: Greyhound Weirdoes | 100 |
| 14 Australia: Get Me Out of Here | 114 |
| 15 Thailand: Meet the Sister | 131 |
| 16 Christmas Plans with Uncle Gary | 141 |
| 17 Teaching English was Superior than the Sister | 143 |
| 18 Trying to Learn Thai | 150 |
| 19 The Harsh Truth and the End of Miss Lucy | 160 |
| 20 How the Sister Saved my Life | 165 |

21 A Full Moon Party Lights the Way 171

22 Bye Bye Bangkok 177

23 Laos: Drifting and Dodgy Shakes 190

24 Cambodia: Angkor Wat and a Nasty Surprise 204

25 Vietnam: From South to North 215

26 China: Adventures with a G-String Obsessed Swede 227

27 Trans-Mongolian: Don't Be Afraid of the Big Bad Babushkas 251

28 Russia: The Last Stint 268

# 1 Ecuador: The Fear of Returning

His dark hand frisked over my groin, centimetres from my money belt and everything I had. His other pressed hard on my upper chest; pinning me against a wall.

"*No tengo nada, no tengo nada*," I said, lying that I had nothing. I had to; I'd been foolish. On my first night in Quito, while looking for a bar in *La Mariscal* area, I was lost. I had my money, cash cards, and passport hidden in my money belt under my trousers.

My heart raced, not because he could injure me; I could cope with a beating. I feared something worse.

He towered over and ranted in Spanish. His breath stunk of alcohol.

"*Momento, momento,*" I said, raising my arms in defence and gazing into his white hungry eyes. He eased off. I fumbled in my pockets and pulled out a dollar coin.

"*Lo siento,*" I said, apologizing. He grunted, huffed, and pushed me back against the wall. I thought back to my life in England. I'd rather take a few punches than return.

"*Por favor, no tengo nada,*" I said, my voice getting desperate. The man let go and glanced around. We were on a side road off the main avenue. Bar lights flickered in the distance but no one else was about. He was safe. He raised an arm to strike. I hunched away.

"*Momento, momento,*" I said, trying to stall him. His face tensed and body trembled. What if he had a knife or a gun? Voices in my head told me not to be stubborn. Even if I got through a battering, he'd find my money belt. I moved my hand towards it, about to surrender, when his hand came down. He patted me on the shoulder, shrugged as if apologizing, and paced round the corner.

I froze. I'd survived. I darted to the nearest pub, sat by the bar, and ordered a beer. My hand shook as I took a swig. An unknown tension filled my heart and stayed with me for my entire journey around the world.

The next morning the incident really hit me. I was already low after getting rejected from tons of language academies while in Mexico. I'd done a TEFL (Teaching English as a Foreign Language) course in London and left for South America without any job prospects. I'd never been away on my own and was still only twenty-three. I'd spent August and September trying to find my first teaching job, but without experience or being able to commit for at least a year, no one wanted to know. My savings were running out so I'd come down to Ecuador, desperate to find a job.

The attempted mugging threw me. I'd not had any problems with locals in Mexico and had presumed Quito safe. *La Mariscal* area seemed fine during the day; hostels, bars, and internet cafes dotted the tourist area, and travellers, mostly wearing hiking gear, roamed about carefree.

However, when the chilly night came, the streets became deserted. After the mugging I stayed safe in the hostel bar, where I met Yan, a giant Danish man travelling across South America on his red motorbike. It was while talking to him when I realised living in Quito was going to be complicated.

"It's more dangerous than people think," Yan said in his hoarse voice. He sounded as if he'd been inhaling motorbike fumes all day. "Last night I had to defend myself with this." He whipped out a butterfly knife and the blade glistened as he waved it in front of his face. The weapon looked tiny in his ogre hand.

"What, did you stab someone?"

"No, it wasn't necessary, in the end." He snapped the knife closed and rested it on the bar. "He was only a kid, about fifteen. He tried to steal my wallet but I grabbed his hand like this." He pulled my hand and twisted me round on the bar.

"Okay, Okay, I get the picture."

"Then I pulled out my knife," he whispered. "And he ran."

"I'm sure. Can you let go now?" He was pushing my arm further up my back.

"Oh, sorry," he said, releasing me.

We sat on the bar stools and sipped beer in silence. Yan seemed tense. He was just as tall as my mugger had been, but his hair, tied up in a ponytail with a green rubber band, was long and greasy.

"Have you had many problems in Quito then?" I asked.

"I have lived here for one month, three times they try to mug me, once with a knife, but I am lucky."

"Lucky?"

"Yes, sometimes they can be angry; if you don't have money, they beat you and leave you lying in the street. There is much poverty here and the police are arseholes! They give no shit. You was lucky last night my friend, maybe best that you leave Quito if you can't handle the danger." He ordered two more beers and some salty crisps.

"I considered leaving. Last night scared the shit out of me, but I'm determined to stay and accomplish what I've come to do."

"What's that?"

"Find a job teaching English."

Yan was fortunate because a Dutch motorbike magazine was sponsoring him to travel round South America while taking photos and writing about his journey. He'd already been through Africa. He showed a photo of him next to his red bike on a wooden raft crossing a muddy river. Young smiling black kids surrounded him and waved.

"That was in Congo," he said. 'It was always my dream to travel and work abroad, if you are keen on being a teacher, then stay and just be careful."

Yan's wise words were inspiring. I brushed away the mugging memories and went job hunting. I loved walking about Quito during the day. The capital was alive with a mixed race of people rushing about. Most of the language academies were hidden among the high buildings in the modern part of the city, but I preferred strolling about the *Centro Historico*. I liked wandering about the uneven cobbled streets and stopping to sit on the wooden benches in *Plaza de Independencia*. As I darted about the thin roads I'd catch glimpses of the tall white virgin monument at the top of a hill in the distance (*El Panecillo*, or, small loaf of bread). I felt safe in the old part of town during the day because there weren't many louts and the locals were always smiling. However, when night fell, I felt uneasy and stayed in my hostel.

Within a week, I'd scoured the city and left my CV at most of the language academies. I was beginning to wonder if I'd ever find a job teaching, when I walked into Princeton Institute.

José, the senior teacher, greeted me as we stood in a bright yellow reception on the fifth floor.

"Well, *amigo*, that is perfect timing. I need a teacher to start on Monday." He spoke in an American accent but seemed Mexican with his dirty Sanchez moustache.

"You do?" I was surprised after so many rejections.

"Yes, the kids are a little naughty, but you will be fine." He patted me on the back. "How long are you staying for?" The dreaded question; whenever I told anyone the truth, that I planned to leave in three months to travel along to Brazil, they normally shut the door in my face.

"As long as I can, I want to stay a while and learn Spanish." He kept a poker face.

"Do you have any experience?" Another fatal question; I considered twisting the truth but he was giving off good vibes.

"I have a qualification from London to teach but no real experience yet."

"That's no problem, you can speak English, can't you?" he said, laughing. When he asked if I could start on the Monday, I snapped up the opportunity, even though wages were only $3 an hour.

"Okay, I have a class: three hours with three, energetic, young students. I'm sure you'll be fine."

I left ecstatic, but unaware of what I'd let myself in for.

Before I started, I wanted to find a place to live to get out of *La Mariscal* area. In an internet cafe I found an advertisement for a flat down Amazonas Avenue in the centre living with an Ecuadorian family. I arranged to meet with the landlady and her daughter.

"*Hola, bienvenido,* - welcome," said a frail, but chirpy, old woman. She opened the flat door further and a strong smell of meat stew wafted out. She seemed delighted to meet me.

"*Maria, Maria,*" she said, smiling, but holding her throat as if in pain. I followed as she clonked up some wooden steps into the open flat. We sat by the dining table in the joint kitchen and lounge.

Maria's red silk scarf was wrapped round her neck like a brace. She grimaced when she spoke. She wet her lips by sipping warm lemon tea, but her weak voice made her difficult to understand.

After a couple of minutes of trying to communicate, a petite, attractive, tanned lady in her early twenties appeared.

"Hello, you are Parry?" she said, holding out her hand after wiping it on her top.

"It's Barry, actually."

"I'm Maria, and this is my mother, Maria." She patted her mother (who I'll call Mamaria) on the arm. "We are nice to meet you. Would you like see the room?"

They led me towards the front corner of the flat next to the kitchen. The room was almost perfect; a double bed, ceiling high wooden wardrobes, an en-suite bathroom, and an amazing view of mountains in the distance. The only problem was the pink duvet, but I could live with that.

"Do you like?" asked Maria.

"Yeah, the view of the mountains is amazing."

"Yes, the mountains are beautiful," she said, moving closer to the window. "Behind is *Pichincha*, a volcano."

"Oh really, where is it?"

"You no can see here, one day I show you."

"As long as it doesn't erupt."

"Erupt?"

"Explode," I said, making the appropriate hand movements and noises.

"I hope that not, the last time was bad," she said, frowning. "Four years ago it open and the city bad, lots of *ceniza,*" she said, unsure of the word in English.

"What is *ceniza*?" I hoped not hot molten lava. I checked my dictionary. "Ash, that's not so bad."

"It was bad. Very hot, and took many time to clean city." Mamaria shuffled her feet and spoke in Spanish.

"How long do you stay?" Maria asked.

"Depends on the volcano," I said. They both raised their eyebrows. "I mean, at least three months."

"Oh, that is good. You be here for Christmas and the New Year. We make you very welcome," said Maria. Mamaria hugged me and we agreed I could move in the next day.

I was keen on learning about new customs and cultures and getting a deeper insight into local people's ways, but during my first weekend I doubted my decision to live with a family.

"My mother want to know what time eat every day and when you come home to sleep," asked Maria, popping her head in my door as I unpacked.

"I'm not sure, I'll eat when I'm hungry, but I won't be out late; I had a problem a couple of nights ago."

"Tell me, tell me," she said, sitting on my bed.

"Well, the other night a man..."

"Wait," she said, leaping out of the room. She returned with Mamaria and they sat on my bed, gazing. "Okay, continue with story."

By the end of the story, Mamaria was sobbing.

"My mother say she sorry for people of Quito. Must be careful outside, never on own."

"It probably won't happen again."

"Hopefully not, but never can be sure." Little did I know that it *would* happen again; and more than once on my travels.

During my first weekend, Mamaria kept lurking about outside my room sipping cups of lemon tea. When I went food shopping she waved goodbye and when I came back she was waiting at the top of the stairs. She trailed behind trying to speak to me as I put the things away, but understanding her voice and accent was impossible.

Maria was equally as nosey. On Sunday afternoon, as I was cooking some tuna pasta, she interrogated me.

"So tell me about your family, you must have girlfriend, and why you are in Quito?"

"Well, I have two sisters, they are both in London with my parents, and my girlfriend is there too."

"But why she no come with you?"

"She has a good job."

"That is sad; maybe she can come and see you here? You no are sad to leave your family and country?"

"Yeah I miss them, but I want to travel and teach." I'd spent ages dreaming about leaving, getting out of my stressful sales career and finding a worthwhile job that didn't involve money. The thought of returning pierced my heart.

That evening, while I was preparing my classes in the dining room, the front door creaked open and someone clonked up the stairs. I was surprised because Mamaria and Maria were in their rooms. I waited in anticipation, unsure whether to dash for my bedroom, when in walked a small man in his early fifties carrying a jacket under his arm. His head was proportionally smaller than his body and his black bushy moustache hung over his lips. I stood up.

"HELLO, *SOY JAVIER,*" he shouted, offering his hand.

"*Soy Barry, mucho gusto,*" I said, unsure of whom I was pleased to be meeting.

"FATTER!" He pointed to his chest, which confused me; he might have had a slight beer belly, but he was trim. "*SOY* FATTER *DE CASA.*" He repeated the phrase three times, each time louder, until it clicked.

"Okay, of course, the father."

"Yes, FATTER, JAVIER."

He was proud and happy to see his family as they kissed and hugged the man of the house.

"Come," said Maria, "sit with him and drink red wine, his favourite program is now."

For a tough Ecuadorian man, I was baffled by his favourite program; Clarissa, a terrible American 'comedy'. We nodded and smiled to each other, sipping the fruity wine. Every now and then he'd burst out laughing and shout something to Mamaria, now sat beside him. She was sipping fluid through a long plastic tube connected to something hidden under a turquoise blanket hanging over her sofa. I presumed it was medicine to help her throat (Three weeks later I discovered she had been sneakily slurping beer).

It was time to discover if I was cut out for teaching, or not. Waking up at six-thirty on a dark Monday morning was a shock to the system, especially when Mamaria startled me in her pink dressing gown.

"They might be a bit crazy," José said as he led me down the dusty smelling corridor towards my class. We passed five empty classes. "But, don't worry; I'm sure you'll be fine." He patted me on the back and closed the door. The window faced out over Quito. The sun had risen and mountains sat in the distance. The view beat the one of a grey wall from my stuffy office in London.

After a few minutes the reception bell rang and three noisy kids ran down the corridor. The door burst open. They were laughing and chatting in Spanish.

"You are new teacher?" said the boy. His legs kicked about as he shuffled in the chair. The two older girls whispered to each other.

"Yes, I am. My name's Barry," I said, writing my name on the board. I took their names

"You are American?" said Mila, the oldest girl. She was only about twelve and wore enough makeup to suggest she was on her way to a Barbie look-a-like competition.

"No, I'm English."

"We want American teacher, English is strange accent, we not like." Her accent was American. Diana, who wore less make up, nodded.

"Really?" I said.

"Yes, really," said Mila, tightening her lips. "When my mother know, she not happy, why are you English?"

"Well, I was born in England, so that makes me English." Pablo laughed.

"This is not funny," said Diana, also in an American accent.

"If you like I can speak in an American accent," I said, in an American accent. Pablo laughed again, but the girls complained in Spanish.

"I like England," said Pablo. "England football is better American football."

"Football is stupid game," said Mila.

"What do you like then?" I asked.

"American English." She crossed her arms and gazed out the window.

Pablo, aged ten, was a joy to teach. He grinned at everything and was interested in the lesson. When he got an answer correct he jumped up and banged his hands on the table. Mila, Pablo's sister (poor chap) continued to huff and grunt at every exercise and complain that she didn't understand my "posh" accent. Diana was an only child.

7

"You can dance?" Pablo said in the middle of the lesson.

"Of course I can. English people can dance better than South Americans."

"No they cannot!" said Diana, standing up. "We best dancers." They chatted in Spanish and agreed on something.

"We can see?" asked Mila, smiling smugly. I preferred not to dance that early in the morning, especially without a beer in my hand.

"Only when we finish the lesson," I said. They moaned, but I changed the subject by asking them about their hobbies and we continued with the book. I thought they'd forget about the dancing but Pablo brought it up towards the end.

"We see dance now?" he said, fidgeting in his chair. I tried to get out of it, but the young Latin women were persistent. I gave them a quick jive, to which Pablo cheered and clapped, and Mila and Diana smirked.

"Good good, you are good," said Pablo.

"Latin dance gooder," said Diana.

Mila and Diana left complaining to each other, while Pablo bopped behind.

"How was that?" asked José.

"Difficult. No one's ever said I speak 'posh'"

"Yeah man, they can be a nightmare. Pablo was happy, but the other two *senoritas* will have to put up with your accent. Anything un-American is posh for them, don't worry, things can only get better."

I hoped so.

## 2 The Secrets of Teaching

The class situation got worse. At the end of the first week, as I was explaining that they had to make a written and oral presentation to the director, Diana and Mila kept going on about my English accent.

"Why you cannot learn speak like American?" said Mila, banging her fist on the table.

"He no American, he English, and you badass," said Pablo, hitting her on the head with his pen.

"Okay guys, come on Mila, how many times do I need to tell you? The important thing is that you learn English, whether it's American or English, they will both help you."

"I think not, Hollywood actresses are all American," said Diana.

"Yes, but they pretty, you badass," said Pablo.

They bickered again and a fight broke out. I lost my temper, banged on the table, and shouted. Diana left the class crying and in came José.

"Look," he said, calmly, patting my shoulder. "You need patience, I know it's tempting but you can't shout."

After the kids left, I asked José for some advice on how to control them better.

"You have to be clever. Study Spanish, then you can scare them by saying you know what they are talking about and threaten to speak to their parents. That always works with me." He winked.

During my second week I got another job. The director of Harvard Institute, Mark, who was built like a heavy weight boxer but was as friendly as a whistling postman, was delighted by my English accent.

"Most of our native teachers are American," he said in his deep voice before sipping a coffee. "It's nice to see some English blood." He smiled as he leaned back in his chair.

"I think I'll keep my blood if you don't mind." Mark let out a low deep laugh and banged on the table.

"Good, good. Well, we need a new conversation teacher to help in class with the other teachers, from three in the afternoon until seven, four classes a day, and also Saturday mornings. You just need to chat with them in English, get them speaking and do some activities."

"Great! What books do you use, what materials?"

"You can do what you want; normally the teachers make up the lessons. Can you start next Saturday morning?"

"Sure."

"You will teach all ages here. You will enjoy it. They are good people." And he was right.

I turned up on Saturday morning with no idea what I was going to teach.

"Your first class is with The Lord," said Mark. I pictured a wise bearded man teaching English through religion.

"Don't look so worried. Alex is his first name. Come, I'll introduce you." I followed Mark as he bumbled down the corridor, kids stomped about and teenagers whispered and pointed at me.

"This is Barry, the new conversation teacher," Mark said, leaving me in the capable hands of The Lord.

"Hey man, nice to meet you, what's up?" he said, lifting his dark shades off his pale face. He wore a black suit, white shirt, and bright yellow tie. He cupped my hand and shook it hard.

"Hey, is it Alex or The Lord?"

"Call me what you want. The ladies prefer The Lord. Welcome to my world." He swung his arm out towards an empty classroom. Being on the seventeenth floor, I loved the view of *El Panecillo* in the distance and *Centro Historical* underneath.

When The Lord found out I was from London, he clapped his hands and pulled his tie.

"Wow! What do you think of my whistle?"

"Lovely, mate."

The Lord had never been to an English speaking country but his English was excellent, and he could control his class. During the lesson, none complained or muttered and all were engaged. Even while I did my part they behaved well, apart from a few random questions at the end.

"You have girlfriend?" asked one girl. A couple of others giggled and the boys jeered.

"Yes, I have a girlfriend."

"Where she is?"

"She's in England with her family, next question."

"Why she no here?" I glanced over to The Lord, who was equally as keen to know the answer. "You love her?" she added. Another jeer broke out from the audience.

"Okay, let's change the subject," said The Lord.

"Can you dance?' said another girl. Maybe it was a mandatory question for all new gimpy English teachers.

"That's enough now, let's continue with the exercise," The Lord said, and they stopped. They listened to him.

"How do you have that control over the kids?" I asked in the break.

"It takes time. I'm Ecuadorian and they respect me, also I know what they are saying. Did you hear them making fun of your accent?"

"Not them as well."

The Lord laughed.

"You need to improve your Spanish, but first you need to learn the *important* words, come by after your last lesson and I'll write a few out."

I thought he was going to give me a rundown of a few ways to cope with the Spanish verbs, but instead he wrote out a list of the top twenty swear words.

"When you hear the kids saying these, send them out. They'll think you know perfect Spanish. One day you'll become as good a teacher as me."

"Great, how can I repay you?"

"With more words like this, but English ones, I love them."

The next morning's lesson with Mila and Diana was delightful. As they came into class I heard Mila call José a 'wanker' so I sent her out.

"How you know what she say?" said Pablo.

"I've been studying," I said, grinning. "Now, who's done the homework?" They got their books out. Mila was quiet all class and apologized at the end.

"Good, let's hope we see an improvement in your English accent next lesson," I said. She stormed out. The next day they'd all started on their presentations.

Teaching at Harvard was demanding without any resources. I used ideas from the internet to keep the lessons fun and interesting with conversation activities. The good thing was that I could repeat the lessons and alter them depending on the level and the students seemed happy just listening to a native speaker.

The level of English of the Ecuadorian teachers impressed me, especially of The Lord, and Marcus, a chubby man with a button nose. He was polite and laughed like Santa Claus would. It's a shame some of his students were less mannered.

"You have sex with Ecuadorian woman?" said one lad from the back. The class roared with laughter. Marcus stood up, fuming.

"That is no way to treat a guest in our country," he said, pacing up to the lad.

The only female teacher was TJ from Argentina. When I first saw her, I thought she was one of the students.

"Where's the teacher?" I asked.

"Oh, that's me," she said, standing up straight. "Why, did you think I was a student?"

"No, of course not, I was just joking," I said.

"You English men are so funny,' she said in her twangy American accent.

The problem in TJ's class wasn't her students, they were fun and behaved; it was her. During the first lesson, she gazed and smiled while I taught, occasionally playing with her long black hair, and fluttering her eye lashes. She wore mounds of perfume and laughed too much at my stupid jokes. At the end, she brushed my arm as I was about to leave.

"Maybe we can go for a coffee one day or something, outside school." I knew South Americans were touchy feely people.

"Maybe; I don't really drink coffee though."

"Ah yeah, I'm sure you only drink tea." She leaned towards me, brushing her pert chest on my upper arm.

"Not really, just water, juice, or beer. Anyway, gotta dash.' I made a sharp exit. I wanted to stay out of trouble with Mark, and my girlfriend.

After the initial cross-examinations with the teenagers, my lessons started to go to plan. Mark's class of adults were my favourite. He used to leave us alone so everyone was more relaxed, especially me. They were a gentle group compared to the highly charged teenagers.

Before classes and in the breaks I used to chat with The Lord and Marcus. They loved to practice their 'street words', as they used to say.

"So you like the Ecuadorian vaginas then?" asked The Lord.

"What? Ha, well I'm sure they're very nice, but I have a girlfriend."

"Ah yeah the polite English man, what other words do you know for vaginas?" said Marcus. He was different outside the class.

"We have a few, here I'll write them down for you." They grunted in approval and practised like two horny teenagers.

"Wow, you have a lot," said Marcus. "I like this one, muff. Lord how is the muff today?"

"Good and you? How is the fanny?" he replied. It was all harmless fun.

Overall, the students were a great bunch. Teaching a mix of ages, levels, and personalities was an experience, even though it was difficult to keep up with their names. Ecuadorians were happy and extremely family orientated. Most of them couldn't understand why I wanted to travel the world and desert my family for so long. Those that did understand made it clear that I was very lucky to be able to travel and have the opportunity to see the world. Most hadn't travelled far out of Quito. I started to appreciate how lucky I was to be able to travel the world.

After a couple of weeks, Mila and Diana had calmed down and I began to enjoy teaching. Days were long but learning how to teach and getting to know the kids and teachers was worthwhile. I was still obviously finding my feet, but I was finally living in another country and experiencing things that I wouldn't have if I was just a traveller. I'd stopped thinking about returning to England.

I started to feel more comfortable walking about on my own as well. Busy with classes, the mugging incident began to fade away. I still paced to Princeton in the morning and home from Harvard in the evening when darkness had fallen, but I rarely had any problems.

Until one night I made another mistake.

## 3 The Buzz of Teaching Overrules

It was a Sunday night when I got my second scare. I'd been to visit the *Cuidad Mitad del Mundo*; a city thirty kilometres outside Quito with a thick white line of the Equator painted on the floor. The only exciting parts were a massive rectangular stoned pillar with a metallic globe on top, and some fried tangy bananas and tender lamb joint I had in a restaurant along the steep hill on the way down.

Back in Quito I popped in for a beer in one of the bars in *La Mariscal* area and got chatting to a couple of expats from Australia. They'd been living in and out of Quito for a year and reminded me of the dangers.

"Yeah mate, gotta keep ya head down at this time of night, don't go walking on ya tod now, get a cab if I were you," said one as I mentioned leaving. I took his advice, but it made no difference.

As usual the streets were empty and silent, but I felt safe in a vehicle. The cabby stopped about thirty metres short of my flat's entrance and I checked to see if anyone was about.

"*No pasa nada* – Don't worry," said the driver. The only sign of life was a harmless looking couple strolling along the side of the pavement nearest the buildings. They must be taking a romantic stroll, I thought.

I was wrong.

I got out and strode near the road to avoid potential danger. The couple had sped up and drifted over. My nerves rose as memories of the last incident crept back. They darted closer, trying to block my path. I continued with my head down and hid my bag. My camera was inside.

"*Escuchame, escuchame,*" said the man, asking me to listen. I looked down and tried to pick up the pace, but it was useless; the couple had trapped me. The man stumbled towards me as he repeated "*Escuchame, escuchame.*"

He put his arm round my shoulders. My legs shook. I gazed up at his dark face, his bloodshot eyes were half closed; his breath stunk of alcohol and cigarettes. He mumbled something.

"*No entiendo, no entiendo,*" I said, stating I didn't understand.

He made it clearer. He glanced quickly behind and then stared in my eyes.

"*Escuchame, amigo.*" I followed his eyes as they peered down towards his hand. He held a bread knife.

"Okay, Okay," I said, panicking. I guessed he wasn't asking if I had some butter for a sandwich. My legs shook even more as the beasty woman frisked my jacket and trousers. She was panting fast. I had no money, just my camera.

"*No tengo nada! No tengo nada,*" I said, remembering the first incident. This was different though; I was worried for my life.

Thinking back, I should have handed over my camera, but the way he was swaying suggested he'd forgotten he was robbing me. The beast had moved back and appeared more concerned about her lover.

"*Lo siento, no tengo nada,*" I said, unsure why *I* was apologizing.

He moved closer.

I was about to give over my bag when he squeezed and shook my hand, patted me on the shoulder, and shrugged in a drunken stupor as if to say, "Sorry mate, my mistake, have a good night now," and they continued on their romantic stroll.

My hands were trembling as I unlocked the huge metal security gate to the flat. No one was up so I grabbed a beer and sat on my bed. Where was I living? How lucky had I been? I'd escaped unharmed again. These muggers needed some formal training. No wonder poor living conditions forced them to rob; what chances would they have in a job where they had to use their brain?

I felt angry and confused. Despite my flat being only thirty metres away, I should have known better than to walk alone at night. Part of me started to doubt risking my life to live abroad and teach.

"What's up man?" said José the next morning. "Why the rush, you're ten minutes early?" I filled him in and he tried to get me to take the morning off.

"I'm better off here at work, that way I can forget about it all."

"You need to be careful round here at night man. I've been mugged twice. I think most people have in Quito. It's not the safest place in the world."

I'm not sure if José mentioned anything to Mila and Diana, or if they could sense I was shaken up, but their behaviour was more civilised.

"Hey, we ready for badass presentation," said Pablo.

"We want you to listen and check," said Mila.

"Yes, they better than before," said Diana.

"But I not speaking in an English accent," said Mila.

I listened and picked out some grammar mistakes. There were lots and I wanted to keep them motivated without putting a downer on their work so I only checked the main mistakes (I found out later that I should have been more thorough).

Maria and the family also tried to cheer me up.

"*Pobresito Barry, lo siento, lo siento,*" said Mamaria, apologizing as she wiped her eyes.

"We are sorry for this action," said Maria. "Especially because happen outside our flat, we can look after you, but you must be careful." They were supportive, but seemed embarrassed.

Despite the morale boost, I left for Harvard and felt the fear again as I walked along the main avenue. I was a bag of nerves when I arrived.

"Wankers," said The Lord after I told him. "I've been in trouble a few times you know."

"You, too?"

"Yeah, everyone has a story. One time I was on a bus during the day and this guy sat down and threatened me with a knife in my side. I gave him everything I had straight away; you never know what these fuckers will do. It can be a dangerous city. You're not the only one who's had problems. It could have been worse."

"Yeah but it seems like they're out to get me."

"You have to be hard when you walk around," said The Lord, slamming his hand on the table. "Don't get paranoid, improve your Spanish more, and don't let anyone push you about. Be mean and they will respect you for it. Have patience."

I was grateful for The Lord's advice. I needed a kick up the arse. I'd always been a shy lad and would prefer to avoid confrontation than get involved in a fight. I considered going home, but thinking about my life in England made my stomach turn. I used to slave away at a sales desk, working only for money, and conversing with city lads who I had nothing in common with. I'd felt like the odd one in the group because I was different.

Now I was living in Quito, learning Spanish, but most importantly learning how to teach English. I was making progress with my classes and refused to let some knob-heads spoil my fun. Giving up was no way forward.

Besides, Princeton had given me the first real buzz of being a teacher and I loved my job. As mentioned earlier, the kids' writing had a few mistakes which I'd overlooked. They were young and had improved so I let some of the errors slide. I handed them to the director on the Wednesday. On the Thursday I witnessed the hot fiery blood of Latin girls.

"*La puta directora*! - That fucking director!" said Mila as she threw her project on the floor.

"*Que puta*! - What a bitch!" said Diana, throwing hers towards the window. "She say we no pass level."

"I no like, she a badass, badass, badass," muttered Pablo as he slumped in the chair.

"What's the problem?" They all spoke at once; throwing their arms in the air and shouting that the director was a crazy bitch. She had scribbled over the assignments in red pen, picking out every single mistake. I felt guilty; she should have blamed me rather than the kids. I spoke with José and explained it was my fault.

"Can't you give them another chance?"

"I need to speak with the boss, she was angry."

"Yeah but the projects are much better than they were, they're only kids."

"I know, I know, but the director's a pain in the ass." He paused. I shrugged my shoulders. "Well, if they can do them again before tomorrow she should be okay."

"Great!" The kids were still annoyed, but they left happier.

The next morning, the projects were perfect and after the director listened to their presentations, in a small class with three other teachers and the kid's parents, she let them pass. The kids jumped up and down and congratulated each other. They'd brought in some chocolate cup cakes, and had made red and black paper graduation hats; including one for me with 'Barry Bad Ass Teacher', on the front.

I felt a buzz knowing that I'd helped them pass.

"We will miss you," said Mila.

"Yes you are badass teacher," said Pablo as he slapped my back.

"You are all badass students," I replied, thinking that the parents didn't know English.

"Thank you very much for your effort," said the mother. "The children have really enjoyed the lessons with you." I was shocked. Either she hadn't heard me or she didn't mind, either way I got off lightly. Everyone shook hands and the kids bounced out the door.

I was sad to see the little monkeys go. Despite my balls up, I'd enjoyed my first teaching project. Unfortunately, the end of the crazy bunch meant the end of Princeton.

"I'd just like to say thanks José, for giving me my first opportunity."

"No worries man, thank you!" He shook my hand and showed me out. "You did me a favour anyway. Now we can have some peace and quiet round here again."

It was then that I realised teaching English as a foreign language was going to change my life. I still wanted to travel the world and looked forward to more adventures, but teaching English gave living abroad a focus. I still had a long way to go, but I was on my way to becoming a world travelled teacher.

# 4 The Highs and Lows of Being a Teacher

Life as a teacher in Quito had its ups and down. Improving my Spanish made me feel more comfortable. Simple tasks such as supermarket visits and eating out in local restaurants became the norm. Living with the family got better. Mamaria was more pleasant than I'd initially made out. She was interested in how my classes were going, often showed me pictures of her son who was living in Guayaquil in the South (perhaps she saw me as his replacement), and stopped lingering about outside my room. She slaved away in the kitchen most afternoons. Everyday a different meat smell filled the flat and she always invited me to eat, but I had to decline because my timetable clashed.

I got on better with Maria too, despite her refusing to speak in Spanish.

"I must practise my English for my career; I will be a successful lawyer one day like my father, but maybe in the States."

Javier normally trundled through the door panting and moaning after a heavy day at his law firm. Mamaria and Maria always greeted him as if he had just returned from a weeklong expedition round the volcano, Pichincha. Conversation with Javier rarely went further than work and Clarissa, but he was a pleasant man and always offered me a glass of red wine.

The students at Harvard were great and I really enjoyed teaching there. The only problem was TJ. She started to pile on the pressure and turned up to flirt with me at the start and end of my lessons.

"We have been watching you," said Marcus as the lift's doors shut.

"Yes, are you keeping something from us?" said The Lord, resting his shoulder on mine.

"What are you guys talking about?"

"You know perfectly well," said Marcus, grinning.

"TJ," The Lord whispered.

"What about her?" I said.

"We think she wants to find out if Barry has special sex power," said The Lord. They burst out laughing and smacked a high five.

"You guys only think about one thing."

"Yeah, but you will be the one getting it, especially next week when the Fiestas of Quito arrive," said Marcus. "You can find lots of minge this time of year."

I dared to ask what the Fiestas of Quito involved.

"It's fantastic!" said The Lord in his most seductive way, forgetting I was a bloke. "It is our independence week and the city is alive with music, food, and alcohol, which means dancing and action for Mr Jackson," he said, clicking his fingers together.

"And what if Mr Jackson doesn't want any action?"

"He can enjoy a ride around the city on a Chiva; a small, colourful bus with no windows, and a musical band on top playing our traditional music."

"The women of Quito go crazy," said Marcus. "It's a perfect time to get laid."

The students kept going on about the festival too, and when Mark invited me on the school's Chivas I accepted. I wasn't going to miss the biggest party of the year. I just hoped to avoid TJ.

After listening to so much hype about the Chivas, I was electrified when one whizzed past as I was in *La Mariscal* during the day. Two Chivas, painted yellow, red, and blue - the colours of the national flag, drove past with a band on top. The sound of whistles, trumpets, and drums made a type of salsa music, but tinnier. Cheerful Ecuadorians stood on the roof dancing, blowing their whistles and drinking, some about to topple over. A few people watching from the street cheered and waved.

"VIVA QUITO!" Everyone chanted. As the Chiva turned the corner, people on top held tight to avoid falling off; their only protection was a knee high metal rail. No wonder people died during the fiestas. Hopefully Harvard's Chiva would have more protection.

The students were unmanageable knowing they were going on a Chiva and The Lord and Marcus were just as excited.

"This is going to be awesome," said The Lord as we gathered with over fifty students by the main road. Two women students were clinging on to The Lord's arms, while Marcus was trying to calm down the youngsters.

"Hey, I was hoping you were coming," said TJ. She greeted me with two kisses; something I was still trying to get used to.

"Hi TJ, what's up?"

"Oh, you know, getting ready for the party, will you dance with me later?" She brushed my arm.

"Maybe, if you're lucky." What was I saying?

"Oh really, hey come with me," she said, dragging me off to check out an artesian goods stand. She bought a green pearl necklace which, when she put it on, slid straight down into her cleavage.

"What do you think?" she asked, shaking her chest.

"Yeah, very nice," I said. "Is that Alex?" I darted off.

After twenty minutes cheering and waving at random Chivas hoping they were ours, the students became restless.

"*Donde estan las putas chivas?* – where are the fucking Chivas?" said one kid.

"Yeah, *donde estan las putas Chivas?*" I muttered, not thinking anyone would hear me.

"*DONDE ESTAN LAS PUTAS CHIVAS?*" they chanted, pointing and laughing at me. Mark became agitated.

"You are supposed to be the future of Ecuador," he said to the kids. "Stop this right now." He threw down his arms. Luckily he didn't realise I'd encouraged the behaviour.

When our *puta* Chivas did arrive on the other side of the road, everyone cheered and bolted across; oblivious to the other Chivas and cars whizzing past.

I went up top with Marcus and we sat at the back, TJ was at the front, and The Lord ran over to the other Chiva. The metal rail was again only knee high but it didn't stop everyone standing up and prancing about.

The band looked as though they had been Chivaring it up all week. Most were in their fifties. One bloke was passing round some booze to the others.

"Do you know *canelazo?*" asked Marcus, opening his bag. "It's a mix of cinnamon, sugar, and *aguardiente*, the secret ingredient. Normally it's hot, but today we drink like this." He held up a bottle he'd prepared.

"Go on then, twist my arm," I said as he poured some in to a white plastic cup. The drink was potent but sweet and fruity.

The two Chivas were full of students and teachers and when the band started everyone jumped up and down on the roof. I remained at the back like a responsible teacher, hiding from TJ. When the engines started, we jerked forward.

The *canelazo* changed my perspective on the dangers of the Fiestas of Quito and soon I was standing up waving to strangers, and chanting "Viva Quito!" When we stopped alongside another Chiva we whistled, waved, and cheered as if everyone was lifelong buddies.

"How do you like it?" Marcus asked as he topped up my crushed plastic cup with his lethal homemade brew.

"Strong stuff; does the trick though." He laughed and slapped me on the back.

We flew about the streets of Quito at fifty mph with screaming students dancing about. As we reached the old town, Ecuadorian flags flapped out the windows, Chivas rammed the roads, and partiers grooved on the pavements waving and celebrating. Fireworks screeched into the sky. It was a once in a lifetime experience.

"Hey Barry, will you dance with us?" asked one of my students.

"Sure why not," I said. The students cheered when I got up and even more when I started to dance. I could feel TJ gazing from a distance.

After about two hours, we were driving through *La Mariscal* to go to a disco when the Chiva screeched to a halt. Everyone rocked forwards onto the floor. A couple of girls screamed and one boy at the bottom of the pile yelped. Luckily no one was hurt and everyone laughed it off, but someone grabbed my hand.

"I feel a little drunk," said TJ. "I have never done before," she added, holding her head. I helped her down, but she dragged me inside. Then she went dizzy.

"Sit down here and I'll get you some water," I said, plonking her onto a chair.

"You are so sweet," she said. I ignored her and went to the bar. When I returned she was putting on makeup; so much for feeling dizzy.

"Thank you, you are so sweet." She took a sip. "Do you want to kiss me?" She looked deep into my eyes, pouted her lips, and lifted up her chest. I was under the influence of very strong alcohol.

"Sorry, I have a girlfriend in England. You are a lovely girl but I can't."

"That is a shame because I would like to kiss you," she said, pulling me closer.

"Sorry, you know how it is." I pulled away.

"Yes but I love you." Her eyes were watery.

"What?"

"I fell in love with you the first moment I saw you." I kept silent. "I think you are wonderful. I have a feeling about you."

"Okay nice, sorry, I need the toilet." I jogged off.

The Lord was in the men's room brushing his hair.

"I see you have found a nice muff," he said, patting me on the shoulder.

"The muff found me, she's crazy man; she just told me she loved me."

"No way, good work!"

"I need to get away from her. Can you go and distract her?"

"Okay dude, I don't mind sloppy seconds." He surprised me yet again with an expression. I hid in the corner with Marcus while the Lord persuaded TJ to get a taxi home. I was safe.

We danced, drank some more, and partied into the early hours and I got a taxi home, without getting mugged. It turned out to be one of the best nights I had in Quito. The Lord and Marcus knew how to treat a guest and show the ins and outs of their culture; something I would never have experienced had I not been living there as a teacher.

The next afternoon I avoided TJ and walked into a standing ovation to Marcus' class.

"They are impressed with your dancing," said Marcus. I wasn't the gimpy shy English man anymore.

At the end of the Fiestas de Quito I had my worst foreign cuisine experience. Mamaria invited me for a "special" lunch. After seeing the results of her excellent cooking before, I was excited about getting my teeth into a delicious homemade meal.

"*Okay, es para Barry*," Mamaria said, plonking the plate before me. A strange rotten smell darted up my nose.

"*Gracias, oh que rico*," I said, saying it looked delicious. I was lying. A grey sickly slop with unappetising stringy meat buried inside oozed over the plate. Normally her cooking looked amazing. I was miffed. Everyone was staring. I must have been pulling a strange face because they seemed offended.

"Is everything okay?" Maria asked, coughing slightly.

"Yeah sure, *que bien, que bien*," I said, forcing a smile. Fortunately, some rice arrived along with everyone else's plates. We were all in the same boat, but the problem was that *I* was heading straight into the iceberg.

They tucked in, making appreciative noises whereas I played around with the rice, scared of the grey substance.

"YOU MEAT, IS GOOD?" Javier shouted.

"The meat, of course, how silly of me," I said, cutting up the scraggly gristle. It was thin and intestine like. I've never eaten shit, but if I had, then I'm sure the disgusting muddy flavour would have tasted the same.

"YOU LIKE, BARRY?" asked Javier.

"*Si, Si, muy bien*," I mumbled with the rubbery meat swishing round my mouth. I managed half a plateful then made an excuse that I had to call England. Three hours later, I was violently sick - from both ends - and couldn't eat for two days. It was the first, and last, time that I ate Mamaria's delicious homemade meals.

Another high of living abroad was that I could travel at the weekends. After the incident I'd put off travelling on my own, but I had to build up my confidence again. A short weekend trip to Otavalo, a charming indigenous village in the Imbabura province about two hours north of Quito, got my travel buds squirming.

The start wasn't that great though. On arrival to Otavalo, I was wandering through a littered plaza when a yelping dog made me turn. The owner had slammed his dog's ear in the car door and was driving round while the poor dog scrambled its legs in the air. The worst part was that the majority of the locals were laughing.

I put it down to a one-off and continued. I spent the afternoon browsing the indigenous markets for Christmas gifts for my family; I was starting to miss them. The stalls were so colourful; shades of red, yellow, blue, and green gave the markets a homely feel. You could get anything from thick woolly jumpers, coats, scarves to giant rugs, panama hats, or blankets. I went for some hand painted pictures of Ecuador (which I wouldn't recommend sending to England, especially as they were made from glass, muppet).

In the evening, I went for dinner in a local family's restaurant. Their speciality was chicken soup. When a chicken's foot bobbled to the surface, I gazed round to see if anyone else had chosen the local delicacy. Most people were nibbling on the bony feet. I gave it a try, but the texture was too rubbery. At least it was better than Mamaria's grub.

The highlight of the weekend was on Sunday at San Pablo Lake. The view of the green hills glistening on the reflection and the fresh river smell gave me peace. A group of mothers were washing their children's clothes in a stream and I thought back to my mother. She'd always complain about doing her Sunday washing, but these women seemed perfectly happy; on a social event rather than on a chore.

As I lazed by the lake, content being outside Quito, Ecuador charmed me with its natural environment and tranquility. I felt safe. I imagined living by the lake, setting up a language school for the families to learn English. Why would they need another language though? It was refreshing to see the locals happy with what they owned; no materialism, computers or T.V, just themselves and the gift of the lake to gaze at each day. I had to get out and see the country more.

An incident that spurred me to get out of Quito took place a couple of weeks before Christmas. I was standing in the lift at Harvard thinking back to San Pablo Lake, when a pale man in his late twenties wearing glasses and a light blue granny knitted jumper got in.

"Hi, you are a teacher here at Harvard?" he said.

"Yes, do you study here?" His face was familiar.

"Before yes, I work in an office on floor fifteen. I am José. I'm looking for a private English teacher to practise a little."

"Oh right, well..." I was about to say I was too busy.
"What about classes then?"
"I don't think..."
"I can meet you after work."
'I'm a bit tired actually."
"I'll buy you a coffee." The lift clonked to a halt and he stepped out. "See you at seven." How did he know when I finished?
"But..." The doors closed. Great, what had I arranged? I hated people pushing me around.
"Maybe he's okay," said Marcus on our break.
"Or maybe he wants to take you to his love palace," said The Lord, giggling.
"Or maybe he wants to hum on your plums," added Marcus.
"I'm gonna stop teaching you fuckers!'
"I am a fucker, The Lord of Fuckers," said The Lord.

Mark was more helpful and looked up José's records. He'd been a good student with no problems. I was wary though. Mark let me leave early, but José was already waiting downstairs.

"Hey," he said, smiling and shaking my hand. His was warm and sweaty. "Okay let's go in my car; I know a good place."

"Your car, what place?"

"It's in the centre where the tourists go; near Papaya net, the internet place." I knew the place so I went along. His car was tidy and smelt of stale cigarettes. He offered me one, but I declined. As the fresh smoke filled the car, I went to open the window.

"Sorry, don't you like the smoke?" he said, opening my window from his controls. The doors clunked locked.

I made small talk to try to suss him out, but he never gave a straight answer. When we got in a traffic jam and he pulled down a dark side road, I glanced over.

"Don't worry, it's a short cut, I know the roads." He smirked. I was sure he could tell I was nervous. We pulled up outside Papaya net and for a moment I felt foolish for doubting him.

We sat at a round table by the window and José ordered a coffee, I a beer. We chatted in Spanish. I talked about my girlfriend and made it clear that I enjoyed the traits of the opposite sex, but he was less forthcoming. He lived with his family and had recently separated from his "partner."

I spoke about football, but he knew nothing about the Premier League, and I mentioned I'd just joined a gym round the corner. He glared, almost flirtingly. I checked my watch.

"So you think I can be your private student?"

"I don't think so, listen, I'm quite busy already and don't have time."

"Well maybe we can just meet and have a beer; we can speak in English and Spanish. We can both practise, your Spanish is good." He was definitely flirting now. I made an excuse that Mamaria was cooking and got up to leave.

Even after all that I ended up giving the flat's number, knowing Mamaria or Maria would answer it. The problem was that he knew where I worked and when I finished.

"Is that a limp I see you walking with?" The Lord asked the next day. "Did you enjoy the love making?"

"Yeah it was great."

"YOU DID?"

"No you dick!" I explained what had really happened and The Lord told me to steer clear.

"There are some crazy guys in Quito that look for gringos, can be for money or other things."

That evening Marcus accompanied me out of the building just to be sure. When I arrived home, Mamaria told me that José had called, six times.

"This man is your friend, no?" asked Maria.

"No, I think he's crazy."

"Be careful with men like that, they are the same to the women here," she said. I felt guilty for getting Mamaria involved, but she assured me not to worry.

Two days later at the gym, guess who turned up? He'd hunted me down.

"I thought I would see you here," he said, grinning and staring.

"Did you?" I said, dropping my weights in anger.

"You are out a lot I see, never in the house."

"Yeah, I told you, I'm busy."

"Great." He stared at my arms.

"Look, what do you want?"

"Nothing, just looking, you are strong, no?"

"Listen mate, I'm here to do some exercise, now if you don't mind." I turned my back on him.

"Can we meet tonight?"

"Are you serious?" I said, scrunching my face in disbelief. "Tonight I have plans, and this weekend too, and the next. I don't have free time!" I'd raised my voice. My new, tougher, side was showing.

"Oh, okay, no problem, here is my number." He handed a piece of paper to me.

"I don't want your number," I said, moving towards the running machine. "Now if you don't mind, I'm busy." He left.

Eventually he stopped phoning the house. I never saw him after the gym incident, but I went back to the old and trusty 'Don't talk to strangers' policy. It was time to move on.

## 5 Feliz Navidad, Año Nuevo, y Adiós

"What do you mean you're leaving?" said The Lord after I'd told him I was heading to Brazil after New Years. "But we haven't been out to find some muff together yet."

"You know I've got a girlfriend, besides, Marcus is more of a charmer."

"Why thank you kind sir," said Marcus, putting his arm round me. "But I am also upset, why do you have to go so soon?"

"My tourist visa is about to run out and I want to travel through Peru and Bolivia for a month and get to Salvador before the Carnival."

"THE CARNIVAL?" The Lord shouted. "You're going to be in BRAZIL for the CARNIVAL? That is the minge paradise. I'm definitely mad now."

They both envied how I could leave without any responsibilities and travel to the other side of South America; neither of them had left Ecuador. Not everyone had the freedom to travel.

Mark was fine about me moving on, but Mamaria and Maria were sad.

"We must make this Christmas special for you, and New Years, you must celebrate here, like a son, and eat with us," Mamaria said, in Spanish. I hoped her Christmas menu didn't involve intestines.

The build up to Christmas was fun. Shops and restaurants put up Christmas trees and lights and played traditional Christmas songs. The city was more vibrant than normal; a lot more tourists were passing through and the locals seemed happier.

Mark organised a combined farewell and Christmas drinks for the students and teachers. With each of the younger classes we had a party, which involved lots of musical chairs, regaetton dancing, and eating cake. For the adult students we drank and danced in the main hall. Everyone petered out until a few of us staggered to a karaoke bar. Marcus and The Lord were secret duet experts. They sang with style, especially compared to my crap attempted in Spanish.

The last few Christmases before I left England, I'd yearned to be away to experience another culture and way of life. However, when Christmas Eve came round all I could think about was my family and mates.

I bought Mamaria and Maria some jewellery, and Javier some chocolate and a bottle of red wine. At midnight, after I'd been to a pub and toasted in England to Christmas, we ate turkey (without intestines) and exchanged gifts. They bought me a new jacket and bottle of rum.

I'd needed one since I arrived and it would help for cold nights on my next trip (the jacket I mean).

The evening was special. I couldn't imagine an English family welcoming an Ecuadorian traveller into their home for Christmas. Mamaria, Maria, and Javier saw me as part of their family and I was grateful.

On Christmas day nothing happened. The family went to church in the morning and then visited relatives.

"Do you want to come with us?" asked Maria.

"No, it's okay. I'm going out for a walk and then I'll call home."

The streets were deserted apart from homeless mothers and children scouring for food and money. It was hurtful to see kids so sad on Christmas Day. One kid tugged on my shirt as I walked past and sniffed the bubbles of snot round his nostrils as he asked for money. I gave him what I could, but it wasn't much.

After I got off the phone to my family, the fact that I was on my own hit me. I felt lost and lonely and kept thinking about previous Christmases and how much fun they had been. The new experience had been interesting and I was very grateful to the family, but it wasn't the same without your own. *I'd* made the choice to leave though; the poor kids living in the streets had no other option. Thinking back, it was nothing compared to what happened the following year while I was in Thailand, but more about that later.

There were three things left to do on my list before leaving Quito: sample *cuy*, Ecuador's most famous pet food; witness the burning of the President, and go on a trip to the beach with the family.

When I say pet food, I don't mean food Ecuadorians give their pets, rather pets that Ecuadorians eat. *Cuy*, or guinea pig, is a delicacy and I promised The Lord and my students that I'd try it before I left. A few adored the special cuisine, while others grimaced at the mention of eating the ratlike animal. I wanted to make up my own mind.

"Go to Baños in the Tungurahua province three hours south, it is best there,' The Lord said after I met him for a Boxing Day beer.

On the giddy trip through the Andes I tried, but failed thanks to cloud, to spot the huge volcano, which gives name to its province. Tungurahua is an active volcano and if ever erupted, would wipe out Baños at its base.

In October 1999, 25,000 people evacuated the village temporarily thanks to the first eruption of the volcano. Mounds of ash spilled out the top and covered the town killing seven people in the process.

Baños was more colourful and vibrant than Otavalo, and the mountains on either side reminded me of Oaxaca in Mexico. I dumped my stuff in a hostel and wandered round. Compared to Quito, Baños was like a miniature village. The only noise came from a few kids playing in the main plaza and the occasional bird chirping. The calmness and tranquillity was spooky after so long in the capital. I wasn't complaining though; I felt safe.

After a nose about, I stumbled on a strange stuffed animal museum. I've never been a fan of the hunting world, but something dragged me inside. The exhibits began reasonably tame: a couple of exotic birds, harmless snakes, and lazy lizards, all kept in glass cabinets. Then I spotted a poor horse's head pinned up high on a wall, and then a couple of baby monkeys, who looked electrocuted. I was unimpressed.

In another glass cage, perhaps trying to put me off sampling them later; were two Ecuadorian guinea pigs gawping, as if stuffed alive. How would I eat *cuy* after that? To top it off there was a deformed baby something (I'm not sure what) floating in a jar of murky green water still attached to its umbilical cord.

After a quick shower and change of clothes, I asked the hostel owner where I could find *cuy*.

"*CUY?*" He frowned at me.

"Yeah, *cuy*, I've heard it's pretty good here."

"Yes, it is," he said, staring. "But not many tourists leave here alive after trying it." I assumed he was joking and wandered off.

I was starving and excited about trying a new dish. Even though I'd had many heated debates with students about eating *cuy*, and after seeing the poor creatures mortified in the museum, I was adamant on giving it a go. I presumed that the chef would carve and present the delicacy on a plate with some salad and chips.

When I caught a whiff of burning meat from a barbeque, my stomach rumbled. Local people sat on tables outside a restaurant, happily tucking into their meals. A full place is a good place, I thought. Then I spotted the grill.

I moved back in shock. Were they the same guinea pigs from the museum? The crispy *cuy* were lined up in neat rows burning away on their backs with a kebab stick shoved through. Their little legs and arms reached out and their mouths open as if crying out in pain as the flames wrapped round.

Had these people no shame? In the class debates no one had mentioned you see them whole and could choose the one you wanted. I thought that was only with lobsters. I couldn't face munching away on the burned domestic animals, and settled for a Chinese round the corner. Who knows, I may have eaten guinea pig anyway.

As if I hadn't seen enough poorly treated animals, the next day I went to the San Martin Eco Zoo. I got up early and didn't shower because I wanted to try out the hot springs first, but they were packed full of grubby little kids and teenagers and half naked old people, probably depositing deadly *cuy* gases.

The people of Baños must have taken a while to build the zoo because it was awkwardly placed on the side of a mountain with a valley stretched below. Inside the zoo were birds, including giant eagles, a few jaguars and tapirs, and some capybaras, which were apparently the biggest rodents in the world. My favourites were the monkeys. Monkeys always make me laugh but these were extra naughty, running about fighting with each other over the food. I imagined their conversation.

"Hey man, why do they keep giving us this leftover food? What is it today?"

"Tastes like guinea pigs again."

"What again! When are they going to learn that it's a domestic animal and we're supposed to eat nuts and things? Who eats guinea pigs anyway?"

The solitude was getting to me. I could have stayed longer in delightful Baños and done a jungle trek or gone hiking in the mountains, but I wanted to save cash for my adventure in January. It had been a pleasant break and I'd regained some confidence about travelling alone.

"What's that then?" I asked Maria and Javier as they sat in the lounge stapling some old trousers and a shirt together.

"This is our *Año Viejo*," said Maria. "We are making Lola, the President." For New Years, every family make a dummy, like a Guy Fawkes, to burn at midnight; a way of saying goodbye to the bad luck or memories. The dummies represent someone they hate, like, or even a close relative who has died.

"Why the President though?" I asked.

"*Lola es una puta,*" said Javier. "HELP, YOU HELP?" he said, pushing me towards the pile of old newspapers.

"My father believes the more people that help the better." I didn't argue.

The bright and sunny New Years Eve morning came around quickly. Locals, who had returned from the beach, and newly arrived tourists, who looked lost, rammed the busy capital. I felt sad that I was away from my family and mates, but I was getting used to it and felt excited about the New Year party.

The family dressed up for the celebrations and Maria looked especially pretty. We had a few drinks and talked about the year gone by. As it approached midnight, we carried Lola out into Avenue Amazonas where a manic chaos had formed. The area was packed with families and friends piling their dummies together ready for the huge bonfire. A strange sombre tension filled the air; unlike back home where everyone was getting two or three drinks for when the bar shut. Some families stood calmly, reflecting, others danced about.

Just before midnight Mamaria warned me to stand back from the bonfire. A bunch of lads fired some rockets to signify that another year had ended. Firework smoke clouded the sky. Everyone kissed on the cheeks and hugged as they said '*Feliz Año Nuevo*'. A few shed tears. The Ecuadorians danced round the bonfires and let off fireworks to burn away the badness. I was lucky to be able to share the night with such a friendly family and still think back to them every year at New Years.

After congratulating random strangers and dancing about while dodging the fireworks, we made our way back in for the dinner, a huge roast chicken. After the meal Javier got out the whiskey and we saw in the New Year in style.

As usual on New Year's Day I regretted drinking so much. Mamaria woke me up for a nine-hour drive through the Andes. No chance of a New Years day lie-in. From when I entered Javier's battered van until we arrived I felt uncomfortable, giddy, and moody.

Javier must have still been over the limit as he drove like a loony. He was fine until we got on the motorway. He picked up the pace and whizzed in and out of the other vehicles. Mamaria and Maria kept telling him to slow down, but he fixed ahead.

When we reached the Andes, the road became thinner and slow trucks blocked Javier's path. He kept overtaking though, even on blind corners. I'd never been as terrified on the road, worried we were going to collide with oncoming vehicles. The only time I enjoyed the views of the trees and surrounding mountains were when we stopped for food.

When we got through the mountains, the traffic died down and I thought we were in for a relaxing drive. No such luck. Javier drove faster and with the bendy roads I wasn't surprised when we hit a bump and almost toppled over.

"*BASTA PAPA!*" shouted Maria, she'd had enough. I wanted to say a few more, expletive, words, but refrained. The van had skidded off the road into a ditch, and we were lucky not to be injured.

He finally calmed down and we arrived to the 'beach house' in one piece.

"*Donde esta la playa?*" I asked as I helped Javier lift back the squeaky rusty gate. We were in the middle of the country.

"*Solo vente minutos,*" said Javier. Twenty minutes, by car. There was no 'beach', and the wooden 'house', which Javier had built on stilts a few years ago, looked unstable and about to squash the squabbling turkeys pecking around underneath.

I was starving, sweaty, and knackered but we had to drive another twenty minutes to get some food. By the time we saw the sea, night had fallen and it started raining.

I'd never been so happy to get my head on a pillow and was asleep in seconds. Peace at last. However, things got worse. An hour later, the squabbling turkeys woke me up and continued yapping all night. I'd only managed a couple of broken hour's sleep, before I was woken up by everyone tiptoeing about on the squeaky floorboards.

I went for a wander outside in the fresh morning air. Javier was picking weeds from his dusty plot and watering the non-existent crops. The turkeys were asleep in the shade under the house. I picked up a small stone to throw.

"*Has dormido bien* Barry?" asked Mamaria, had I slept well?

"*No, muy poco,*" I said, gazing at the guilty culprits. "*Los pavos hacen mucho ruido, no?*" I said, saying they made a lot of noise.

"*Ruido? Que ruido?*" she said, patting the deceiving bastards.

I wanted to maintain the good relationship I had with the family so I tried to forget about the disastrous start. I helped Javier clean the plot and bag up the rubbish, but we didn't set off for the beach until early afternoon. I had to be patient.

Maggie announced we would be doing the rounds before the beach.

"*Vamos a ver la abuela,*" she said. The grandmother, no one had mentioned a grandmother.

"NO SEA, NO SEA," Javier shouted, confirming what I thought. We drove for about half an hour and pulled up by a small house in a village nowhere near the beach.

"NO SEA, NO SEA," Javier repeated as he laughed. Then it became clearer what he had meant to say.

"This is my grandmother," said Maria, introducing me to an old, frail, and blind, woman sitting out on her patio.

"NO SEE, NO SEE," Javier repeated. After some juice and cake, and a two hour chat, we headed for the beach, arriving just after four in the afternoon.

Despite the nightmare journey and chores, getting in the refreshing sea and marvelling at the mountains across the bay had been worth the wait. That evening we ate fresh fish by the beach and downed a few whiskeys back at the house. Javier must have given a couple to the turkeys too as they were quiet and I managed a decent sleep.

We spent the next day by the beach. It was fun hanging out with the family and just chilling. I had time to reflect on my experience in Ecuador. I had changed. I was less naïve and more aware of the dangers of being alone. I'd enjoyed teaching and learning a language and living in another country was rewarding. I'd become stronger and the fear of returning home had faded, for the moment anyway.

What made the real difference were the people I'd met. Apart from the obvious crooks, Ecuadorians were an open, funny, and charming bunch. The family were generous and The Lord and Marcus had become decent friends. I was sad to be leaving, but glad to be going on a new adventure.

I had to wait longer than I'd anticipated. The journey back to Quito was equally as gruesome. Javier was desperate to return before dark and, thanks to the thick rain and lack of warm clothes, when we arrived in Quito, we were all frozen. The next morning I couldn't get out of bed; I'd caught a nasty cold and my whole body ached.

When I gathered my strength a couple of days later, I caught a bus up to *El Panecillo* to take a few last minute photos of the capital. I'd saved the best views till last. The centre of town seemed tiny, surrounded by white, brown, and ochre buildings stretching out to the green hills and mountains in the background.

Down at Harvard I chatted with Mark for a while and thanked him again for giving me the opportunity. I stuck my head in a few classes (apart from TJ's) to say goodbye to the teachers and students. Then I went out for a farewell greasy fry-up with The Lord and Marcus.

"Don't forget us man, we are your children," said The Lord, banging his knife and fork on the table.

"Don't worry, how can I forget you guys?"

"I'll miss your vocabulary," said Marcus. "I need to find a new dirty dictionary."

"I think you've got enough for now," I said.

Saying goodbye to them was emotional; they'd welcomed and helped me settle down in the difficult capital. If it hadn't been for them,

I might have taken off earlier. I was glad I could teach them a few swear words.

I left on the 6th of January, almost three months after I arrived. I planned to be in Salvador for the 1st of February. I'd lost almost a week of travel time being ill so I'd have to cut out some places.

The family gathered in the lounge to say goodbye and I thanked them for their hospitality and promised I would look them up if I returned.

"Thanks for your humour and smiles," said Maria, translating for Mamaria, who had tears rolling down her cheeks. "We hope your family are well, good journey," she added. I said goodbye and wished them luck.

"WOMEN BRAZIL YES, GOOD, GOOD," Javier shouted as he shook my hand for a final time. He looked more excited than I was about the across trip to Brazil.

## 6 Peru: Tension on the way to Machu Picchu

If you were an explorer, let's say Indiana Jones, and were with your troops in the depths of Peru on an expedition, and someone came up to you and said.

"Would you like to see a hidden city?" Would you believe them, or run away thinking they'd boil you up in a steaming black cauldron? Then, if you discovered a lost Inca world, would you keep it a secret or tell the world?

Hiram Bingham, an American historian, explorer and re-discoverer of Macho Picchu faced these dilemmas when he was strolling around near Cusco in 1911. Hiram introduced Machu Picchu (or 'Old Mountain' in Quechua) to the world, and made it one of the Seven Wonders.

The Lost City of the Incas had always been a mystery to me ever since my auntie Carrie showed me pictures in an encyclopaedia. I promised her that I'd snap photos at Machu Picchu with Harry, the guardian teddy bear she'd given me. The question was whether the little guy could last the four day trek, especially with the stormy weather and high altitude.

The journey down from Quito to Cusco was madness. After being in Quito, I wanted to save some time so I did the 1,600km journey in three bus trips spread over four nights.

The Peruvian border crossing was chaotic thanks to sweaty hounding locals, but I managed to find a decent taxi driver who took me to get my passport stamped and then dropped me off in Tumbes, where I caught the next overnight bus to the capital.

I failed to do Lima justice. Two nights without proper sleep had battered my senses and I was delirious. While I was resting on the steps of the cathedral in Plaza Mayor, munching some bread and sipping orange juice, a dwarfish woman with long black hair and a thick monobrow sat next to me. I told her I was living in Lima and was going to meet some teachers later that evening, in case I needed to escape.

"And you? Are you from Lima?" I asked.

"*Si*, I live there," she said, pointing beyond the square. "Today I free!"

"Lucky you, free? Why, where do you work?"

"I don't work. I am free from my husband." Maybe she was confusing her English. "He is working, and I have come to the square to see the people and take the air." Maybe she wasn't.

If I'd had my wits about me, I probably wouldn't have agreed to go on a tour of Lima with Marta, especially when she started stroking my wispy blonde arm hair. She led me along the busy streets up towards a museum, which she refused to tell me the name of, and seemed genuinely shocked when it was closed. Cautiously, I continued with her to an Art Museum near *Parque Italiano*, but that's where the fun stopped.

"You think how I look with no clothes?" she asked, standing by a naked female sculpture. I hadn't, but I bet she was hairy all over.

"Err, that's a bit…"

"Do you like these?" she said, pointing to the statue's nipples.

"Not my type really, bit small," I said. "Is that the time?" I peered at my watch. "I really must be going now Marta; I'm meeting a friend at six. It was lovely for you to show me round."

She insisted on guiding me back to Plaza Mayor. I let her, but with wary eyes.

"Can I ask you something?" she said as we got back to the steps. Here we go, I thought, how much did that cost? "Can we be in contact on email; I like to practice my English."

"Yeah sure," I said. A light get away. Maybe I had been too harsh.

Once we'd said goodbye I darted back to my hostel and slept until I had to get up for my bus to Cusco. I'd have to return one day to Lima and see it properly.

The twenty-six hour bus trip to Cusco was a bloody nightmare. To start with the poverty in the miles of shanty towns outside Lima made me feel guilty for being able to travel the world. A huge mass of flimsy wooden huts with a thick carpet of litter engulfed the suburbs. The faces of the poor kids running about were heartbreaking.

After a few hours we approached the mountains and it was clear that the driver was mental. All through the night he screeched round the bended corners and refused to pull over for a pit stop when everyone complained about the shit and puke covered toilet. The stench was unbearable and my bladder felt as though it was going to burst every time we turned a corner. When he finally gave in and stopped, about twenty-hours into the journey, everyone piled off the bus hurling abuse.

I'd never been so relieved to see a destination as I was Cusco.

"Cusco, Cusco," said my robust travelling companion as she pointed towards the orange and brown roofed houses in the village protected by the Andes. Lucia was Cusconian and gave me a business card of her sister's trekking company.

"*Mucha magica, mucha magica,*" she said, referring to Machu Picchu.

The rain lashed down as I walked up the steep hill towards the centre and I wondered if trekking for four days was going to be a good idea. I dumped my stuff and tracked down the hiking shop just off Plaza Armas.

"When can I leave?" I asked Carmen, Lucia's sister.

"Can tomorrow, walk four days, the first day easy, then very hard the day number two, up, up, and up," she said, moving her hand higher. "Then the day three no problem, the day four you can to see the Machu Picchu." She pointed to an enlarged familiar photo of the Old Mountain.

The four-day trek included all food, an English-speaking guide, tents, and porters to carry the gear. I stocked up on essentials: water, chocolate, black sacks for waterproofs, coca leaves for extra energy at high altitudes, and a small bottle of rum.

I disliked Cusco. Had there been less travellers and hiking shops then I might have enjoyed being in a, previously, secret location, but the hordes of tourists had ruined the quaint village. The further I travelled from Quito though, the safer I felt, or maybe I was learning how to handle myself better and my courage was growing.

I'd never been slung in with a group of strangers on a four-day trek before. On the first morning I realised there was going to be tension. Our group of nine were at the starting point, KM 88, by an old railway station. The Urubamba River whooshed by on the left.

"What's up Doc?" said Ted, a loud mouthed Texan kitted out in camouflage gear to Borne, a wise, white bearded Norwegian man in his sixties.

"Sorry?" said Borne, taking out the raw carrot he was gnawing.

"Got any spare carrots old boy?" Ted said, winking at his English sidekick, Chris, who smirked, but not for long because he was trying to adjust the straps on his huge rucksack.

"Yes if you like," Borne said, innocently. "I have plenty. It's good energy."

"Nah, you can keep them,' said Ted. "Ya nancy," he muttered without Borne hearing. I'd never met a Texan, but I knew Ted was going to be a handful.

"I'll take one," I said; I felt sorry for the bloke.

"Okay everybody," said Javi, our guide. He was a stocky black haired Cusconian with legs the size of a baby elephants'. He'd hiked to Machu Picchu over twenty times. "That is where we start." He pointed to a wobbly footbridge with a valley of tree covered mountains behind.

"If anyone falls in they're a gonna," said Ted, laughing on his own.

"We are going to walk for about four hours in the Urubamba canyon before we stop for food," Javi said. "I will lead the way, but stop now and then to make sure everyone is okay and explain some history of the Inca trail. Good luck. Any questions?"

"When can I go fishing?" asked Ted.

"This is an Inca trail, not a fishing competition, but you may have a chance tonight. Please keep to the path everybody."

"Yeah right," Ted muttered. Borne tutted and walked away.

"Let me introduce the guys," said Javi, waving his arm out to his compact, solid, and happy smiling crew. The seven small but tough indigenous Indian lads from Cusco, all in their twenties with the same size legs as Javi, shot off with the majority of the gear to set up a base for lunch. Their Spanish was limited as they only spoke in Quechua (the official language spoken by Incas and now by over ten million indigenous people in South America), but Javi was fluent in both.

"I'll give you a couple of minutes before we leave," said Javi.

As everyone checked their gear and stretched I wondered why they were carrying so much. I had the bare minimum: one spare pair of clothes, sleeping bag, torch, binoculars, camera, the essentials I'd bought in Cusco, and Harry. Some looked as though they were carrying their grandmother's knickers collection. Chris was the most uncomfortable; he almost fell over when he put on his rucksack.

Everyone stood waiting eagerly to get started, we were a complete mix of characters and I wondered how things would pan out, would we make it as a team or would there be fights? We had the same mission in mind, to get to the ancient city of Machu Picchu. Whether we liked it or not, the nine of us, me, Javi, Ted, Chris, Borne, a French couple, a blonde Danish girl, and two Argentinian lads, were stuck together for the next four days.

The first morning was light going compared to the rest of the trek. The French couple shot in front and I stayed at the back with Chris and Ted as we wandered along the mud trail. Overhanging trees protected us from the drizzling rain. Apart from our panting and puffing, the only sound was the river rushing by and the blabbering Texan. He could be funny at times, but arrogant.

"Yeah, my Spanish is good, it should be, I've been studying it for ages, GOD DAMN," he said, swiping at a tree with his walking cane.

We caught up with Carla, the blonde girl from Copenhagen. She had been training for the trek around Cusco and studying Spanish while living with a family.

"It's been great fun, so different to boring Denmark," she said. When I told her that I'd been teaching in Quito and was heading to Brazil she envied me.

"That's the life I'd love to live, it sounds so exciting and interesting."

"Yeah, I guess it is." That compliment may not have seemed much to anyone, but it filled me with joy. I thought back to London when I used to be the boring and dull one and felt proud I'd survived the tough times in Quito.

We stopped high and deep in the mountains by a flat grass area so we could see back down the valley. I enjoyed looking back and seeing how far we'd walked along the Inca trail.

"When are one of those funny little Inca men gonna cook me a big steak," said Ted as we entered the camp.

"I don't think you're in Texas now, mate," said Chris.

"Yes," said Carla, firmly. "Can you please respect the others, they are carrying all our stuff, you know."

"I'm hungry," said Ted. "If I can't get a steak I'm gonna catch me a big trout."

After a short wait, we crammed up in the marquee, Javi brought round bowls of steaming spaghetti bolognese. Everyone waited, but only eight bowls turned up.

"Don't wait for me," said Borne said as everyone stared at him. "I'm having something different."

"I didn't know there was a choice," Chris muttered. Everyone started to complain, until Borne's food arrived.

"Oh, that's wonderful," he said.

"What in the God's name is that," asked Ted, "rabbit food?"

"It's healthy food Mr. Meatball," he said. "I'm a vegan now, I used to eat meat, but I got too fat and decided against the cruelty of animals," he said, crunching on another carrot stick. His plate was full of raw vegetables.

"Well I love meat man. I dunno how you can eat that shit," said Ted.

"This *shit* is actually very good, you should try it."

"Yeah, many people in Scandinavia are vegans now,' added Carla. The French people spoke in French, tutted, and began to slurp their food down. I chuckled with Chris. Things were going to get hot in the Big Picchu House.

Shortly we were on the trail again, refuelled and raring to go. The crew stayed to clear everything up. We offered to help, but Javi insisted we got a move on. I headed in front with the Argentinean guys, Andre and

Victor. They were from Buenos Aires and loved football. We talked about the Hand of God and they were surprisingly embarrassed.

"We know he cheated, everyone knows that. Winning the cup was not like the best," said Andre.

"I'd have to agree with you there," I said. "That was the first time I cried over a football match, I was only six."

"I am sorry for that," said Andre, "but it's a funny old game."

"How do you know that expression?" I asked.

"We lived in London for three years and watched a lot of football. I love the Arsenal and Andre the Tottenham," said Victor.

"I'm sticking with Andre then. I'm a Spurs supporter," I said. Typical, I was on a four-day trek in the middle of nowhere and I was stuck with an Arsenal fan. Had we been elsewhere we'd probably have spoken more about football but we never mentioned it again.

Time flew by that afternoon (as did the crew running past); we bumbled along the flat path, chatting and enjoying being out in the open. Now and then we'd stop and take photos, enjoy the silence, and marvel at the acres of green mountains.

When we got to the evening campsite, the crew had already set up the tents and marquee on a small flat grass area surrounded by tall trees and a river gushing along. I shared a tent with Ted and Chris, who had been the last to arrive because Chris had been struggling with his ankle after carrying such a heavy load.

"I'm going to die tomorrow man," he said, taking off his sock to reveal his swollen ankle. Javi suggested the crew take a few kilos the next day.

Ted went off to catch a 'massive whale' but returned soaked after he'd fallen in.

"So you didn't catch any dinner then?" asked Borne.

"No, there weren't any vegetables floating around, I'm afraid."

"Maybe next time you should take a gun and shoot them."

"Shut it dickwad," said Ted. His face had tensed and he was moving closer to Borne.

"Okay guys, dinner in twenty minutes," said Javi, keeping the peace

After vegetable soup and potato salad, everyone bombarded Javi about Machu Picchu.

"So what is Machu Picchu all about then?" asked Ted.

"Well, there're a lot of stories of Machu Picchu, so you may have heard different, but it was basically a city built in the fifteenth century by the Incas."

"The fifteenth century?" asked Victor.

"Yes, it is thought that Pachacuti, a powerful Incan leader, built Machu Picchu for his family to live and to spend their holidays."

"Crikey, that's a bit of a walk to go for your holidays," Ted said.

"Yeah, why didn't he just go to the beach?" Chris added.

"Pachacuti is not a man to joke about. His name means 'He who makes the world' and he was a Sapa Inca, or God Emperor, who turned a tribe in Cusco to a huge empire across South America. He didn't have time to go to the beach on holidays," Javi said, calmly.

"So then what happened?" asked Carla.

"Francisco Pizarro, a Spanish conqueror, came with his army to Peru. The Incas were already fighting a civil war, and their army was weak thanks to smallpox. Pizarro conquered the Inca Empire and the Incas fled Machu Picchu leaving it hidden from the world."

"Wow, what no one lived there?" asked Chris.

"It is thought a small group of people lived there, until Hiram Bingham re-discovered it in 1911."

"And now he must be a millionaire," said Ted.

"Well his family maybe," said Borne. "He died in the 50's." He smirked at Ted. Borne had done some reading (unlike the rest of us) and was full of interesting facts.

Javi got us talking about our travel and trekking experiences, but Ted always tried to go one better than the rest. Most of the group retired to bed when Ted stated that he'd bungee jumped off the Grand Canyon. I didn't want to get involved with the petty competitiveness and offered round some rum to the only ones left: Ted, Chris, and Javi. Chris pulled out a litre bottle of vodka too. No wonder he'd been struggling with the weight.

The second day's plan was to reach the highest pass; Warmiwanusca or Dead Woman's Pass, at 4200m.

"With a name like that I reckon we're gonna be in a right mess when we get to the top," I said to the Argentinean lads as we set off on a relatively easy path. It was 7 a.m.

"Don't worry, we will help each other," said Andre, patting me on the back.

"Yes, come on, we are a team now," added Victor.

As usual, the French shot off, but with Borne this time; he was getting sick of Ted. I walked with the Argentinean guys and Carla whereas Javi helped hung over Chris and Ted.

As we got deeper into the trees the path became steeper and more groups of trekkers were battling along. The path turned into wide steps, which became narrower and more difficult to climb and keep balance.

At every corner was a new steeper surprise. The higher we went, the more my legs strained and tighter my lungs felt; the air was fresh, but thin. After an hour of step climbing we paused by an opening so everyone could catch up.

"That's amazing," I said to Carla as we stood looking out over the lush green mountains.

"Yeah, but look up there," she said, pointing towards the next challenge.

"Jesus," Victor said.

"Are they people?" I said. It seemed like small ants wearing backpacks were walking round another mountain. Ted and Chris were unimpressed with how much was ahead.

"Okay everyone, listen please," said Javi. He looked serious. "Now is the hardest part of the trail, what you can see now is nothing, you are going to have to be careful. Don't rush. After this peak you will see another and another until we finally get to Warmiwanusca." Everyone let out a gentle cheer. "We meet there. It's about two hours up hill. Please, be careful, this is where we have most of our injuries. I will stay with Chris. Good luck."

The French couple and Borne were stretching, the Argentinean lads munching on chocolate, Carla was taking photos of the views, and Chris and Ted were slogging back the water. The next bit was going to break all our balls, even the girls' ones.

There were no trees to protect us as we battled along the thin, steep mountain path against the strong wind. I focused ahead, not looking down or over the sheer edge. My calf muscles killed and my back asked to chuck my bag off the side, but I ploughed on. Walking alongside the Argentinean guys and Carla helped numb the pain. We supported and encouraged each other, especially when we thought we'd reached the peak, only to find another long trail.

After climbing a couple of hours, the cloud began to clear and Dead Woman's Pass appeared. Groups of trekkers waved down from the peak, but I had no energy to wave back. As we approached, I felt a mix of relief, joy, and hunger. I'd never climbed so high before. Over fifty trekkers cheered and whooped us to the finish line.

I took a moment for myself and gazed down. The morning's trail headed down into the darkness of the valley and a long line of trekkers were still on their way up. We were, 4,200 meters high, half of Everest.

"Why's it called Dead Woman's Pass anyway?" Ted asked Javi once we were all together. The French couple and Borne looked capable of doing it again, but Chris's ankle was wrecked.

"Its name comes from that part of the mountain there," he said, pointing to a strange bump. "What can you see?"

"A rock," said Carla

"A doughnut," said Ted.

"A tit," said Chris, to which the lads giggled.

"Yes Chris, well done," said Javi, much to our surprise. "That," he said, sprawling his arm out, "is a woman's breast, and is the reason for the name." Carla and the French lady disapproved as we took photos.

The steep walk down was easier, but my legs shook most of the way. The campsite was bigger and noisier than the previous night. We were next to the stinky washrooms and toilets. The amazing crew had already set up camp and tucking into a hot pasta dish over the other side was heaven.

We spent the rest of the day recovering from the morning's hike and getting ready for the third day. It got dark early and most of us were asleep by 9pm, apart from a couple of late night drinkers, present company included.

Despite the rain I loved walking on the original Inca trail on the third day. The path changed and looked more like I'd expected; unevenly bricked grey blocks slammed together with mud. Strolling along the ancient path was more romantic, and the smell of rain reminded me of home, which seemed further away than ever. I was glad to be on an adventure though.

Trekking was less straining as we ploughed our way through the beauty of the trail. We stopped at various ruins where Javi told us about the history, and Ted and Borne argued about the facts.

I spent some moments alone reflecting on the experience, but also time practising my Spanish, and teaching skills, with Victor and Andre. They were top class lads and made the walk interesting.

The only problem was the rain. Thunder and lightning made for some exciting moments, but my shoes and trousers got soaked; the black sacks kept my upper body and bag dry. In the late afternoon the rain eased up when we were about to go down the Inca steps.

"Okay everyone, we are nearly at the end of the third day," said Javi. "Now, you must please be careful on this next section, we are going down the Inca Steps."

"Oooooooooooh," said Ted.

"Yes Ted, especially you," said Javi. Everyone muttered with approval. "These steps will be extremely slippery due to the rain and they are steep. I suggest sticking in pairs or groups. Watch out for each other. We don't want any nasty accidents now do we?"

"I don't know, one would be nice," said Borne, staring at Ted.

"Better watch your back then," said Ted.

"Okay guys, thank you," said Javi. "Good luck, see you at Winay Wanya, the last ruins before our camp for the night."

"Ah yes, Winay Wanya, one of my favourites," Chris said, sarcastically.

As usual, the French were off, leading the way down the steep stone steps, which weren't that slippery, but I still held on.

When we arrived at the last set of ruins, 'Forever young', the sun beamed down on the best sight so far. Green rows of terraces surrounded another ruined city. We were close to camp and everyone was in an ecstatic mood and run about the ruins like a little kids playing hide and seek, apart from Chris whose ankle was still giving him a hard time.

After three days battling through the mountains there were signs of normality: buildings with doors and ceilings, an even and flat floor, and trekkers sat round in a bar drinking beer. The queue for a hot shower was twenty smelly travellers long and I figured another day wouldn't hurt so I went for a hot meal and a pint.

Seeing everyone in a bar was strange. Most looked fresh and clean, the French were sitting still, and Ted and Borne were chatting to each other without angry faces; they'd given up quarrelling.

After a couple of drinks and some food, we chipped in to thank the crew. They were not continuing to Machu Picchu but taking the gear down to the local town, Aguascalientes where they'd catch a train to Cusco. Javi organised an emotional procession. The crew stood in a line outside as we shook hands, cheered, and thanked them. For me, the smiles on their faces said it all. Whether it was because they were happy we were saying thank you, because they'd made it in one piece, or they were getting away from Ted, I was unsure, but they were chuffed.

Getting up at 4am was a struggle, especially after a few beers. I felt knackered, dizzy, and sick. I put it down to the early start and lack of sleep and tried to shrug it off. Machu Picchu waited.

Chaos formed on the final walk; at least two hundred trekkers rushed to arrive at the Sun Gate for sun rise and see Machu Picchu light up. It was still dark, so we were hoping for a clear day, but when we arrived at the Sun Gate thick cloud blocked what was supposed to be one of the best views. It wasn't to be.

As we ploughed on, a long trail of tired trekkers followed behind. As we approached the ruins, the cloud started to lift and a familiar mound *Huayna Picchu* - or young peak in Quechua – stood in the distance. I felt relieved we'd arrived.

I turned and smiled at Andre, who grinned back. Victor and Carla noticed we'd arrived. Everyone was beaming.

"Look at that," I said as we stood on a ledge over the ruins. "We've made it." Machu Picchu stood in full glory, and we'd even beaten the French.

The four of us posed for photos with Harry, he'd done well for a little guy, and I thought back to my auntie.

The site was massive and there was so much to see. Huayna Picchu, the dark mound in the centre, was hypnotic, especially with the wispy clouds racing round. I stood staring for some time before Javi gave us a guided tour. He explained that the site divided into three main parts, the Priest and Noble District, for priests and royalty, the Popular District for the lower class people, and the Sacred District dedicated to the Sun God. The three parts were separated into different sections of terraced ruins sitting on the grassy floor. We followed Javi round, stopping to look out over the valley or at other sections of the Inca Empire.

Then my climax came to a sharp end. I started to feel faint. Javi was doing an excellent job, but my attention span was fading along with my vision. My back started to ache and I felt spaced out. My body was rebelling against the overnight journeys, lack of sleep, and late night drinking sessions.

I forced myself through Javi's two hour guided tour, but by the end I felt totally drained. Most of the group were knackered too, and everyone, even the French, declined the option of walking up Huayna Picchu. It was an anticlimax after such a long trip, but our bodies couldn't take anymore. We just wanted food and to get back to Cusco. It wasn't going to be that easy though.

We caught a bus down to Aguascalientes; a Machu Picchu souvenir town appropriately named for its natural hot springs, and were in a restaurant when Javi dropped the bad news.

"Sorry to stop your fun guys," he said, "but we have a bit of a problem."

"What, no meat?" said Ted.

"No, worse," said Javi. "There has been a landslide and the train track going back to Cusco is blocked. We have to wait until the morning. Go and find some accommodation before the other trekkers find out." Mutters and moans followed as everyone disappeared. I stayed with Javi. My vision became blurred and my back ached more I sat with my head in my hands.

"I think you may have altitude sickness," said Javi.

"You reckon?" I said.

"Yeah, don't worry. You just need food, water, and a good sleep. No beer. You'll be okay tomorrow." I felt terrible.

"You missed a big night," said Ted as we waited for the train back to Cusco the next morning.

"I thought as much, I was out of it though, I slept for almost fifteen hours." I'd missed the final party in the bars in Aguascalientes, but I was revitalised.

Back in Cusco we all said our goodbyes, (apart from the French), swapped emails (even Ted and Borne did, apparently they'd been seen sharing a pint), and I thanked Javi for the excellent tour.

"It was a pleasure," he said as we hugged. "Take it easy next time, not so much beer, you crazy English."

I considered seeing more of Peru, but anything after Machu Picchu would have been an anticlimax. The trek had been an adventure and my confidence had grown. Seeing where the Incas had lived had been interesting, but the highlight had been hiking with people from all around the world.

The trek had taken one more day than I'd expected, so I needed to cut back somewhere. I had to get a move on. That evening I jumped on a bus heading for Lake Titicaca.

## 7 Bolivia: A Mere One Night Stand

I'd heard good things about Bolivia: hospitable locals, cheaper accommodation and food, a bustling historical capital, and an excellent place to visit the Amazon. I was excited about seeing a new country and wanted to relax and fully recover from the altitude sickness. However, just as in Ecuador and Peru, my first day in Bolivia had complications.

"*Donde esta un banco* - Where's a bank?" I said to the hostel owner in Copacabana, Titicaca's lakeside town. I felt drowsy after another sleepless overnight journey, this time because the bus driver's loud trashy pop music had kept me awake. The white haired hostel owner stared and frowned. "*Un banco por favor?*"

"*No banco, no, no,*" he said, wagging his finger. Was he saying there wasn't a bank in Copacabana? I hoped not. After leaving Cusco in a rush I had no money.

"*Banco, no tengo dinero,*" I said, showing him my bank card.

"*Ah, okay,*" he said. I sighed and waited for him to signal where to go. "*No, no banco; problema. No hay luz.*" I thought *luz* meant lights, not electricity. A power cut had struck Copacabana, which meant even the cash points were out of order. What was I going to do?

Luckily, he let me off paying until the next morning, and even leant me $3 worth of *Bolivianos*. I was starving after not eating since Cusco, but settled for some bread so that I could have an evening meal. I refused to let the power cut ruin my day and went down to the lake.

Titicaca is the world's highest lake at just over 3,000 meters above sea level, also known as 'Rock Puma;' *titi* – wildcat or puma, and *karka* - rock. The map of Titicaca is supposed to look like a puma chasing a rabbit - to me it's like a Tyrannosaurus Rex chasing Bart Simpson - either way it's massive.

As I walked downhill passed the red, yellow, and green houses and souvenirs shops, the deep blue reminded me of San Pablo Lake in Otavalo, but a few hundred times the size. The enormity of Titicaca was daunting.

Copacabana was like a beach resort town by the sea: gringos sipped beer outside the bars while enjoying the mild sun, a handful of stray dogs ran about barking and biting each other, and a few tourists dressed in shorts and t-shirts were out on a pedalo.

A couple of Bolivian ladies dressed for winter in colourful shawls and funky little bowler hats were parked on a red stone wall, pointing and laughing at the silly gringos on the funny boat-bike. I sat up from them and ate my bread discreetly so the stray dogs wouldn't come running, but something worse came my way.

A spicy meat smell drifted past. Shaded by a large yellow umbrella, an old guy had sparked up his special Titicaca Kebab stall. Next to him a group of four kids quarrelled as they played table football. Their parents stood waiting for succulent kebabs. The rich smell was too much. I felt poor and hungry, but nothing compared to the many people I'd seen on my travels. Suffering would do me good.

I spotted a few tourists walking up a small hill by the side of the beach and went to explore. In ancient Spanish, Copacabana means 'to see the lake,' which I did from the top of Mount Calvario. The hour stroll up was a breeze after Machu Picchu, and the view over to Isla Del Sol reminded me of Greek islands. The hill is one of the most important religious places in Copacabana and is a popular Christian pilgrimage point.

A group of tubby local women with plump round happy faces gossiped by a wall. I imagined their conversation.

"So what did he say, dear?"

"You'll never guess, apparently the tubby look is back in again."

"How do you know?"

"It was in last week's *Hola* magazine."

"Finally, that will stop him moaning about me losing weight."

"It's about time too, eh? Poor old Javier's Titicaca Kebabs was about to go out of business."

"Yeah, I heard that one of his friends cut the power to force everyone down to get a kebab."

"I'm not complaining, let's get going before he runs out."

The hunger was getting to me.

After traipsing round mountains in Peru, Copacabana was an invigorating change. Seeing water was calming and, even without power or food, the lakeside town was turning into one of my favourite spots.

Back down in the village, I ambled round the grid like streets, took a few photos of the bright white Basillica church, and browsed the many colourful markets. Not once did I feel threatened being alone.

With the mid-afternoon heat, the local's choice of clothes surprised me. The men wore jumpers and jackets, and the women long skirts with a jumper or shawl and a traditional bowler hat. Were they expecting a sudden snowstorm? And why were most of them overweight? I thought Bolivia was one of South America's poorest countries.

I finished my afternoon by Titicaca. Sitting next to the highest lake in the world was a strange sensation. How had a lake like Titicaca arrived to the middle of South America? It would have been interesting to put the scene into rewind and watch Copacabana form around Titicaca, a marvellous natural sight.

As a reward for starving myself all day, I stumbled on a restaurant that accepted credit cards using the swipe system. Fresh trout with potatoes, salad, and a couple of cold beers sorted me out; no wonder the people in Copacabana were a little on the heavy side.

The electricity was back on in the morning. I settled with the owner, gave him a few extra Bolivianos to say thank you, and then squeezed into a small van heading to La Paz, the capital, about four hours away. I would have stayed longer, maybe just to try one of the delicious smelling kebabs, but I had to move on.

In La Paz, which means 'the peace' in Spanish, I had a miserable experience. The journey out of Titicaca was uncomfortable. I was cramped up in a van full of hefty Bolivianos wearing too many clothes and blocking the view with their bowler hats (In the 1920's railway workers from Britain set off the bowler hat trend in Bolivia). The only person not wearing a hat was Vincent, from Geneva.

"Where're you off to?" I asked the short, dark haired chap. We'd stopped by a river formed by the edge of Titicaca to cross over on a long canoe.

"Le Paz," he said in a French accent. He told me he'd been travelling round Bolivia and Peru for a couple of months and had already been to Le Paz. He was going back to meet friends.

"You can stay in the same hostel as me if you like; there is a great night life in Le Paz."

Once over the river, we squeezed into another tiny van and scrunched along the rocky roads to Le Paz. Over the jerky four-hour drive, the sky turned greyer and more shantytowns appeared. I felt sorry for the lost looking Bolivianos, who were skinnier than those blessed with the luck of living by the glorious trout filled Titicaca.

As we circled down into the capital, the size of Le Paz startled me. The snow capped mountains in the distance made me feel romantic, but as we declined into the pit of shacks and battered buildings I feared what lay ahead.

When the driver pulled up in a small, dirty, hectic plaza I was relieved Vincent was there; I had no idea where we were on my map. Fear memories of Quito crept back. I wish I'd known then I was going to have a shit time.

Le Paz was hectic and I took an instant disliking. Perhaps it was the moody cab driver, the thick polluted air, or the dirty residence we stayed at near *Calle Zoilo Flores*, but I'd hoped for a more peaceful capital after Titicaca. At least the hostel was only one pound per night.

Vincent offered to be my Le Paz guide. I thought back to Marta, the dwarf-like woman in Lima, and hoped he had different intentions; from what I'd seen of Le Paz I preferred not to walk alone.

As we walked down Sagamaga Street, stopping at a few textile and leather markets, I felt unsafe as strangers brushed close. Since Quito I hadn't worried about muggers, but when we got to the chaotic Plaza San Francisco, Vincent put me on edge.

"Don't speak to anyone here," he said, looking around as if on the run. "There are a lot of tricksters who will try to fool you." He told me that pranksters would flash a fake policeman's badge and ask to see my passport and nick it.

"It happened to a friend of mine. He was stuck here for almost three weeks." I gazed around the plaza; the brown San Francisco church was on one side, cars and buses whizzed round tooting and parping, dodgy blokes strolled about casually glimpsing at us. In three weeks I wanted to be in Salvador, not stuck in mental Le Paz.

"Come on, I'll take you to Plaza Murillo, it's safer," he said, seeing I was anxious.

Plaza Murillo was less chaotic with less potential criminals and we could hear ourselves think. On one side was the yellow and white congress building, the main political hub of Bolivia. On another side were the Burned Palace and Cathedral.

"That has been burned down many times," said Vincent, pointing to the darker yellow and white President's Palace. The Union monument in the centre surrounded by pigeons flapping about reminded me of Trafalgar Square. A few local families and couples strolled round, enjoying the slightly warmer afternoon. It seemed a sociable place; but I could think of a better one.

"Fancy a beer?" I asked.

"Sure, why not? I need something to eat first."

He stopped at a street stall to get a kebab, but the meat looked undercooked.

"You sure about eating that," I said.

"I am used to it now," he said, taking a bite. Grease oozed down his hand. "I've been eating from the street for two months, no problem," he said as we walked off. I sounded like a sissy, what would Ted have said? But I made the right decision.

A few beers later Senor Tough-Guts was having doubts about his digestive abilities.

"Let's get a cab back to the hostel," he said.

"What? It's only seven, the night is young," I said; keen to have a few more beers.

"I don't feel too good, you can go out near the hostel," he said. He did look white, so we left. When we got back, Vincent rushed into the loo and returned ten minutes later holding his arse.

"That was sick, I'm going to bed."

The beers had reduced my inhibitions and I fancied checking out the nightlife. Vincent recommended the streets behind the hostel, but after a quick walk up and down Sagamaga I realised there was more nightlife at the top of Mount Calvario on a cold winter's night. I ate a creamy lasagne, downed a couple of beers, and went to bed, feeling fine and hoping to explore Le Paz more the next day.

But I got sick again. I woke up in the middle of the night hot, sweating, and my back ached; just like after Machu Picchu. Had the lasagne been dodgy, or was it altitude sickness again? I took a couple of paracetamols and went back to sleep.

In the morning, I heard Vincent telling someone how much his arse hurt. I couldn't face peering from under the covers, what if he was showing him? I went back to sleep.

When they left I tried to sit up but felt dizzy, nauseous, and my back ached even more. I finally got up sixteen hours after I'd gone to bed. I dragged my weak body into the shower, got dressed, and went out to get some food and water. After a slow dizzy walk round the back streets and suffering on emails trying to sound jolly to my family back home, I went back to bed.

"You have altitude sickness," said Vincent that evening. "We are three thousand five hundred meters high. It is common here, many people get sick."

I was annoyed at getting ill again and being further behind schedule. I desperately wanted to do a jungle trek, but that meant going north and I felt unfit.

"That will be a bit crazy," said Vincent. "Go in Brazil, you will be ready then."

So that was the end of Le Paz. I never found out if the mental capital had any charm. From the little I had seen I was unimpressed, and for a capital whose name actually means 'the peace' it was far from tranquil.

The following morning, still feeling dizzy and weak, I caught a bus to Cochabamba, five hours away. By the time we'd arrived via a valley after an action free bus journey, I felt better. The sun glistened off a small lake and there was a hill towards the right, the rest of the land was flat, finally. Taxi drivers waited outside the bus, but they smiled and nodded when I declined. A hostel owner welcomed me as if we'd been pen friends for years.

"How nice meet you finally," he said, almost pulling me over while shaking my hand. "England England, David Beckham."

After crazy Le Paz, adjusting to the calmness of Cochabamba was easy. As I strolled round Cochabamba's grid like streets, I had a bizarre feeling of relief, as if I could finally relax after being on the go since Quito. The city was still 2,500 meters above sea level, but the air seemed less dense to breathe.

Cochabamba is famous for its year round spring temperature, and the trees and flowers in bloom at Plaza 14 de Septiembre filled the air with a sweet fragrance. Like most squares in South America, a cathedral stood in the corner and old locals gossiped as hungry pigeons pecked for scraps.

Round the back streets a group of attractive, perhaps posh, younger adults waited outside an English Academy. I was tempted to see if the director had any jobs; maybe I could have stayed a couple of months.

I must have been missing climbing because I wandered towards the Cristo De La Concordia; a statue of Christ on a hill outside the centre. A cablecar was available but I trekked up the spiralled stone steps. The dry and hot afternoon made tough climbing; I was glad it had been raining at Machu Picchu.

Just as I was beginning to wonder why Cochabamba was so safe, three flustered German tourists paced down the steps. A rock clanked against the floor and another flew past my foot. Rather than turn back, which I would have done a month before, I continued. I felt stronger and refused to believe danger existed in Cochabamba. Another rock whizzed past my foot and I caught a glimpse of young boy's head ducking behind a bush; he looked harmless.

I pushed on to a bend where three ten-year old lads stood holding rocks. The wide smiles on their grubby faces suggested they were just having a laugh. I held my hands up in defence and they smirked. One lad asked for money but I just smiled and continued. I turned back a few times, but soon they'd run off. In Le Paz, they probably would have had knives and guns.

I was sweaty and thirsty at the top, but glad I'd battled up and squeezed among the crowds. The huge white statue of Christ stood proud with his arms stretched out as if summoning rain. The Christ is a smidgen taller than the one in Rio de Janeiro. They are both thirty-three meters to represent Jesus' death age, but Cochabamba's is a bit taller because Bolivians believe Jesus died slightly older than thirty-three. That's why it's the largest statue of Christ in the world.

The statute might have been taller, but the view in Rio had to be more inspiring. Maybe if I had seen Cochabamba before Machu Picchu it would have been more impressive, but all that caught my eye was the lake on the left.

After I'd chilled by the lake for a couple of hours and got lost in some dull markets, I headed back to the hostel. I wanted to liven up my time in Cochabamba. I took a long hard look in the mirror. I was hairy. My dodgy travellers beard had gone past the irritating itchy stage, but the rise in temperature was making it annoying. I hacked away with my tiny mirror and blunt scissors until I had a moustache.

If I had been in England, I wouldn't have lasted five minutes with my mates. I looked like a smarmy porn star, or worse, one of the 118 guys. Fortunately, I was in a peaceful town in Bolivia where no one cared if I looked like a seventy's disco freak. The tash stayed and I went for an evening meal.

I felt cocky walking through the cobbled streets. An elderly lady stared as I bowled past her stall.

"Got your number," I said, clicking my fingers and winking. She smiled back, oblivious to my terrible impersonation.

A fine breeze blew as I reached Plaza 14 de Septiembre, and the locals of Cochabamba looked as though they'd been to a wedding. Men in suits and women in long dresses waltzed round while their children ran about playing. Grandfathers wore ties and accompanied their elegant better halves. Even the dogs and cats looked groomed.

I found a place to eat behind the plaza where a young waitress smiled as she showed me to a table in the corner. Maybe she was partial to facial hair. With her dyed red locks, blue eyes, and long legs she looked more Russian than Bolivian. This had the making of a corny porn movie. My imagination slipped into a naughty frenzy.

"Good evening Sir, how may I be of assistance on this hot night?" she said, huskily.

"Well Señorita," I said, stroking my *bigote*. "I need something strong. I am very hungry and need to eat something to boost my energy." She giggled.

"Well Señor, I can recommend the sausage; I am a big fan of the sausage," she said, gazing me up and down.

"In that case, I shall have...," then a voice snapped me out of it.

"*Si Señor*," said her old and wrinkled mother. "*Que te pongo*," she added briskly, wiping her wet hands on her dirty top.

"*Pescado, por favor.*" I stuck with the fish.

After my meal, the plaza was bustling with dolled up locals. A large crowd had gathered around a young magician dressed in a white suit.

He too had a hairy handle bar and performed the usual stunts: flowers from his sleeve, card tricks, and a finger guillotine stunt. He finished by pulling a tiny black kitten from under his coat and gave it to one of the kids.

On the other side of the square a different crowd had formed around a small group of teenagers performing a funky dance. They were dressed in 80's clothes dancing to 90's dance music. The audience bounced about and clapped. I joined in for a bit, but tiredness kicked so I retired to my room and fell asleep watching Lethal Weapon 2, in Spanish. That was my excitement.

The next morning the tash came off and I was relieved to see my upper lip again. I chilled out on emails, read in the plaza, by the lakes, and in a restaurant. By the end of the day I was ready to leave. I'd enjoyed quiet Cochabamba and felt safe, but I preferred more action. Brazil had to be more exciting. I was determined to continue my quest to Salvador and settle down again.

The highest hurdles were still to jump though. The bus journey to Santa Cruz began well. We stopped at a few delightful towns and I dozed off while watching an orange sunset light up an open field.

Then the problems began.

The noise of commotion and panicking voices woke me up. We'd stopped by the side of the road and the driver was ordering off the passengers. People shone torches outside. I thought about the guidebook's gangsters warning. Travellers had been kidnapped on the way to Santa Cruz before. I panicked, hid my money belt, and followed the crowd off the bus.

Outside, dim moonlight lit up the chaos. Furious Bolivians were moaning and shouting at the driver while snatching their bags from underneath and darting along the road away from the bus. No threatening gangsters with guns were in sight, but I remained on edge. I strapped on my rucksack and followed the crowd along the road until we came to what felt like a field.

"*Donde vamos* - Where are we going?" I asked a young lad.

"*Por alli* - Over there," he said, pointing into the darkness.

"*Donde vamos?*" I asked another lady.

"*El rio,* - the river," she replied. I kept slipping on the wet grass. I was confused, tired, and irritable. A river trickled past in the distance. A queue formed and everyone put down their bags and waited. We shuffled forward occasionally, but it was bewildering.

After half an hour, the sun started to rise. I craved water for my dry mouth. The huge queue of angry bus passengers started moaning when they noticed the bridge had collapsed. A large heap of rumble was on either side (there were no dead bodies). Luckily, a few thin canoes waited at the river bank to transport everyone.

The speed with which they transported us in the canoes and loaded us up on the new bus was impressive. You wouldn't catch National Express doing that if there was a problem with a bridge in England. As we drove along the final flat stretch the long line of palm trees gave it a tropical feel. I slept.

I started on bad terms with Santa Cruz, but it was my fault. Despite a warning from the bus driver that the centre was over an hour walk, I tried to head in the vague direction to save the cab fare. After thirty minutes traipsing in the blistering heat along a noisy main road I gave in. I was lost, roasting, and in a foul mood.

The taxi driver dropped me off outside a hostel with a courtyard out the back where travellers were hanging out smoking gear and sunbathing. Normally I might have chatted, but I hid in my room and tried to wind down. The broken fan, lack of cold running water, and lumpy bed didn't help. To top off my bad temper, I realised I had to get to the train station, a couple of kilometres away, in order to reserve a ticket to Brazil for the following day.

An hour and a half later, after a hot and stuffy local bus detoured round Santa Cruz's circular streets, a large group of tricksters waited at the train station's entrance. Did I want a cheap ticket? Did I want to get a first class seat half price? Did I know that the ticket office had closed down? Well the answer was "No I didn't, and go screw yourself." I'd become wiser and stronger. I bought a ticket to Corumba, Brazil, refused to speak to any of the tricksters as I came out, and caught a cab back to the centre.

That was when I started to like Santa Cruz. I calmed down and was up for exploring so headed straight for Plaza 24 de Septiembre. I'd ranked up a number of plaza visits, but this square was unique. Not because of the cathedral, sheltering green trees, or spotlessly clean pavements, but the women (come on, I'm allowed some shallow moments).

As I walked past a café I gazed inside and had to double take.

"Nah, that can't be true," I thought. "Not in Bolivia." The women were amazing, and if I had been a woman, then the men wouldn't have been bad either. A group of mid-twenty year olds dressed in white, perfectly tanned, and remarkably good-looking, were chatting and flirting with each other. The group of gorgeous women were like something out of Beverly Hills 90210, a type of Boliviawood. Perhaps I *could* stay and set up a school.

Since then, I've read that Santa Cruz is one of the wealthiest cities in Bolivia and the major fashion and modelling area. The women have a special beauty pageant in which the rest of Bolivia aren't allowed to enter (not that they'd stand a chance) and they call their town *La Capital de la Belleza Amazonia* - The Capital of the Amazon Beauty; slightly arrogant, but deserved.

I didn't want to get arrested for gawping so I continued. As it was a Sunday, there was little to see in the quiet centre. I walked round a couple of dull markets and the deserted circular roads, but the heat got to me so I went back for a siesta.

In the evening I went out for my last night in a Spanish speaking country (for a while anyway). The plaza was alive with kids shouting and running about, and the good-looking gang were still posing, proud of their beauty. Had they ever seen the shantytowns in Le Paz or the bowler hat people in Copacabana? I doubted it. Maybe they were happy in their own little world, who was I to judge.

In a restaurant just off the square, I sat surrounded by exotic plants and white candles in a blue patio and enjoyed my last meal of soup with chicken and rice, washed down with some cool beers. I hoped I would be able to use Spanish to communicate in Brazil. Spanish had become my friend and protector and I was enjoying being away from England. My previous life felt like a distant nightmare.

The next morning, I made the most of Spanish and got my haircut. I'd felt fine getting it cut in Mexico and Ecuador, but awkward in the flashy Bolivian barbers. The swanky male hairdresser kept stopping and cracking jokes to the other lads waiting. I couldn't understand them. I guessed they were laughing at the unfashionable gringo with the funny accent, but I cared not.

After one final walk, some emails, and lunch, I caught a cab to the station. A few Brazilians lingered about. They seemed louder, more confident, and their nasal accents were strange. Chilling on the wide train seat and stretching my legs was a relief after the bus journeys. As the train departed, I thought back to The Lord and Marcus and imagined what they would have been like on a train to Brazil. No doubt making rude comments about how many Brazilian women they were going to pull.

I only knew Bolivia on a mere one night-stand basis. I was disappointed I'd got ill and had to miss out the jungle. The highs were the views at Lake Titicaca, recovering from Le Paz in Cochabamba, and seeing the best looking women in Boliviawood.

I was craving something more exciting and, Brazilian. I'd been looking forward to the exploring the biggest country in South America and embarking on a new adventure. I was aware of the dangers and conflicts, but, naively, felt more prepared.

## 8 Brazil: Rio de Janeiro – From High to Low

I travelled non-stop from Santa Cruz to Rio in two days. Once at the roasting Brazilian border in Corumba I caught a modern, powerfully air conned bus to Campo Grande. As I waited for my next bus in the stuffy station, I noticed a distinct change in the people. Brazilians were super hyperactive. A group of lads and girls in their late teens were prancing about practising for what I imagined were their carnival dances. They spoke and laughed louder than anyone I'd seen in South America. They seemed high on life, excited about their overnight bus trip. Luckily I was on a different bus to the manic group and slept for most of my journey to Sao Paolo.

I only saw Sao Paolo from the bus window, but I wasn't bothered about skipping through the massively built up city made up of four lane motorways and enormous skyscrapers. The traffic was horrendous and the smoggy grey sky aided my decision to whizz on.

The closer we got to Rio de Janiero, the more excited I felt. Until we drove through a rundown and corrupt black market outside Rio's *rodoviaria* (bus station) and those gutsy nerves came knocking. Rio had a nasty reputation for being dangerous, with drug and gun trafficking problems.

Once off the bus, I ploughed through the hectic crowd of sweaty Brazilians shouting at each other and headed for the information desk, where the assistant persuaded me to splash out on a hostel in Ipanema.

"A special bus will take you to the door. You can get it from there," he said, pointing a few metres away to a bus stop; anything to avoid the dodgy market outside. "There's a special caipiriña night tonight, free drinks from 8pm." Sold.

Rio seemed much safer away from the station. Parents strolled about with their kids, young couples in love walked hand in hand, and there were no gangsters wearing bandanas patrolling the neighbourhoods. Cruising through Rio's modern streets was uplifting and a glimpse of the sea boosted my adrenaline further.

The hostel in Ipanema was trendy. Smart white and brown leather sofas dotted round the pine floored reception, plush tables and chairs were set out for the buffet breakfast, and the rooftop pool was rammed with gorgeous ladies wearing thongs. Okay, they weren't in the pool, but they were on Ipanema beach.

I was unsure where to look first: at the view across the bay towards the cliffs in the distance, far out across the rough, cold sea, or at the amazing Brazilian women showing their pert bums. I'll leave you to guess.

Ipanema beach was active. Toned up and tanned young women lounged around listening to their ghetto blasters while Brazilians dudes strutted about in their tight Speedos doing aerobatic stunts. Heaps of reggae style lads selling bracelets and necklaces marched up and down pestering sunbathers.

The fresh sea looked appetising but a few crafty lads lurked about so I lay on my towel; sweaty and hot. I felt out of place on such a hip beach with my pasty white body. I'd get a tan though; I'd be in Brazil for a while.

I went back to the centre and strolled round the streets behind the beach. Flashy convertibles whizzed past with smart couples behind the wheel wearing designer sunglasses, women shoppers tottered about wearing skimpy clothes, and there were no suspicious characters. I began to relax.

Then I went from an absolute high to a disastrous low.

**The High**

I ventured back to the hostel and spruced up ready for the free caipiriña. I arrived early, ordered a beer, and stood by the bar. The only other traveller waiting was a short chubby balding lad reading on one of the sofas.

"Hi, can I sit here?" I said.

"All right mate, sure," he replied. That was odd, his accent sounded familiar. "How you doing?"

"Yeah, not bad, mate, you?" I said.

"Yeah, wicked." He grinned and chuckled. Wicked? No one had said "wicked" to me since home.

"Wicked yeah, where you from?" I asked.

"London, well, Watford."

"Don't fuck about," I said. "That's just up the road from me."

"Where're you from?" He sat up and rubbed his forehead.

"Harrow, well, you know Eastcote?"

"Don't fuck about, yeah, I know. Shit that's quite close to me," he said, laughing. We were miffed. Nish had also been working in sales in London and was on a round the world trip. We'd even travelled to the same places and had a similar on-going itinerary. The coincidences became weirder.

"So what Uni did you go to?" he asked.

"Southampton."

"Don't fuck about," he said. His jaw dropped.

"Why, did you?" I said. He nodded. We were both laughing. "What's your name?" I asked.

"Nish," he said. I told him mine and we shook hands again. We had been in the same year at University; Nish had studied Politics while I studied Economics.

"I spent most of my time in a bar called Avondale," I said. "I worked there."

"You worked in Avondale House?" he asked.

"Yeah for two years. Why?"

"I worked there for a bit too?"

"Don't fuck about," I said. Then it clicked. We'd worked a couple of shifts together and knew half a dozen of the same people.

Nish was also intending to go to Salvador for the Carnival. There was a reason that we'd met again. Perhaps it was fate.

After I'd sunk a few caipiriñas, and Nish a couple of guaranas, we went for a drink by the beach. The night breeze had become chilly, waves crashed down on the shore and bars along the promenade were full of locals and tourists. A group of lads were playing Foot volley on a section of the beach lit up by some small floodlights.

"How do they keep the ball up like that?" said Nish, sipping his coconut through a stripy red straw.

"They're Brazilian, aren't they? This isn't Watford, you know, mate."

"Very funny smart arse."

The coincidence of bumping into someone I'd worked with at University was incredible. After travelling on my own for five months, meeting someone with a similar background was comforting. For the first time in a long while I remembered who I was. I'd missed that British banter of being able to take the piss and not feel insulted. We decided that the next day we'd explore Rio together.

"Come on you lazy bastard," I said, waking up Nish.

"What time is it?" He groaned.

"Rio time," I said, smacking him on the back.

After a fruit cocktail breakfast and some advice from the chap on reception, we caught a local bus to the base of Corcovado Mountain and then a taxi to the top to see *O Cristo Redentor* – Christ the Redeemer.

As we whizzed round the sheltered mountain roads, glimpses of the city below flashed through the trees.

"This'll probably be one of the best views of our trip mate," said Nish. As we got out of the taxi at the top behind the giant white statue the wind rustled my hair. We ignored the hordes of tourists pushing and barging each other and followed the path round the statue towards a patio in front and squeezed into a decent spot along the wall so we could gaze over Rio. Down below the sun reflected off the buildings, glorious beaches glistened, and the dark blue sea sparkled.

"This is wicked mate. Now I feel like I'm in Brazil" said Nish, grinning. "It's a magical place, but not as good as Machu Picchu."

"I agree, there was no challenge to get here, but Rio must be an amazing place to live."

We stayed for a while and defended our place from a bunch of nervy Italians. I felt glad I'd met Nish; travelling alone was challenging, but some places were better with a companion.

"Good to share this moment with you, Nish."

"Yeah."

"It's been tough travelling on my own."

"Yeah, I know what you mean."

"Yeah, I've had no one to take any photos of me, do the honours."

"Cheeky git."

Half an hour's taxi ride later we were in a cablecar rising up to the top of *Pao de Acucar*, or Sugar Loaf. The four hundred meter high mountain is a monolith; a single mass of rock.

"This is pretty unstable eh?" I said as the carriage creaked along the thick wire cables.

"Yeah, it's packed too. Imagine if it snapped now."

"Don't mate," I said, slapping his bald head. Half way up, we changed cablecars and then arrived at the summit.

"Copacabana is supposed to be one of the longest commercial beaches in the world," said Nish as we lent on a wall gazing along the beach. Along the right were hotels and flats, sunbathers dotted the sand, and the sea stretched out towards the left.

We walked around the enormous loaf of sugar, stopped for a drink, and breathed in the fresh air.

"Why don't you stay here and find a job?" asked Nish.

"It's more expensive and I think you need the right papers. I've heard it's easier to get work in Salvador."

"I love it here though man; it's like London but with a beach and fitter women."

We caught a bus back to Ipanema, changed, and went down to the beach. The same hip and trendy young crowd were baking in the sun.

"Now you're here I can take a dip," I said, running off. I hadn't been in the sea since Ecuador and the temperature on this side of South

America was a lot bloody colder. We chilled out like a couple of beach bums and waited for the sunset.

"That's gotta be one of the best sunsets I've seen man," Nish said as the orange sun dipped behind a small cliff face at the end of the beach leaving behind a trail of dark orange.

Compared to the previous day alone on the beach I felt much more relaxed. I tried to imagine travelling with someone all the time, but that adrenaline edge would have disappeared. Nish agreed that some places were better to travel alone, but Rio, with its dodgy reputation, was definitely one to explore with someone else. If only he had come with me to the bus station the next day.

That evening we settled in a swanky bar along from the beach and sat in the corner by a round wooden table.

"You sure we're allowed in here with sandals?" I asked.

"Chill man, we got in, didn't we?" Nish said, sipping his third coconut of the day.

"Yeah but look," I said, pointing to the immaculately dressed clientele. Everyone was dressed in designer gear. "I feel out of place."

"Shut up and get another drink down ya," Nish said. "If we were in a flashy bar like this in London you'd only be able to buy a quarter of a pint for the same price. You'll soon forget that you look like a trampy traveller anyway."

We spoke about the Carnival; we were excited about seeing the madness in Salvador. We'd heard the music was less commercial, atmosphere more bohemian, and prices cheaper than Rio. We needed a place to stay and I promised to help out Nish.

"We better not end up in some dodgy shit hole," said Nish.

"How much do you wanna pay though?" I said. "You know the prices are gonna rocket. All I want is a floor and a bed."

"Trust me to meet Mr. Pikey to sort out my accommodation."

"Don't worry mate, I've never let you down before."

"You haven't needed to, yet."

I wanted to stay in Rio longer, but my money was running low and I needed to find a flat and a job. We walked back to the hostel because I had to get up early to catch my last bus to Salvador.

"I'll see you in a couple of weeks then," I said. Nish was planning to travel some more before joining me. "Have a good one."

"Yeah, good luck with the jobs."

"Cheers baldy, take it easy on the coconuts."

"Yeah I will. And you be careful," Nish said, laughing, "don't get mugged."

If only he'd known.

**The Low**

I woke up buzzing. I had company for the Carnival, Rio had been fantastic, and I'd *almost* made it to Salvador without any major problems.

"No way, I'm not getting out here!" I said to the taxi driver. He was insisting I get out next to the nasty black market. "Take me to the bus station entrance."

"*Nao, Nao,*" he said, pushing me out the door. I haven't paid up front for a taxi since.

Thinking back he could have set me up. I kept my head down and paced along the pavement past the rotten smelling market. Men were shouting from behind the wired fence on my left. I felt someone behind. I daren't look and trotted to the station. Once inside, I checked behind. I was safe.

After buying my ticket to Salvador I had twenty minutes spare. I relaxed, put the ticket in my bag, not wanting to draw attention to my money belt, and bought a ham baguette from a quiet cafe at the back of the station. There were a lot of free seats and I chose a high circular table in the middle of the waiting area. I rested my rucksack against the leg of the table and put my smaller bag by my feet (I normally kept my small bag hanging from my front, but there were only a couple of harmless families about, or so I thought).

I was excited about getting to Salvador. The journey from Quito had been fun, but I was ready to settle down again and find some work. On the final trip I'd planned on catching up on my diary, which I normally kept in my rucksack.

"Pssst, pssst," said a voice from behind. The quick sound startled me. I kept my head down. Why would anyone want to speak with me? I continued eating.

"Pssst, pssst." Don't look back, don't look back, I told myself.

After a minute, I felt a tap on my shoulder. My heart started racing. I turned my head. A small white lad with a bum fluff tash wearing a blue baseball hat smirked. He was only about thirteen.

"You, you," he said, waving a note in my face.

"*Nao, nao,*" I said, about to turn round.

"You, you," he said quickly, pointing to the floor. Had I dropped some money? I'd just put a note in my pocket so maybe I had. He forced the note in my hand, smiled, and walked away.

Strange kid, I thought as I put the note on the table and bit from my baguette. I looked at the note; ten Euros? But I was in Brazil. I glimpsed down. Something was different. My large rucksack was lying flat on the floor.

I'd been done.

I felt nauseous, tense, and my heartbeat sped up. He couldn't have? I didn't? No. The little wanker! My small bag, which I'd put down for the first time in three weeks, was gone.

I span round. The boy was pacing off round a corner.

"OIIIIIII," I shouted, putting on my large rucksack and legging towards him. There was no use; more people had filled out the walkway and I lost him as I turned the corner. My fucking camera!

I realised that someone else must have nicked my bag as he was distracting me so I sprinted back to the café. I asked the waitresses and families sitting about but no one had seen anything. I was extremely hacked off.

How could I have been so stupid? Everything had gone in a flash. What hurt most was losing my diary and the photos of Machu Picchu, Bolivia, and Rio. My Auntie would never see the photos of me and Harry. I'd have to email someone from the trip, but wait; my address book was gone too, and what about my bus ticket?

I'd been done good and proper.

I bolted up to the ticket office. Surely they'd let me on anyway.

"*Perdona, alguien me ha robado, mi mochilla, mi billete,*" I said frantically, trying to explain to the distraught assistant.

"Ah, okay, okay," she said, looking behind for someone with authority.

"*Necesito nuevo billette, por favour,*" I said, asking for a new ticket. She told me how much.

"*Que?* I'm not paying again," I said. "Don't you understand; someone has nicked my ticket?" It was no use; I needed proof from the police.

The police, of course, maybe they could find the fucker. I had to get some sort of document for my insurance anyway. I kissed goodbye to the bus heading to Salvador, the next one was in eight hours, and went in search of a copper.

An old acquaintance helped me.

"Hey mate, you remember me?" I asked the lad at the information desk.

"Yeah sure, how's it going?"

"Bad."

Within five minutes, he was translating everything to two sturdy coppers.

"You need to go with them to the tourist station and fill a report, and then maybe you can get your bus ticket," he said. "I'm sorry man, this happens all the time round here, it's not a nice place."

The coppers whizzed me round the streets of Rio to the tourist police station and within two hours I was back, pleading for a new free bus ticket.

"What, *porque no?*" I said to the bus company manager showing him proof that I'd been robbed.

"Company policy; it's not our fault," he told me, in Spanish. I bought another ticket.

The girl who dealt with me must have felt sympathetic as she never put through the credit card transaction (which I found out a month later after it failed to show up on my bill). Not everyone that day was being a wanker.

I felt the lowest on my trip so far. I had to wait six hours for the next bus and another twenty-six hours until Salvador without anything to listen to or read. The worst part was that I'd arrive in Salvador at night without a map or any idea where to go.

I was furious and kept retracing my steps. The mugging had happened so quick, who nicked the bag? Had the cabbie been in on the scam? It was probably better I had lost bum fluff boy; god knows what weapon he could have had.

I'd been done by the pros of Rio.

For the first time in six months I wanted to be home. I wanted to be safe. I still felt revved up when I boarded the bus; book-less, music-less, soul destroyed and thoroughly pissed off. I saw everyone as a threat, even other passengers. I trusted no one. What would Nish say? Don't get mugged indeed. Forget the fear of returning home, I had a new fear; Brazil.

## 9 Salvador: The Hectic Build Up To Carnival

I spent the journey gazing out the window trying to get a grip. It was difficult though; if I'd been a bag of nerves after Quito, how was I going to be in Salvador knowing how quickly your life could change?

The thought of arriving at night worried me. I had no cash, no guide book, and no idea where the bus station was with respect to the centre. After the incident in Rio I felt like a lonely boy who'd lost his mummy.

When we stopped for petrol I was having a stretch when a tanned Brazilian looking lad with long brown hair approached me. I'd seen him on the bus chatting up some Italian looking woman. Not more hassle.

"Got a light, mate?" he said in a Mancunian accent.

"Sorry?" I said. Surely he was Brazilian.

"A light, do you have a light, mate?" he said. He smiled while the fag hung out his mouth.

"Sorry mate, no. Are you English?"

"Yeah man, you too?"

"Yeah, I thought you were Brazilian, who's that Italian girl you're with?"

"That's Lucy, my bird; she's English as well, mate."

"Blimey," I said, offering a hand. "am I glad to meet some English people."

"We thought you were some irritable French bloke, you looked well pissed off yesterday."

"Yeah I was, still am; someone nicked my bag."

"That explains it."

Joe and Lucy were also heading to Salvador for the Carnival. They were a top couple and lent me a guidebook for the remainder of the journey and also promised to share a cab to the centre. Things were looking up.

When we arrived in Salvador night had fallen.

"I'm not getting on another bus in a hurry, I'll tell you that," said Lucy as she slammed the taxi door shut. She was also from Manchester, in her late twenties, blonde, and seemed a good match for Joe.

We left the bus station and sped along a motorway. As we approached the centre I felt relieved I'd met them. We pulled off the main road down some cobbled streets and the taxi vibrated.

"So where're we heading?" I asked.

"The historical centre," replied Joe. "It's supposed to be the best place to stay, it's called Pelourinho."

"Not sure if I like this," said Lucy as a few rough looking blokes peered in the window.

"Don't worry love, the book says its fine," replied Joe. I shared the same sentiments as Lucy; the bag incident had put me on edge.

Pelourinho, which means pillory or a form of punishment, was, not surprisingly, dark and menacing. We stopped at the bottom of a wide steep plaza, which acted as a crossroads to the dimly lit streets. All the buildings had their doors shut and lights out. The only people walking about were homeless men getting comfortable for the night.

"You sure about this area?" I asked Joe.

"Yeah, apparently this is the happening place, it is Sunday don't forget, you hungry?"

We were starving, but after we'd checked into the hostel and ambled up the steep plaza, along one of the cobbled side streets to another extensive, flatter plaza with a spooky cathedral to the right, we realised that everything was shut. I was glad to get to bed, even if I was in a dorm with five others.

The 1st of February, and I'd made it in time to start job hunting before the Carnival. Nightmares about getting mugged in the dark streets of Pelourinho left me crabby and anxious on my first morning though.

Joe and Lucy were tucking into the buffet breakfast of fresh strawberries, cubes of mango, chunky bread, and sweet orange juice.

"Have you been outside yet?" asked Lucy. She seemed radiant.

"No not yet," I said, dreading returning to the quiet spooky plaza. I downed a cold glass of juice.

"Well, you'll love it. It's not as bad as last night," she said. "The plaza is alive, it's so colourful, and there's a great feeling in the air. I can't wait for Carnival." She kissed Joe on the lips.

"All right luv," he said, elbowing her off. "It's still ten days away, calm down, will ya? What you doing today, Bazza?"

"Finding a job, I need to get sorted before the Carnival starts, my money's running thin." Joe showed me the nearest tourist office and his map and we arranged to meet up back at the hotel that evening.

Pelourinho had transformed. From the bottom of Praça - plaza - José de Alencar the dark dreary buildings had turned into bright yellow, blue, green, and even pink vibrant shops and flats. They looked ancient though, and with the cobbled streets Pelourinho seemed a century behind Rio.

A group of taxi drivers pestered me and a couple of lads wearing tattered clothes asked me for money as I paced across the plaza. Carnival music poured out the clothes and souvenir shops while happy smiling black men wearing white cotton trousers and colourful shirts waved me in. I smiled shyly and ploughed on to the tourist office.

So where exactly was I? Pelourinho was at the top of the bay, or Bahia as Salvador is better known. The surrounding area was much larger than Quito and I felt intimidated about finding a job. I went back down to the hostel and borrowed the yellow pages, dotted out the language academies, and set off.

The walk back up the steep slopes in the sizzling heat made me sweat. I sat on the steps of the cathedral and gazed over the pretty *Praça da Se*. A spiked metal fence surrounded a fountain in the middle. Foreigners bumbled about as if inside a weird fairytale square. Brazilian women, or *Baianas*, wearing long white dresses, making their bums look chunky, tottered after the tourists to get their photos taken for money.

A group of athletic black guys wearing only white tracksuit bottoms with green, yellow, and red stripes up the sides were doing a peculiar type of martial arts. The African style drumming drew me over. The energy was inspiring.

A pair of toned and muscular artists battled in the centre while others sang and played on drums. The strongest man strummed a long twangy instrument, like a bow, with a rattle sound. The pair jumped about, threw flying kicks and did back flips, but never touched. They tagged out and others entered the circle. The drums, singing, positive energy, and rapid movements of the men were hypnotic. It was the first time I witnessed Capoeria.

As I strolled away from the plaza, remembering I was supposed to be searching for a job, I drifted over a modern plaza and gazed down at the deep blue sea from an elevator, *Elevador Lacerda*. Seeing water and breathing in the salty air relaxed me. I'd always wanted to live near the sea. I began to feel a connection.

I walked for a while along shopping streets, past clothes shops and markets blasting out Carnival music. I had a shirt and trousers on and felt out of place as the tough local lads with shaved heads wearing shorts and vests stared. I kept my head down and continued on to a more modern and wealthier part of town where I met Murphy.

In an American run language academy, the receptionist turned me away because I didn't have work papers. A tall black man followed.

"Hey you," he said in a firm burst. Oh shit, what does he want? I felt tense.

"Sorry?" I said, briskly. At first his face appeared mean, but then he smiled.

"You are a teacher of English?" He had a strong African accent and spoke aggressively.

"I might be. How did you guess?" He let out a deep laugh. I relaxed slightly.

"I am an English teacher, you know." His huge muscular hand shook mine. He smelt musky. "That school is shit; they want all the papers. Listen," he whispered. "I'm looking for a job, too."

"Oh right, where are you from?"

"Nigeria." Murphy told me he had been living in Salvador for two years because he'd met a 'good woman.'

"You need place for the Carnival? Yeah, the Carnival is coming soon, and the women will be crazy." He grinned and poked out his thick pink tongue.

"Maybe," I said. I had to keep up my guard.

"I have room, in a flat, very cheap, good room for the Carnival, you want?"

"I dunno. Where is it?"

"Pelo."

"Pelo?"

"Pelourinho. One hundred and twenty *reais* a month, cheap, if you want, call me." He wrote his number down on my pad. Thirty quid for a month was a bargain, especially during Carnival. Murphy shook my hand again and we clonked knuckles. Then the lanky bloke ambled towards Pelo and I continued job searching.

By the end of the day I was desperate to live in Salvador. I'd spoken to a couple of directors in snazzy academies along the beach front and felt a buzz imagining teaching there. Most of the directors gave positive vibes, but would only know student numbers until after Carnival. Living by the sea and working for a decent academy would be a dream come true.

My first night out in Pelo inspired me even more. Pelo was heaving with locals and tourists that evening as I strolled towards Praça da Se with Joe and Lucy.

"What's that drumming?" said Lucy.

"I don't know, but it's loud," said Joe. We tapped our feet and wiggled our hips as the group of black drummers dressed in white linen jived past. Each whacked their drum in perfect rhythm as the older and wiser leader with dreads flapped about energizing the performers. Their faces beamed as the crowd formed round, everyone bopping and dancing to the deafening thumps as they built up to a mind blowing climax and then stopped, silent. The audience applauded.

"That was amazing," said Lucy as we sat down to eat our 'pay by the kilo' buffet. We'd grabbed a range of meat, salad, and vegetable dishes.

"You haven't eaten anything yet," said Joe, grinning.

"Not the food, the music," she said, hitting him on the head with her fork. "I've never seen such an energetic band before, the Carnival's gonna be excellent."

That was just a taste of the bands we followed round practising for Carnival that night: each one dressed in different costumes and whacked their drums as they bounced round the dimly lit streets of Pelo.

I loved the music and atmosphere, but, despite having Joe and Lucy by my side, I still felt on edge. A few aggressive lads kept asking me for money. I tried to remain positive though, soon was the Carnival.

"We're heading to a beach tomorrow," said Joe as we got back to the hostel. "We'll be back in a week. We've found a flat round the back streets."

"Jesus, that was quick." I told them about Murphy and they advised me to call him. "Listen, thanks for all your help the other day," I said. "You really saved my arse."

"No worries mate," they both said and we arranged to meet up in a few days before Salvador really got lively.

After a couple of days traipsing round Salvador I realised two things. Firstly, I was probably going to have to wait until after the Carnival to find a job; most of the directors were welcoming, but unsure of student numbers so they couldn't promise me a job. Secondly, Pelo was probably one of the coolest, but dodgiest parts of Salvador. I was determined to stay but had to find a flat. The only person I knew was Murphy.

"Hey man, good to see you," he said in his aggressive tone. We met at the bottom of Largo do Pelourinho. He gave me a sideways high five and whacked his knuckles on mine.

"Yeah, you too, so - where's the flat?"

"Up there," he said, pointing up a street sloping away from Pelo. I had purposely kept away from that deserted side of the city.

"So is it your flat?" I asked as we walked along the quiet cobbled back street. Houses were even more worn down than the centre of Pelo.

"No man, my flat?" he said, laughing deeply. "I am staying there, you know, it's a Brazilian woman's. She has fifteen rooms."

"Fifteen?"

"The flat can be busy, but it's safe, you see now," he said, wiping the sweat off his brow.

Thinking back, Murphy could have been a malicious gringo murderer leading me to his den. I'd taken a risk, but it paid off. We walked for ten minutes, past a local supermarket and a small internet cafe, and into a house that stank of spicy meat. We waited in the square lounge.

"Come, this is the owner," said Murphy, introducing a dazzled lady with black frizzy hair.

"*Hola, tudo bem?*" she said. She was about forty, plump, and wore a dirty stained apron. Her smile seemed friendly and trusting. A little skinny naked kid ran through the lounge.

"FABRIZIO!" the lady shouted. She whacked him on the bum, pushed him into a bedroom, and slammed the door.

We followed her past the untidy kitchen and onto the outside patio. On the left were the ten rooms, or cells, in a prison block, five up and five down. On the right were the two, stinky, communal bathrooms.

"Here is the room," said Murphy. I peered in. Two single beds took up most of the length of the cell and were separated by a dusty chest of drawers with cobwebs hanging off at the back and a small pile of ants scurrying around the base. Burgundy metals bars protected the window, which had no glass.

"She clean before you come," said Murphy, trying to sway my decision. "I live here," he added, pointing to a similar cell next door. "We can be neighbours for the Carnival." He grinned and stuck out his pink tongue.

Frizzy seemed delighted when I agreed, especially when I told her I had a friend who wanted a room. Nish was going to kill me.

The next morning, Murphy escorted me to my clean cell. The view out the bars towards the toilets was less romantic than the mountains in Quito, but it would do.

The set up of the house was confusing so I separated everyone into three groups: The Royalty; those that lived in the house, The Servants; those who helped The Royalty, and The Prisoners; those that lived in the cells.

The Queen of the house was Frizzy and her son Fabrizio was the main Prince. The King, at least I think he was the husband, was a weird middle-aged pasty white man. He looked European, was constantly mumbling to himself while drunk, and lived in the bedroom.

I decided the young muscular Brazilian lad with a completely shaved head was also a Prince, and a pretty, young, and skinny Brazilian girl was a Princess. I was unsure how, or if, the Prince and

Princess were relations of Frizzy, if they were brother and sister, or a couple.

The Royals' servants included a chunky female cook with massive breasts, and a short tubby bloke who looked like a big friendly Teddy Bear. Teddy Bear was the odd job man and lived with the Royals, whereas Big Breasts lived somewhere else.

The Prisoners were Murphy, I, soon to be Nish, two dark Brazilian lads: one with huge buck teeth who watched too much television, another with a strange small head who never flushed the toilet, and a short white curly haired girl learning the funny string Capoeria instrument.

Of the twelve, Murphy was the only one I understood (at least until Nish arrived). I had to get cracking with the Portuguese.

By chance I found a job. I'd almost given up hope of getting something before the Carnival when I telephoned an academy, P.E.C, a few kilometres out of the centre and Marcus invited me in for an interview.

Despite arriving two hours late after catching a wrong bus and ending up in a slum area, Marcus seemed happy with my experience and offered me a job straight away.

"It was lucky you called," said Marcus in his serious tone. He wore a white short sleeved shirt and black trousers. He was only about twenty-five and had a number two shaved head and sticky out ears. "I was beginning to think I'd lose my students."

"Yeah, I guess we both got lucky," I said, feeling good that soon I'd be back teaching. We had a chat about Salvador and the Carnival.

"I hate the Carnival," Marcus said abruptly. "It is very dangerous. All the bad people from the neighbourhoods go looking for fights and also there are a lot of drunken foreigners, will you go?" he asked quickly. Considering I'd planned on being one of those drunken foreigners, I chose my response carefully.

"Well, I'm interested to see it yes, it's a new experience for me, something to tell my grandchildren," I said which made him smile briefly.

I had to mould the truth about how long I was staying for, I knew I'd be heading to Australia in May, but I said I'd stay and see how things went. I guess he was pretty desperate for a new teacher. Classes started the Monday after the Carnival.

Marcus toured me round the four classrooms and kitchen area, and introduced me to his mother, the director, and his wife, the receptionist. His mother was a small grumpy old lady whose name I missed, she spoke no English. His tall and chirpy wife, Rosy, was attending to their new baby boy who was bouncing around in a pram next to reception.

Marcus gave me a copy of the student's books and a CD Rom, both of which he'd produced, so I could plan some lessons. On my way out I thanked him again for giving me the opportunity.

The only setback was the neighbourhood around P.E.C. Dark had fallen and the streets were crowded with rough looking lads. As I waited for the bus, I felt uncomfortable in smart clothes while the majority of men wore vests and shorts. They stared, but I kept my head down. I was relieved to get back to the house.

When I told Murphy about where I was working, and where I had to walk back from once the bus dropped me off, he warned me to be careful.

"Cars don't stop at the lights there, have you seen? They drive through because people will rob them. It's better if you walk fast."

After the incident in Rio my self confidence had fallen and I was slowly gathering myself. However, after another sordid event, my balls of steel took a beating.

It was a Sunday and I was walking down *Av 7 de Septembro* towards the beach. All I had was a clear plastic bag with my towel, sun cream, a bottle of water, and a couple of bananas. The streets were deserted.

About halfway down on the other side of the avenue an aggressive local lad was giving grief to an old European man. The old man started shouting and the lad gave in, but he discovered his next victim. Oh shit - here we go again, I thought as the lad came towards me.

"Hey, hey, hey," he said, crossing the road. His face was gaunt and arms were thinner than my wrists. His skin was a peculiar faint purple colour. "*Dinero, comida,*" he added, holding his bony hand to his mouth; he was asking for money and food. I felt sorry for him, but also wary of the way he gazed.

"*No tengo nada,*" I said, and picked up the pace. My heart started pulsating faster as he trailed behind. He kept putting his hand on my shoulder, but I shrugged him off.

"*No tengo nada,*" I said harder and began to jog across the road. He scampered behind, almost tripping me up. I stopped and turned round.

"*Comida, comida.*" He put his hand on my shoulder again and his eyes seemed sad. Sod it, I thought, I'll give him a banana.

"Okay, okay," I said, taking a banana from my bag. I held it out. He smiled weakly as I handed it to him. Thank god, I thought, and I started to calm down, but not for long.

His kind and grateful face changed into a mean and destructive one. As he took the banana he clenched onto my other arm and held onto my cheap plastic watch.

"Oi, what the..." I said. I'd never seen such anger in someone's eyes before. He grimaced and wrenched the watch clean off my wrist. "Oi, you fucking...," I blurted, but it was too late, he'd turned and run away.

I stood frozen and outraged, trying to comprehend what had happened. There was no way I was sprinting after him for a crappy ten pound watch, but I was fuming. What more did the tossers want from me? He'd even stamped on the banana. The most disturbing part was the look of anger and hatred in his face, as if I'd stolen the watch from his mother on her death bed.

I was relieved when Nish arrived a week or so later.
"How's it going you ugly bastard," he said as we met at his hostel.
"Not bad fatty, how's you?"
"Good, yeah wicked. Mate, sorry to hear about your bag."
"No worries, you haven't heard the latest though, have you?"
"Why, what happened?"
"Some bastard nicked my watch off me the other day while I was walking to the beach."
"You're joking?" he said, laughing. I laughed too, for the first time since the incident; I'd felt defensive and couldn't see the funny side alone. Nish made everything seem less serious.
"Come on; let's take you to the palace I've found."
"It better not be dirty."
I felt relaxed walking with Nish in the local area.
"I've been living in fear mate," I said. "My confidence has really gone down, especially after the watch incident. It's good to see your ugly mug."
"Yours too honey."
I introduced Nish to Frizzy and she showed him to his residence.
"Well I'm glad it's cheap," he said, trying to sound upbeat.
"That's the spirit. It's not too bad, eh? Come on I'll show you the toilets," I said, taking him back downstairs.
"King Barry, who is your friend?" Murphy asked, greeting us with his usual knuckle hurting handshake.
"This is Nish."
"Your lover? You like the men and the women?' he asked Nish.
"Me? No, just women thanks," he said, laughing politely.
"Like me," said Murphy. "I like the Brazilian women. I like to hit them." His face became serious.

"What?" Nish asked.

"Hit them, you know, like this." Murphy thrust his hips as he pretended to slap someone's arse.

"Ah, so you don't actually hit them?" I said.

"That depends," he said firmly as he and went into his cell.

"Nice friend you have there," said Nish as we walked back to the centre.

"Yeah he's all right, sorted us out with the flat though, didn't he?"

"Yeah lucky that, what would we have done without him?" he said, sarcastically.

# 10 The Carnival in *Bahia*

The Carnival in Bahia originally started as an idea to create utopia, an ideal community, and bridge the gap between social classes. A week's celebration where poor and rich could join, forget about their pomposity or poverty, and mingle in a huge street party.

In 1950, two Brazilian blokes, Osmar and Dodo, changed the face of the Carnival. They drove an old Ford T car through the streets blasting out music through some speaker boxes, pulling along a massive crowd. The next year the '*Trio Eletrico*' formed when Osmar and Dodo asked a friend, Aragao, to join in and play through the streets, this time in a Chrysler. From there they created The Electric Trio.

Nowadays, in Salvador, up to a dozen huge trucks (*Trio Eletricos*) with powerful sound systems attached to the sides are the basis for one of the largest street parties in the world. Bands clamber on top as they drive round and blast out their music to the wild crowds dancing in the streets. Having only experienced Notting Hill Carnival we were eager for the Brazilian one to get started.

Part of me was still on edge though, especially after Frizzy told me she hated the Carnival and to watch out for groups of thugs causing trouble.

"Don't be a sissy," said Nish. "We'll be all right." We were sat on the steps outside the cathedral in Praça da Se a couple of days before Carnival. Baianas in their white dresses were flocking after groups of tourists and a bunch of five men were showing off their capoeira skills.

"Yeah I know; I'm just on tenterhooks at the moment."

"Maybe we can get some clothes to blend in."

"Murphy suggested getting some vests."

"Vests, what string ones?"

"Don't be silly. Look, all the blokes are wearing them," I said, pointing to a clutter of lads each dressed in a different coloured sports vest.

Eventually Nish agreed.

"I look bloody skinny," I said to Nish as I stood in front of a mirror in the shop. I'd never worn a vest before.

"You are bloody skinny," he said. He did have a point; six months out of England had trimmed me up.

"At least I don't have tits." Nish had never worn one either.

"Are we really going to blend in or stick out like a couple of dickheads?"

"We'll soon see." Wearing the vest made a difference; I felt safer, as if one of the crew.

In the centre, I almost failed to recognise Joe and Lucy because of their dark tans and Joe's braided hair.

"Why don't you get some braids?" said Nish.

"My hair's too short," I said, "although it might help me seem less foreign."

"I was winding you up, mate."

An hour later, three bubbly, gabbling Bahian women were standing round me struggling to style my short and awkward hair. They managed, but the tightening hurt.

"I'm not walking round with you like that; you twat," said Nish, pissing himself laughing.

"You're just jealous baldy." I thought my new hairstyle looked cool. They had platted squares into my head and attached coloured beads at the base of each spike. Now I'd surely mingle in.

"I don't think your plan has worked," said Nish as we tottered through the busy plaza.

"Why not?"

"Cos everyone is looking at you and thinking; what has that twat done?"

"What ya talking about?" I said. A group of young girls pointed and laughed. As we walked back to the flat everyone in the street stared at my new sonic style haircut.

"It'll be different when Carnival starts," I said to Murphy as he laughed outside the prison blocks.

The first day of Carnival was mental. Murphy suggested we start at the beach in Barra (pronounced Baahaa). We met Joe and Lucy, and one of Nish's travelling friends, Simon, a lanky Scottish man who had dropped his high profile job in London to travel the world, by the cathedral in Pelo and headed down.

Pelo had transformed into a Carnival goers paradise; bands were warming up around Praca da Se and there was a lively buzz in the air. I'd made up a potent concoction of rum and sweet peach juice, which went straight to my head. Nish was the first to notice.

"Mate you're pissed already. Stop prancing about."

"Come on man, it's Carnival," I said, slapping him on the head and bouncing round.

On the way to the beach, a carnival band appeared from a side street. Everyone cleared a space as the proud posse whacked their drums, tooted their trumpets, and jived through creating a wave of energy. We bopped along, smiling and gazing at the artists performing in their Carnival costumes.

"That was mental," said Simon as the band made their way towards Pelo.

Trio Eletricos with speakers bigger than large church doors lined up along Baahaa's beachfront getting ready to crank up the party. We topped up with some beers off a guy strolling round with a white cool box and sat on the beach wall. Dark had fallen but streetlights lit up the road packed with excited English, American, and Australian tourists, who stuck out among the hoards of Brazilians.

"Why are they all wearing the same colour?" I asked Nish as a group of Brazilian women in red t-shirts shuffled past.

"They must be doing a dance or something later," he said.

"It's part of the Carnival," said Simon. "Each truck has a group of followers, and each member will have paid for the t-shirt to allow them entry."

After an announcement, one of the trucks began to move and the crowd cheered.

"It's starting," I said to Nish.

"Yeah baby, come on let's go over there," he said, pointing to the other side of the street. We barged through the crowd wearing red t-shirts.

Along the beachfront, the Trios edged out as masses of energetic Carnival goers collaborated round. The Trio next to us cranked up the base and everyone cheered and danced. We managed to push through to the side as some tough bouncers pulled a rope around about two hundred people in red t-shirts. If you didn't have the t-shirt on, then you weren't going in.

We bounced alongside the slow moving Trio as the band on top blasted out their samba songs. The atmosphere was electric and I was ecstatic; hundreds of frantic partiers bounced up and down in rhythm to the pumping music. Goose pimples ran down the back of my neck. We were at the Brazilian Carnival.

"Here we go," I said to Nish, holding on to his shoulders. I felt pissed.

"This is fucking mental," said Joe, shaking his plaits about. Everyone went crazy; screaming and jumping around in unison.

After a while, the crowds started to get manic. Everyone seemed to be pushing and shoving and we kept losing each other. Lucy felt uncomfortable and we waited on the side.

"It's lucky you've got that stupid haircut," said Nish. "I'd have probably lost you otherwise, where's Simon?"

"He's up there," I said, spotting the lankiest bloke in the Carnival, but he was in trouble. A party of young thugs were pushing against the flow towards him.

"Oh shit," I said to Nish. "Look, they're going for Simon." As Nish climbed on the wall, the hooligans surrounded Simon. As the aggressive mob pushed him about, panic rose up inside me.

"They're just looking for trouble," said Nish. "Typical bad boys; individually they're wimps, but as a group lethal."

The louts vanished and Simon clambered through the crowds and waited on a hill on the corner of the beach. We tried to reach him but we got caught behind a Trio and had to wait.

A few policemen with helmets and batons were controlling the crowd when a group of thugs bowled along, smacking into innocent people. One pushed into a copper so he smacked the lad in the arm with his solid black baton. The bone cracked. The policemen clobbered the hooligans with their rock-hard truncheons. Eventually they dragged one lad away, presumably not for a cup of tea and a slice of carnival cake. Maybe Frizzy and Marcus had had a point.

Simon was unharmed but shaken up. From the hill we felt safer, less cramped, and we could watch the bands on top of the Trios. We were glad to take a breather. The locals were generally vibrant and happy, but a few were spoiling it, including yours truly.

"Fancy a drink?" I asked Joe.

"Nah man, we've still got some of this vodka, have you seen that brown shit everyone is drinking?" he said, pointing to a couple of lads holding an odd brown bottle. I bought one.

"Jesus, it's strong stuff," I said, taking a sip.

"Blimey mate, it's like paint stripper," Joe said after a swig. "You gonna drink that?"

"When in Rome my friend, when in Rome."

I'm not sure who invented that expression, but if 'Salvador' happens to be 'Rome' and you're faced with drinking some potent brown liquid, then don't feel obliged to finish the bottle. Things, quite literally, went downhill.

"Mate, watch this," I said to Nish as I got in position to roll down the slope.

"What are you doing? Wait…" he said, but it was too late. I was already rolling through a gap in the crowd. The world spun around as I headed straight for a woman's drink stall. I felt a thud, heard a crash, and got up dazed, confused, and in jeopardy.

The irate woman was staring at the floor wondering how her cool box had just been knocked over and her merchandise was sprawled everywhere. She shouted at me as I tried to mend her stall, but she was pissed off and my constant apologizing in English and Spanish only frustrated her more.

"You twat," said Nish in hysterics when I got back. "What were you thinking?"

"I dunno," I said.

The rest of the night turned into a blur.

The next morning, well afternoon, I woke up with a thumping headache and my bed was drenched in sweat.

"You were an idiot last night," said Nish as we sat outside on the patio.

"Yeah I guessed that by the state of my room; my stuff's everywhere, what happened?"

"After you rolled down the hill and smacked that poor lady over, you were dancing with loads of random people and shaking their hands. Joe and Lucy went back because she was getting groped, we lost Simon, and then came back to Pelo where you refused to go home and wanted to continue dancing with the bands in the square."

"Sorry mate."

"Yeah whatever, don't worry, it was funny. That brown stuff was lethal though; stay away from it."

After a couple of gallons of water and plenty of rice I'd sobered up and it was time to continue the party. We'd tried to persuade Joe and Lucy to come but they wanted to have a quieter night in Pelo.

"My hair's getting a bit itchy now," I said to Nish as we walked through the crowds towards Campo Grande.

"Your hair is looking a bit shit now," Nish said, laughing.

It took a while to push through, but we found a decent spot next to a park full of restaurant stalls and bars and had a drink. I stuck to the beers.

"Maybe it won't be so crazy tonight," said Nish. "Everyone might calm down a bit after last night." Or not; the streets were equally as rammed. The base boomed in the distance. Adrenaline passed through the crowd. We waited.

By the time the first Trio thumped along, followed by their special t-shirt gangs, I'd topped up on beer and Nish was high on guarana. We were in the groove again but in a tight avenue with hundreds of Carnival lovers jiving and waving to the bands on top.

"Mate, do you remember this tune from last night?" asked Nish as he bounced up and down.

"I don't remember much about last night."

"Listen to it," he said. It was a funky tune and easy to sing along to.

"Zoom Zoom Zoom Zoom... Zoombaabaa... Zoombaabaa... Zoombaabaaa..." The crowd loved it and went crazy at each chorus (At the time we were unaware, but that song, *Maimbe*, is famous because Daniella Mercury, from Bahia, sings the song).

For a while the atmosphere was friendly; genuine people having genuine fun. It was difficult to tell who was rich or poor, apart from the men carrying round the white cool boxes, but even they were jumping about having fun. The rich were in disguise, forgetting about their egos and joining the masses. We were creating utopia.

Some muppets had to ruin the *alegria*. Groups of aggressive lads pounded down the sides of the Trios, but now with their beasty girlfriends, spoiling the harmony. Before long, solid rows of police with protective helmets and batons were patrolling up and down whacking anyone who caused disorder. Some innocent victims got smacked for doing nothing so we kept back.

The lads had shattered the utopia. Many were beaten and taken away, bloody and bruised. No girls were though. Despite the mayhem, we stayed in our groove until the Trios passed; we weren't going to let a few nutters spoil our party.

On the way back, litter covered the streets and drunken people, mainly tourists, were stumbling about.

"That was you last night," said Nish pointed to an English lad singing the Zoombaabaa song trying to dance with a group of Brazilians. I was relieved not to have touched the brown goo again.

We stayed in Pelo the following night. Joe and Lucy had had a good time as there was no groping and they felt less life-threatened. The atmosphere without the Trios and hoards of people was more tranquil. Parents strolled about with their children and there were no ruffians colliding with snotty policeman getting baton happy. We chilled out in the square, had a couple of beers, and then joined the parades as they showed off their fantastic musical skills.

The most memorable part of the night was a drumming band of fifteen kids. They played just as well as the adults. One eight-year old kid dressed in a red and white tracksuit stood at the front with a tiny drum leading the parade. The happy-go-lucky boy was the star of the show. Everyone watched in awe as he led the energetic crew, smiling like a true champion.

"The future of Salvador," said Nish. The pride in the young musician's faces showed the importance of the Carnival and music.

They'd practiced and waited all year for that moment. It was soothing to see the real spirit of the Carnival.

I felt a lot safer that evening, there was no need to stand back or worry that a stampede of naughty youths were going to trample us. Pelo was normally a dodgy area, but the Carnival made it a pleasant, inspiring, and magical place to enjoy the motions of what makes Bahia such a famous place to visit.

"How goes it King Barry and King Nish?" said Murphy the next day as he arrived to his cell. He could barely manage a sloppy handshake.

"Good mate, you look tired," I said.

"Yeah, my woman is a beast; we have been hitting and hitting for three days. I can no more, I need rest and ice on my balls; they are like melons."

"Thanks for sharing," said Nish.

"You have been to Baahaa?" asked Murphy.

"Yeah, the first night; it was crazy though," I said.

"Yeah very crazy," said Murphy. "You have been inside with the people?" He was referring to the special t-shirt gangs.

"No, we watched from the side," said Nish.

"NO? Not inside?" Murphy put his hands on his head. "That is the best, you need to do it. Everyone does it, trust me." I looked at Nish expecting him to say no.

"Simon sent me an email saying he'd be in one today."

"Why didn't you tell me?"

"I dunno, it's expensive and you're a pikey."

"You need to go get tickets quick before they sell out," said Murphy.

I'm unsure why we hadn't spoken about paying to be inside the ropes before, but we had the best night. We caught a taxi to Pituba and managed to get the last couple of yellow t-shirts for the same Trio as Simon.

We felt safer on the other sides of the ropes; everyone was in high spirits and there was less chance of getting a smack. With the t-shirt we were part of a massive international gang. I spoke with Americans, Australians, Europeans, and a few Brazilians; everyone was in an amazing mood. We stayed in the middle away from policemen and the occasional line of thugs battling past.

The night was bloody hard work. The Trio rarely stopped and we were on the go for seven hours, jumping and dancing along the coast from Baahaa up to Pituba. Each of the ten times the band played the Zoombaba song the crowd went wild.

As our Trio passed the crowds of onlookers I felt superior, as if part of a protected Royal parade. I tried to imagine how the thugs felt as they barged along the sides; perhaps they hated the organised barricades. Were they even allowed to buy tickets? Maybe the expensive Trios were damaging the utopia, separating rich from poor, and even teasing those less-able Carnival fans by demonstrating their superiority.

If you can look beyond the trouble, the Carnival is an amazing experience. I loved everything about that night; the rush to buy tickets, the crush in the crowd, and the challenge of staying on my feet all night. At 3am we were relieved to stop and get a cab back to Pelo, knackered.

Nish and I spent the last night in Pelo not wanting to dance or move. I couldn't even think of alcohol; my body needed rest and recuperation before I started work again.

"Mate, it's been a wicked party," I said to Nish as we sat drinking guarana.

"Yeah a classic, we'll have to meet up again in Oz, how about that?"

"I'm up for it, baldy."

"You'll have to take out those stupid plaits though; you'll get beaten up over there."

"Mate, they're out tomorrow; my hair's dirty and itchy," I said, scratching my head.

"That'll teach you for trying to blend in," he said. I'd been stupid to think there was a need to blend in with so many different types of people.

The next day Joe and Lucy headed north to do a boat trip along the Amazon to Peru. I never heard from them again, nor Simon.

The Carnival had been fun, exhausting, but most of all educating; seeing the whole of Bahia come alive and try to bond together was an experience. Whether or not the Carnival achieved its goal of creating a better society, in my eyes, was dubious. Brazilians knew how to entertain though; they were energetic and gifted people who put on a fantastic show and proved that the Carnival in Brazil was no doubt one of the best parties in the world.

## 11 Settling In

A few problems arose at P.E.C. I had two classes. The intermediate male class was fun; the older men and boisterous lads were keen to chat in English and had a decent level. However, the female beginner class was awkward. Daisy, a short eighteen-year old student, acted as the translator to the other two women, Jacira, a mature but shy lady, and Rosa, an energetic twenty-year old who had massive eyes. Only Daisy understood my accent and the others gossiped about me in Portuguese.

Daisy was intense. She stared at me all lesson and when I asked her a question she blushed. The others would giggle and encourage her to speak. When the room was silent, Daisy would put on a calm and serious face and speak in her deep voice. The others would clap when we finished a conversation but they rarely spoke in English.

At the end of the first week, I made the mistake of asking what they were doing at the weekend. They nattered and smiled as if I'd asked Daisy on a date. I was just being polite.

"But why do you want to know?" Daisy asked, grinning to show her perfect white teeth.

"Err, I was only asking, you know, a bit of conversation." She translated and everyone smirked and winked, obviously thinking otherwise.

Not only were there problem in class. After two weeks I received my first pay packet, but the brown envelope was rather thin. I thought they were paying me R$5 per hour, but it was per (hour and a half) lesson. When I confronted Marcus and his mother, she started ranting in Portuguese. Marcus calmed her down and settled the tension. I was unhappy with her reaction, but let it go, unlike her. She began to scowl when I entered in the evening and stopped replying when I said goodbye. Marcus was fine and realised we'd misunderstood each other, but the mother turned into a witch and made sly whispering comments about me.

The worst parts of the day were the late night bus trips back. Even though I had a tan and wore vests and shorts to blend in, I felt threatened as local rough lads chatted and glanced over as I waited for the bus. A few times I was asked for money to pay for their bus, but I only ever carried the correct change.

In Quito I'd felt scared, but the feeling was more intense in Brazil. Murphy helped me see why.

"But if you don't know what everyone is saying then how can you feel comfortable?" he asked as we had a beer in the patio. "You are paranoid that everyone is talking about you and thinking about robbing you because you are the only white man, but if you knew how to speak and understand them, then maybe you would feel better."

Just like in Quito, I had to learn the lingo if I was going to boost my confidence and understand what my students were gossiping about. I spent my free time studying Portuguese. Reading was easy after learning some Spanish, but understanding and speaking the nasal language was much harder.

My luck changed when I met Anderson.

I found another teaching job with A.E.C over the other side of Pelo. The director, Charles, a well dressed Brazilian man in his late forties, offered me two hour conversation classes after an 'English by Singing' event on Friday evenings. Those nights became my favourite moments in Salvador.

On my first night, I was surprised how many trendy young adults and teenagers turned up. Over fifty eager learners were rammed into the outside hall covered by a white canopy. Didn't they have anything better to do with their Friday night? This would never happen in England, I thought. I sat at the back next to a small pine tree and observed.

"Right everyone," said Charles on his microphone. "Today we have two new songs for you, but first I'd like to introduce our new conversation teacher." Oh shit, I thought; he never said he was going to introduce me. "He's Parry, come here please Parry." Fifty smiling students turned to look at me. I blushed as I walked down the aisle and stood next to Charles.

"Would you like to say something?" Did I have an option?

"Well, hello everyone, err, I'm from England. I've been in Salvador for a month, it's a great place, the Carnival was a bit crazy," I said, waving my hands in the air. The students must have been thinking, what a plank. "And now I'm here to teach you guys some English, hopefully speak to you soon, thanks." The crowd applauded as I took my seat.

"Okay, great, thanks Parry, and now we have our first song for tonight, Prince, the most beautiful girl in the world." I felt like a right plum.

Each student had a copy of the lyrics in English and Portuguese and after we'd listened twice, they sang along. The students loved singing and the majority joined in. I was relieved that Charles didn't summon Parry to sing.

"Hey, I'm Anderson," said a tall late teenage lad after the choir practice had ended. "So where are you from exactly?" His English was the best I'd heard since Nish's.

"London, and you?"

"I'm from Salvador, of course. My uncle lived in London for seven years. He loved it there; one day I want to go there and make money." Anderson's sociable smile was catching. He beamed when he spoke English and his eyes gleamed with passion.

"I am a voluntary English teacher at another school, you know," he said. "Eventually I want my own school."

Charles dragged me away and introduced me to a group of ten happy students; I'd almost forgotten I was there to 'work'. I spent an hour chatting with the students about the Carnival, which most of them loved.

"It was very nice to speak with you today," said a young lady student at the end. She was a pretty girl with cute dimples and a bright smile. "I hope to see you again," she said, stroking my arm as she left.

"The women here will be crazy for an English man," said Anderson, smiling down. "She's head over heels for you already."

"Nah, she's a student," I said. "Anyway, where did you learn that expression?"

"Like I said mate, my uncle was in London. This is Junior." He introduced me to his taller cousin. They looked like a couple of pro basketball players.

"You having a beer Parry?" said Charles. "I'll get it." It was the least he could do after getting my name wrong so many times.

Anderson reminded me of The Lord; he was equally as keen to learn expressions about women, but not as crude.

"So a good looking bird is a fit bird," I said.

"A fit bird?"

"Yeah, but don't say this directly to a girl, unless you are on good terms."

"What about ugly girls?"

"Minger or munter are the most popular, but be careful."

"Cool, can you write these down for me," he said. Lads wanted to learn the most useful vocabulary first in any part of the world.

The academy closed late so Anderson and Junior walked out of their way to take me back to Pelo; they knew the area was dangerous.

The following week I chatted with Anderson again and told him I'd been having problems learning Portuguese.

"Oh I see, so you want to chat up some birds?" he said.

"Nah, I have a bird, but I do need to learn the language. I could teach you and you could teach me."

"Sounds like a deal."

We met on Saturdays by the cathedral in Praca de Se and spent all afternoon chatting. I taught him expressions and he corrected my pronunciation. Anderson talked about London. His dream was to go there and follow his uncle's footsteps.

Junior often came along but would sit and listen rather than participate. They were only about seventeen and had to be home early so we never went for a beer. Back in England I would never have done that, just sat with mates chatting all day without alcohol being involved.

Anderson and Junior became friends and when you know people in a place you feel protected. Their passion for English inspired me to learn Portuguese and over time my confidence grew, not only with the language, but in Salvador as well. When I walked through Pelo the locals recognized me and instead of asking for money they'd say hello.

Learning Portuguese also helped me control the female class.

"Have you been studying Portuguese?" Daisy asked after I said that I'd bought my trousers from Mexico. They'd been discussing my clothes in Portuguese.

"Yes, and I know that you're talking about me." Daisy translated and they all looked at the floor like guilty school children.

The gossiping stopped, but a new problem arose. Ever since I'd confronted the mother about the pay, she'd been off with me. She wouldn't let it go.

"Barry, can we speak with you for a moment please," said Marcus one evening before class. His wicked mother hunched by his side. We entered an empty classroom.

"It has been brought to our attention that some of the students are not happy with the grammar you are teaching," said Marcus.

"Oh, right," I said. What grammar? I thought. "They say you have not concentrated enough on the grammar and are doing more speaking exercises," he said after the Witch had spoken.

"Yeah that's true," I said. "I've been doing a lot of speaking. I asked them before and everyone seemed to want to concentrate on that." The Witch muttered to Marcus, but little did she know my Portuguese had improved. She said that she didn't believe what I'd said, or that I was a teacher. She trusted her students and her own people. I tried to remain calm.

"One student said you are too relaxed in the class." Don't blow, I told myself.

"Oh right, sorry, which class is it? Maybe I can change things." The Witch shook her head and muttered something about certificates. Marcus nodded.

"Are you sure you have done a course in teaching? It's just you don't have much experience do you?" He'd crossed the line.

"WHAT?" I said, angrily. "I showed you my certificates and references, I don't understand. I checked with the students before and they wanted more speaking and less grammar. It's just a misunderstanding, surely."

I was irate. They seemed as shocked as I was. I'd never spoken like that at work before. Brazil was toughening me up. No one was going to push me around. The Witch backed off and we agreed that I'd concentrate more on grammar.

I never found out who had been unhappy, but the majority seemed bemused at the sudden increase in grammar exercises and homework.

Living with twelve tested my patience. The toilets were sometimes full of crap, my cartons of milk would disappear, and squeezing in the kitchen to cook my own food past Big Breasts was a nightmare. She slaved away all morning, preparing her special stews for everyone. When I asked if I could make my lunch she'd tut and huff. I preferred not to interrupt her feast preparations, but I had a different timetable from the rest of the house.

I found the other Prisoners difficult to communicate with. I only ever saw Small Head and Buck Teeth watching TV or coughing up phlegm in the patio outside. They both smoked constantly and we rarely spoke. I used to nod and say hello to the curly haired girl, but all I ever saw her do was practise her funny squeaky instrument.

I'd spend most of my time in my ant ridden cell. I ate in my room and if I ever spilt food on the floor, I'd have to sweep up before ants scurried from the hidden corners. Most mornings a trail would be lined up outside, ready to pounce. At night, as I was reading or studying, small lizards scrambled about the walls and ceilings. Sometimes I was glad for the company.

Despite my progress with Portuguese, I still only got on with Murphy.

"WHAT? You have TWO jobs now?" he shouted. I'd forgotten he was looking for more hours.

"Yeah, but it's bad money, and one is voluntary," I said, playing it down. I felt guilty.

"You lucky English man, you can get some money now and hit some women."

"How many times do I need to remind you Murphy? I have a girlfriend."

"Yeah, but now you're in Brazil, the rules change. I see the cook has been looking at you. You like her big tits?" He grinned and raised his eyebrows.

"You're sick; she must be over fifty."

"Yeah but look at those tits, and her arse, it's a real *Pompozuda*."

"A what?"

"*Pompozuda* - a big arse; good for hitting."

"Mate, you only think of one thing."

"YEAH."

The first person I began chatting with in Portuguese was Teddy Bear, the odd-job man. I started running in the morning and every time I got back Teddy Bear would normally be helping Big Breasts in the kitchen or fixing up the house.

"*E ai?* – everything all right?" he'd say.

"*E ai,*" I'd reply. "*Beleza* - beautiful."

"*Beleza.*" He'd shake my hand and flex his biceps. Over time we'd chat about the weather and football. He always wondered around the house, whistling, eating, and pretending to work.

One day I found out why he was so happy.

"You know about the French husband, don't you?" Murphy said one morning as we took turns to wash our clothes in the outside wash basin. In the house, Frizzy was yelling at the drunken pasty white King. I'd never seen him sober.

"Yeah he's a drunk, isn't he?"

"Yeah, that's right. But you know why, don't you?"

"Because he wants to go back to France and he's stuck here with you?"

"No King Barry. He can't get it up, you know, he can't hit women." Murphy punched his fist into the air.

"Maybe cos he's always drunk?"

"Nah, he's got a problem; he is ill. That's why the landlady has that guy working for her." He pointed to Teddy Bear, who was pealing some spuds.

"What? You mean he's her lover?"

"Yeah, they're always banging and hitting when the old man is out of his head."

"How'd you know?"

"He told me," he said, referring to Teddy Bear. "She goes all night, like a train, yeah," he said, grinning, as if fantasising. Frizzy had hired her own odd job / sex slave; the saucy minx.

Now that Murphy was in a telling mood, I asked about the rest of the house.

"So whose is the kid?" I asked, referring to Fabrizio.

"He's the young girl's," he said, referring to the Princess.

"But she's only what, sixteen?"

"Yeah and the kid is three," he said. "You do the math."

The Prince and Princess, who I thought were a couple because they slept in the same bed, were nephew and niece of Frizzy.

I felt like I was living in my own soap opera: The Brazilian Royal Family.

## 12 - Falling in Love with Teaching and Salvador

I was beginning to forget about the dangers of Salvador. I still dreaded the evening bus trips back from P.E.C. and rarely walked in the dark on my own, but my confidence grew as I picked up Portuguese. Knowing what my students, the Witch, and locals were talking about made a real difference.

My savings were running low so I led a simple life. I kept on a strict budget, spending money only on essential food and not doing much outside of work. Compared to my money obsessed mind in England, I became content with the free things in life such as studying, running by the beach, and hanging out with Anderson and his mates.

I'd enjoyed teaching in Quito, but I fell in love with it in Salvador. Teaching was rewarding and I got a buzz from helping students. Friday nights at A.E.C was still my favourite part of the week. The music sessions were an innovative way to entertain students while teaching and the atmosphere was uplifting. I became closer to the students. Some needed English to improve their lives and get a job in tourism, others simply loved the language, and some just wanted a couple of hours to get away from their wives. Charles was a good boss, despite continuing to call me Parry, and the students were always grateful after the lessons.

Hanging around with Anderson showed me real passion and belief that anything was possible. He'd never left Salvador but his English was amazing. Every time I taught him an expression he would use it when we next met. He was obsessed with pronouncing his words like a Londoner and when I met his uncle I realised why.

"All right mate, how you doing?" said Ruben. Anderson and I had caught a bus out to the outskirts of Salvador to his uncle's house.

"All right mate, yeah good."

"Come in, come in."

Ruben was a slim man with a neat and short haircut. As we chatted outside in his patio covered with over hanging trees his sisters clonked down massive plates of salad, meats, and typical Brazilian casseroles on the long oak table. After scrimping and saving I was pleased to tuck into some decent homemade food.

Ruben had worked in London for seven years and had saved up enough cash to return home, buy a house, and set up a small commerce business. He'd been lucky enough to make it in London; something few of his colleagues had been able to do.

"It's because I learnt the language so well, the others were lacking in the pronunciation. I would practice every night," he said, proudly.

"I can see," I said. "You've got the best accent I've heard in South America."

"I want to do the same one day," said Anderson.

"You will nephew, you will," said Ruben.

After lunch, Ruben got out his guitar and huge black folder of music. He and Anderson took turns to strum while we sang along. They were delighted to have an English person singing, albeit badly. I'd never sung so much before in one day, especially without a beer. They made me feel extremely welcome; Ruben was a kind and generous man, and I felt honoured to meet him.

My original plan had been to return to England after working in Australia, but life as a TEFL teacher was rewarding; I could help people. The thought of going back to the rat race in England made my stomach turn. I'd changed since England and wanted to make a go of being a TEFL teacher. Australia was next on my list, after that I'd have to wait and see.

Knowing that I would be away from England longer than I expected, I had to finish with my girlfriend. Finishing with her was difficult and I felt like an arrogant, selfish idiot, but I had to let her get on with her life too. Making the decision was tricky, especially with no family around, but Murphy helped lighten the mood.

"Don't worry King Barry; you can hit some women now," he said, slapping his hands together.

"I think I'll wait a while."

"But the cook is still looking at you, the other day I saw her touching her tits."

"Yeah right."

"Listen, when you are ready to hit women, you must be careful."

"Why?"

"I like women as you know; I like to hit them when possible, but you need to choose well," he said. "I heard a story that one man, a white man like you, went back once with a girl from Pelo."

"Yeah, and what happened?"

"Well, they were getting down with the hitting, when her boyfriend crashed through the door."

"No way!"

"Yeah, and the next thing he knew he woke up in the morning, frozen in a bath, and they had taken out his kidney."

"Where do you get these stories man?"

"It's true."

I'll leave you to decide.

As time went on, Murphy asked about England.

"I have heard that if I get my woman pregnant we can go to England and they will pay for everything, is that true?"

"Well, I don't know, you can get some benefits I think, I couldn't tell you."

"Yes, I'm sure I have heard the true. When you return England, you can be my sponsor and help me come to the country?"

"I'm not sure it's that easy. Besides, I don't know when I'll be back; maybe Nish can help you."

"Yes, good idea, great, you can give me his email," he replied.

"Sure, no problem," I said. Nish would be pleased.

Sometimes I wondered why I stuck out living with the Brazilian Royal Family. The house was manic, dirty, and stinky. Life was never dull though. In the evenings, I sat with everyone in the lounge and watched Brazilian Big Brother to try to improve my Portuguese. Like in England, everyone was obsessed with the program, apart from the drunken King, who slept on the sofa breathing out hot alcoholic fumes.

Frizzy would sit with Fabrizio sleeping on her lap while the Prince and Princess shared an armchair and Buck Teeth and Small Head shared the sofa. Everyone was glued to the screen.

Brazilian Big Brother was much raunchier than the English version. Brazilians weren't camera shy and most of the attention was on who was shagging who. When something controversial happened, everyone in the lounge started shouting about who they would evict. Watching the Royals and Prisoners get hot tempered was entertaining.

One evening, as I was sitting next to Buck Teeth, he got up to get something from the fridge. I checked he stayed clear of my milk. He grabbed something and sat back down.

"Crrunncchhh," I heard. He must be eating an apple, I thought. "Crrunncchh," he went again. I caught a strong whiff of something. He can't be, I thought. I glanced over on the sly. He was munching raw garlic.

When he wasn't sleeping through blazing rows about Big Brother, Fabrizio ran about the house causing carnage. He would play with his toys in the lounge or do some colouring in, but never for long. Sometimes he'd come into my cell to show me his toys and mess up my things. I didn't mind, but he drove Frizzy round the bend.

"Faaaaabbbbbrrrrrriiiiiizzzzzziiooooooo," she would call out if he was missing. Fabrizio would panic, peak outside, snatch his toy, and then run off to receive a smack on the bottom.

One Sunday he came running up to me with a football.

"A Brazilian asking an Englishman for a game, well I never," I said. He shrugged. I went to grab the ball but he darted away. He placed the ball on the floor, took a run up, went to strike it, completely missed, and fell flat on his arse.

"Don't worry I won't tell anyone," I said, helping him up. He positioned the ball again, took another run up, and smacked the ball straight into my nether regions. I grimaced. He laughed.

When he realized I was up for playing he shoved me in goal. He was a determined little chap, and even though the ball only came up to his knee, he'd give it a go. Football was in his blood. Perhaps he was a future Pele.

Even though I was getting to know the others in the house, no one was up for coming out on Saturday night to Pelo. Murphy was always with his lady, I preferred not to ask Buck Teeth or Small Head, and Teddy Bear was waiting for everyone to go to bed so he could have his wicked way with Frizzy. I used to buy a cheap bottle of rum to make my own caipiriña and shared the lethal potion with Teddy Bear.

I'd always end up strolling to Pelo on my own though. I was braver and worried less about getting mugged. The Carnival atmosphere continued all through the year in Pelo. I was normally inebriated and used to jump on the back of the parades, dance round the square, and end up in a bar. There was a funky joint with an outdoor dance area where I got chatting to passing travellers. I danced with Brazilian women a couple of times, but they normally asked me if I wanted to pay for the night. Murphy's story about the kidney kept me on my toes.

On the way home, I'd usually end with an *acaraje* (not a secret code name for a Brazilian woman). You have to try an *acaraje* if you're in Bahia. The delicious ball of dough made from black-eyed peas is fried, cut open, and stuffed with either spicy prawns or vegetables; the Bahian replacement for a late night kebab.

Back at P.E.C, the women class were speaking more in English, but Daisy had become extreme. She always arrived first and left last, grinned and stared at me during class, and kept inviting me to the beach. When Jacira and Rosa realised Daisy fancied me they pestered me to go to the beach too. They were pleasant students and I wanted to go, but I worried that Marcus and the Witch would find out and fire me.

Brazilian women are resilient though and I finally gave in, as long as everyone went. What harm could it have done anyway?

One Sunday morning, Jacira's boyfriend, Fernando, drove us to a calm and much less crowded beach past Baahaa. I was expecting us to lie down near the sea and sunbath, but that was 'an English thing' to do and instead we gathered around a red table by one of the many shack beach bars pumping out music.

Fernando was a huge man with only four fingers on one hand. He was charismatic and a joker. Every waiter, or person trying to sell snacks or handicrafts, left the table in stitches. He kept us all entertained, even if he did go a bit far.

"What's the problem Barry, don't you like women?" he asked me in Portuguese.

"Sure, but I have a girlfriend." I took the easy route out.

"Yeah, but she's in England, you can go with Daisy now, have a quick jiggy jiggy and wham bam. You can even borrow my car." Daisy hid her face behind her towel. I just laughed it off.

It was great to be out with people having a laugh and a beer. We ate, drank, and joked all day; apart from Daisy who sat in silence because of Fernando's comments and face gestures. She was unimpressed.

I thought a day at the beach would have calmed everyone down, but instead they invited me out every weekend. I hung around with them a few times, but after an incident at Daisy's birthday party, I stopped.

Daisy and Jacira were overly excited when we met that Sunday lunchtime. I thought we were going to have lunch with her parents, but, oh no, the whole family squeezed into her house. I felt like the guest of honour as Daisy introduced me to everyone from her baby niece to ancient grandfather. I thought my Portuguese had improved but everyone spoke so quickly that I just grinned and laughed at appropriate moments.

When Daisy's mother struck a huge gong, everyone sat round the long dining table. I was at the head. Normally I'm good with new food, but that meal reminded me of the intestines incident in Quito.

"The guest eats first," Jacira told me as Daisy's mother slid me a multicoloured mound of grub.

"Wow, great," I said. I recognized the chicken and a yellow paste thing I'd eaten at Ruben's, but a strange frog spawn type of goo wobbled on the side.

"Try this first," said Daisy, pointing to the slop. Everyone along the table gazed and smiled. The tension reminded me of the scene where Indiana Jones had to eat a strange gunk with flies buzzing round; the one where he nearly gags.

"My grandmother's recipe," said Daisy. Her grandmother nodded and flashed her bare gums. I smiled, took a small spoonful, and raised the slimy, pond water smelling gloop to my mouth. The audience clapped as it slithered down my throat.

"What do you think?" Daisy asked.

"*Que rico,*" I said, saying it was delicious. Everyone cheered and repeated what I'd said. I took a swig of beer to wash the vile taste away and everyone ate.

They were a jolly family. The conversation revolved around Big Brother, learning English, and how skinny I was. Daisy's mum kept piling up my plate; luckily the frog spawn had run out.

After lunch, a few of us sat on the terrace and continued drinking. It was the first time that I had a half decent conversation in Portuguese without Anderson and his mates. The beer helped. Jacira talked about drug and violence problems with local young thugs.

"It's not safe outside after nine." I felt sad to see such a lovely family living in fear. Then Jacira left the room.

"So Barry, do you like me?" said Daisy. What could I say? I thought carefully.

"Of course, you are one of my best students."

"Oh thank you," she replied. Her smile dropped and she moved closer. She looked serious. "But, you know, do you LIKE me?" She touched my arm.

"Like I say, you are a very good student." She rubbed her chest on mine.

"But, you know, more than a student?" She moved her hand towards my face.

"Err, well," I said. Jacira walked in. Daisy hit the wall in anger. I'd escaped.

Lessons became weird after that. Daisy spoke less and the others sensed the tension. I tried to liven up the situation but when Daisy realised that I was not interested she became difficult. I was glad to be leaving soon.

Despite falling in love with Salvador and teaching, I had to move on. My visa was due to start in Australia and a new adventure waited. I had mixed emotions about leaving.

**What made it easy?** When the rain season arrived, Salvador was gloomier, as were the Bahians; they hate the rain just as much as we do.

Classes at P.E.C were too tense. Daisy was on the war path.

I was down to three hundred pounds. I'd enjoyed living a simple life, but my money was still vanishing. I hadn't helped by making a huge cock up. I needed to get to L.A to depart for Sydney, but there was a special offer flight to Miami. I read that a Greyhound bus from Miami to L.A took eleven hours (Yes, I know I'm a plank). So I booked the flight with enough time to see some of Miami and L.A.

How long does the bus from Miami to L.A? Three days and eleven hours = Muppet.

**What made it difficult?** My Portuguese was finally improving. On one of my last evenings in Pelo, I was sitting on the cathedral steps, remembering the fun I'd had, when a lout sat next to me.

"*Hola, tudo Bem?*" he said.

"*Sim, Tudo Bem.*"

"Chocolate?" He grinned.

"Chocolate? What, for eating or drinking?" I asked him in Portuguese. He laughed. The conversation continued in Portuguese.

"No, you know, for smoking," he said, holding a bag of brown hash by his side.

"But how do you smoke chocolate, won't it melt?"

"Your Portuguese is good, you sure you don't want some?"

"I don't smoke, but thanks anyway," I said.

"Okay, man. Take it easy." We shook hands. Three months before, I probably would have got angry and walked off.

I'd miss the music. Carnival style nights in Pelo were amazing, even after all my travels those nights were still the best. I was even lucky enough to see Olodum in Pelo, one of Brazil's most famous samba reggae bands.

Mostly I'd miss teaching Brazilians. I haven't met such fun, polite, and enthusiastic students since.

Charles and Marcus were fine about me leaving. I think the Witch was glad to see me go. When I told the female class, Daisy caused a stir.

"What? But why?" she said, getting angry. She was about to blow.

"I know, I'm sorry, it's been fun though," I said. She stormed out.

Saying goodbye to Anderson and Junior was emotional.

"Man, when I'm in London we can meet up, you need to stay in contact, mate," Anderson said as we hugged on the cathedral steps.

"Yeah no worries, keep practicing those expressions, you never know when a fit English bird might pop through Pelo."

"Yeah I will, keep safe," he said. We shook hands and they disappeared through the crowds in Praca da Se. They were good honest lads and had showed me the highs of Salvador.

On my last day I was sad. Two lizards watched me pack my rucksack and clean the cell. When I left, a small pile of ants waited outside, as if waving me off. I'd told Murphy the time I was leaving, but he wasn't there.

"See you in the World Cup one day," I said to Fabrizio as he crashed about with his matchbox cars. The King was asleep on the couch, and Buck Teeth and Small Head were playing cards. I gave Big Breasts a hug (yes, they were firm) and thanked Frizzy for everything.

As I paced up the road, I bumped into Teddy Bear.

"Good luck man, take it easy with the landlady," I said, winking.

"What? How did you know?" he said, laughing. I waved goodbye to the ladies working in the supermarket and the Prince and Princess came out of an internet cafe in Pelo to say goodbye.

While I strolled through the plaza that I'd been frightened of, taxi drivers didn't give me hassle when I declined their lifts, homeless lads who had asked me for money nodded their heads knowing I was leaving town.

"Not running today?" said a Portuguese voice, a policeman.

"No, not today."

"Good journey," he said. I'd never noticed him before.

As I reached Praca da Se, I stopped for a second to watch a group of lads practising Capoeria and I saw my oldest Bahian friend.

"Hey King Barry, I thought I was going to miss you," said Murphy, sweating and panting.

"Me too."

"Give me your bag, I'll help you. I can't believe King Barry is leaving. This is a sad moment for me. You will go now to hit some Australian women, you are a lucky English man."

"Not really," I said.

"Yes you are! I want to get out of this shit-hole; when you are in London, you can be my sponsor okay? Get me a job and things."

"Yeah sure Murphy, if you ever come over."

He walked me to the bus stop.

"Don't forget about London man, tell me when you're there and I'll come over," he said as I got on the airport bus.

"Sure mate, thanks for everything; you're a diamond geezer."

"A what?"

"A diamond geezer, a good man."

"Okay you too, diamond geezer," he said, laughing as he shook my hand for the final time. "Good luck King Barry! Hit those women!"

"I'll try." The driver ushered me on.

As I waved goodbye to the tall lanky man who'd helped me, I felt a lump in my throat. Murphy was a kind person with a good heart and if he was ever in London, I'd repay the favour. I glanced at him one last time, was that a tear in his eye? Nah it can't be, I thought, but it was.

As the bus travelled along the coast, I thought back to the hard moments. Brazil had taught me to be tougher, more street savvy, and less naive.

I checked in and browsed round the duty free section. A soundless video of the Carnival played. I put on the headphones.

"Zoom Zoom Zoom Zoom, Zoombaabaa Zoombaabaa." I smiled.

The chapter in Latin America was over and a new one was about to commence. That was the beauty of being a travelling TEFL teacher.

## 13 USA: Greyhound Weirdoes

"If you're in America, then be careful of the Greyhound Buses; they're full of weirdoes," my auntie had said to me before I left England. I'll get to my three-day bus trip from Miami to Los Angeles in a second, but first I'll tell you about the weirdoes I met in Miami.

As I strolled through the arrivals gates, flight announcements and rotating billboard signs in English made me think of home, but there was a funny American accent.

"Yes Sir, how may I help you, Sir?" said the chirpy brunette woman at the airport's information desk. She shuffled her podgy hips on the swivel chair and grinned. No one had called me 'Sir' for a while, and never twice in the same sentence.

"Do you have a map of Miami?"

"Yes, I sure do Sir, why here you are, Sir." She reached over the front of the desk and handed me a pocket map. "Anything else, Sir?"

"Yeah, where can I get a bus to Miami beach?"

"Why Sir, you can catch the bus from over there, Sir." She pointed towards some huge double doors. "Number thirty-one, okay have a nice day now, Sir," she said, turning to attend the next Sir in her bizarre over-friendly manner.

I strolled through the doors, over to the stop, and waited.

"Is this going to Miami beach?" I asked the driver, who took up most of the driving space behind the protective plastic screen. She lifted her shades so they rested on her mono brow and revealed a piercing stare.

"Now what does it say on the front there?" she said, pointing up.

"Miami beach."

"Well there you go." She released her shades so they slipped back on her podgy face and looked ahead. When she saw my ten-dollar note, she flipped.

"WAT?" she shouted when I asked if she had any change. "You're not from round here are you?" I refrained from asking if many arrivals were 'from round here' and rustled in my bag for change while the other passengers got on. Luckily, I found a dollar that Nish had given me.

"Sorry about that," I said.

"Next time you'll know, Sir," she said, grinning smugly.

"There won't be a next time," I muttered as I paced past. The doors hissed shut and she bolted off before I could sit down.

Miami was enormous compared to Salvador. As I gazed out the bus window giant billboards flashed through the gaps between the cargo lorries. Cars had doubled in size since Salvador, as had some passengers. The accent of the Spanish speaking Latinos took me back to my adventure in South America. I already missed Spanish and Portuguese.

As we whizzed over the huge iron bridge towards Miami Island, high hotels, which mirrored in the deep blue sea, stuck out in the distance. The pure size of everything was astounding; even walking across the road to my hostel made me feel like a midget.

The hostel was in pristine condition but I missed my prison cell in Pelo. The toilets seemed too clean, and where were the ants and lizards?

If I thought the first two Americans I'd spoken to were a tad weird, then the next was bonkers.

"Hey dude, jeez," said a pasty white American man as he hunched in the corner of the dorm room. He wore pale green boxers, and nothing else. "You scared me then, man." As he stood up, I caught a whiff of stale piss. He was in his forties with long ginger hair, an untidy beard, and a hairy back. He belonged in Teen Wolf.

"Hi mate, sorry," I said as I dumped my bag on the bed.

"Yeah man, you see I was just waking up and, well, you know, sometimes I get scared real easy, ya know." He glanced round the room as if checking for ghosts.

"Ah I see. It can happen to all of us."

"Yeah, you too man, you get scared of spiders and things too buddy?" He shook his arms by his side.

"I'm okay with spiders, but one of my best mates has Arachnophobia."

"He has a what buddy, a rack of who?"

"A phobia of spiders."

"He does? Why me too. I must get back to bed buddy. You have a good day now." He dived back in his sleeping bag and zipped it up to his neck.

The list of weirdoes was going up rapidly and I still had the Greyhound bus journey.

As I strolled along Miami Beach, sweaty joggers panted past and I giggled at the number of dog owners who looked like their dogs.

Just one of the many luxurious yachts in the harbour on the other side of the island were probably worth more than a dozen houses in the street I'd been living down in Salvador. What would Murphy say? Probably that the boat owners hit many women, and try to guess how many days it would take to sail to England. Hearing and seeing

Porsches and Ferraris whizz about made me feel sad for those less fortunate in Latin America.

I went in a small grocery shop to get some snacks and a bottle of water to wake me up from the morning heat. The door buzzed as I entered. Inside smelt like a musky sex shop.

"Can I help you?" said a croaky female voice. I looked around the tightly packed shelves and wondered who was responsible for the neatly organised stock. "Over here," she added, lowering a copy of the Miami Herald to reveal her wrinkled face and messy auburn hair.

"Oh hi, sorry, I just want a bottle of water."

"A bottle of warta."

"Yes, a bottle of warta, please."

"Wait a second." She groaned as she snatched a bunch of keys and hobbled towards two fridges, her flowery dress scraped along the floor. Either she'd bought a size too long, or she'd shrunk.

"Anything else?" she said as she struggled back.

"Do you have any Twinkies?" I asked, in an American accent.

"Twinkies?" she said, sternly. "Are you trying to be funny sonny?" She tapped the tip of her finger on the glass counter.

"No, sorry, I just want some biscuits or something." I tried not to laugh.

"Biscuits over there," she said, pointing into a dark corner of the shop. "Twinkies *aren't* biscuits. Twinkies are here." She signalled next to the counter where a box of Twinkies hid under a thick layer of dust. Perhaps she bought them the same year as her dress.

"Just the warta thanks."

"$4."

"What, for a bottle of warta?"

"Yeah; it's cold."

"You're having a laugh. Don't worry then." I handed the warta back.

"Why you tourists are all the same; come in here, wasting my time never buying anything." She waddled towards the fridges.

"Maybe you should look at your prices Maam," I said, under my breath.

"Fucking jerk."

Up the road, I bought a more reasonably priced bottle of warta and a fresh packet of Twinkies and continued exploring. I wandered along a parade of shops where dolled up American women tottered past chatting about their new gym routines, strolled round a neighbourhood of detached houses with gardens blooming with flowers, and stopped on a bench in front of a basketball court where lanky giants were shooting some hoops. I felt like I was in a movie and tried to come to terms that I was in North, not South, America.

Then the weirdest, but in a good weird way, thing happened. I returned to my hostel to chill out by the pool. No one else was about when I fell asleep. A splash woke me up. Four athletic women in skimpy bikinis were topping up their tans on the other side of the pool and another woman was swimming. A light green towel draped over the lounger next to mine. I half closed my eyes and felt nervous as a glistening toned blonde chick climbed up the pool stairs and plonked down next to me.

"Oh hi," she said as I sat up. "Have you been to Salvador?" She squeezed her long wet hair and the water splattered by her feet. Was I dreaming? How was a pretty America lady lying next to me, and how did she know about Salvador?

"My mom used to visit Salvador regularly," she said. "She would always bring me back a bracelet like that." She pointed to the red and yellow strands tied to my bag.

"Oh right, you had me going for a minute," I said. She sat up straight.

"Had you going where?"

"It's an expression."

"Are you English?" She seemed keen.

"I guess you could say that."

"Wow, that's so cool. You sound just like Hugh Grant and you look like Sean Penn." She clapped her hands together quickly.

"Who's Sean Penn?"

"He's an actor," she swivelled her lush legs round to face me, "and he's quite cute."

"Oh, right," I said, smiling, but unsure what to do, or where to look. What was happening? Was I being set up? After living where every other girl seemed to be a prostitute, sexy women chatting me up made me feel apprehensive.

She introduced herself as Gigi, and I told her I was Jimmy, using my traveller's name. She was an L.A chick and had been working in the film industry. She had a flat overlooking the beach where they filmed some scenes of Baywatch, but was sick of all the pompous superficial imbeciles.

"Everyone is so false, that's why I've come to Miami; it's more bohemian. I'm working in a bar now," she said, proud of her new life. "It's my night off, maybe I can show you round; we can gatecrash some expensive hotel parties."

The situation was a bit much to take in. I didn't believe everything she said, but I was up for hanging around with a fit American woman who thought I was "cute".

A couple of hours later I popped up to her room. She opened the door in only a skimpy pink towel. Her hair wet. Her body shone.

"Hi," she said, as if I'd seen her half naked a million times before. I just had by the pool, but in a towel was different, underneath she had to be completely naked.

"Oh sorry, err, shall I wait out here."

"The polite English man, I love that. No it's okay, come in." The room smelt of her strawberry shampoo. Chillout music played from her CD player. She went into the bathroom and left the door open so we could chat.

"I feel so much better after a cold shower. Gets you in the mood, don't you think?"

"That depends," I said, chuckling nervously. "What are you getting in the mood for?" She slid out from the bathroom in a short green boob tube and white high heels. Her hair was still wet and hung over her slender shoulders.

"What did you say?" she said. "Never mind, do you like pizza?" she added.

"Sure I do."

"Great, let's go, I'm starving."

"I'm Jimmy." She cracked up.

"Oh I love funny men."

"It wasn't that funny," I said, trying to play down one of the oldest jokes in the book. Maybe I could tell her some 'Knock-Knock' jokes over dinner, or maybe not; I really was out of practise.

Miami was buzzing. Loads of young, hip, good-looking people were out to party. Gigi took me to where she worked because she could get free drinks. After a couple of beers and tequilas, we danced to salsa in a marquee out the front and then walked arm in arm to her favourite pizza place.

When I told Gigi that I had to get the local bus at midnight because I was catching the Greyhound to L.A she nearly choked.

"What? Are you shitting me? You're going on the Greyhound to L.A? Why?" She laughed hysterically. I told the long story and she seemed impressed. "I've never heard of anyone who has travelled that far on a Greyhound before. It's full of weirdoes, you know?"

"Yeah, that's partly why I'm going."

"You're crazy. Have you ever considered writing about your travels?"

"Not really."

"I'd like to be a writer one day. I think you have special energy," she said, stroking my arm. "Something is telling me you have to write." She grabbed my hands and caressed my palms. That was the first time I thought about writing.

"So, are you ready to gatecrash a party?" she asked as she wiped pizza from the side of her mouth. Everything she did was sexy.

As we strolled down a street full of multimillion-dollar hotels, I thought back to where I'd been walking twenty-four hours previously; how life changes when travelling.

"So remember," Gigi said as we turned into a path towards a lush hotel, "we have been invited. If anyone says anything, then look shocked and let me do the talking." Numerous flashy cars parked out front and a couple of beefy security guards protected the hotel door. We glided through the lobby, into the gardens, and round a side entrance into the crowd of partygoers dancing to the soft house music. Most guests were too smashed to notice we'd slipped in. Gigi even managed to get us a free glass of champagne.

"You've got balls, I'll give you that," I said as we chinked glasses while chilling on a leather sofa.

"Thanks. Hey, if you're going to L.A, you can meet one of my girlfriends and even stay in her flat. I'm sure she won't mind; she's just split up with her boyfriend and could do with some company."

"Oh really," I said, sipping more champagne. Was Candid Camera hiding behind one of the palm trees ready to pounce?

"I could meet her for a drink if you give me her number."

"Great idea! I feel you have good energy. We'll have to keep in touch." I agreed, glancing at my watch.

"You need to go soon, right?" she asked. I nodded, gutted I couldn't get to know Gigi better, but I had to catch the local bus; I couldn't afford the $40 cab fare. Sometimes I could be such a miserable scrooge.

As we walked back, I wondered if she was going to rob me as she said goodbye. How was it possible that such a pretty girl had taken me round Miami for nothing? Latin America had made me wary, but perhaps over-wary.

After I checked out, we grabbed another beer in a bar near the bus stop and swapped email addresses.

"Don't forget to phone my friend, she's VERY friendly," said Gigi.

"What, as friendly as you?"

"Well almost," she said, leaning and kissing me softly on the lips. Her hair smelt fresh and sweet. "You'll have to see what mood she's in." Was I making a mistake? Maybe she was just an average girl looking for some fun.

"I'm gonna miss you," she said as we stopped for breath.

"Yeah," I said, gasping. It had been a while.

As we waited outside for the bus, I felt as if a two-week holiday romance was about to end. I considered staying with Gigi and paying for a cab, but something inside was telling me to go.

"Oh, here it comes now," she said as the bus came into focus. Damn, I thought, but I had to be careful; what if she went for my wallet as I got on the bus?

"Okay then, it's been short and sweet. Thanks for a great night," I said.

"The pleasure was mine." As she kissed me again I pulled myself away and got on the bus. We drove off. She waved goodbye.

My wallet was still in my pocket.

What an idiot.

She never intended to mug me. What would my mates back home say? I'd been a fool, a scrooge, a blatant muppet. Living in fear in Brazil had dented my trust levels. If anything, I was the weirdo.

On the first stint of the Greyhound journey, trance music blasting from someone's headphones woke me up. I'd spent four hours waiting at the deserted bus station, cursing my decision to abandon Gigi, and when we eventually set off I'd zonked out.

Sensing movement, I peered across the aisle, not wanting to stare, where a man was bouncing up and down using the seat in front as reigns, as if he was in the final sprint of a horse race; my first Greyhound lunatic.

He wore a navy blue tracksuit and a dirty white baseball cap facing backwards. His pointy ginger beard flapped about and pink shades rocked on his brow as he squeaked in his chair.

"HEY YALL," he shouted. Bus passengers often wave at passersby, but no one had ever waved at me across an aisle, at least not with such enthusiasm.

"Hi," I said, softly. His eyes beamed and jaw grinded. I caught a whiff of what seemed like a used nappy. I smiled nervously, held my nose, and then pretended to sleep.

He wasn't the only weirdo. Next to the seat the Elf was shaking, was a mysterious looking person. I say person, because at first I thought the person was a man. He had a short haircut and firm jaw line, but when he turned to high five the Elf, he rested his saggy breasts, covered by his thin white t-shirt, on top of the seat. He was a she, and looked dangerous.

When the bus pulled in an empty service station (I'm not sure where; I was in a tired daze), they jived down the aisle, left the bus, and stood below my window sharing a cigarette. The nappy smell got fainter.

After they'd checked that no one was spying, the Elf held out a bunch of white tablets. Hewoman took two, popped one in her mouth and swallowed, and then put the other in and snogged the Elf. They came back on the bus grinning like two spaced out jesters and plonked in their chairs.

Still knackered, I tried to sleep, but it was useless.

"Hey this sure is a fucking long trip eh?" said the Elf after we'd been travelling for half an hour. I wondered exactly what "trip" he was referring to as he was still jiving in his seat. The nappy smell was getting worse.

"Yeah man," said Hewoman, now sat in front of him.

"Hey you boy," said the Elf. He was talking to me, but I ignored him. "Hey buddy, where you going man?" Please leave me alone, I thought, but he kept pestering. I faced him with my eyes half closed.

"Sorry, what's that?" I said.

"I said where you going boy? We're going to Atlanta."

"I'm off to L.A."

"L.A! You hear that lady, we got ourselves a road honky here," he said to Hewoman, who sat up straight.

"Why that a long way, man," Hewoman said. When I told them I was from London, I had to confirm that it wasn't an American State.

"Why you hear that, we's got ourselves a little England boy now," said the Elf.

"We sure do Hon, why, welcome to America."

When their pills really kicked in, they drifted into their trippy worlds and I finally got some doze.

I slept most of the afternoon and when I came round the sun was setting behind a line of trees on the highway. I felt sweaty and hot and my face pressed against the warm window. My elbow was resting on a something firm, but cushiony. The nappy smell was stronger.

"Hi there Hon," said Hewoman, nudging her breast into me slightly. "You were sleeping like a puppy there," she added, squeezing my leg. Where was the Elf? What was she doing next to me? She stank.

"You looking for my friend?" she said.

"Err, yeah, I thought you were going to Atlanta?"

"That was the plan, but he gets restless, you see. He got off at the last stop." She winked. "I'll see him later anyway." She smiled; the sort of smile that petrifies blokes stuck next to a stinking psychopath on a Greyhound Bus. The bus was full so she must have been forced to sit next to me; at least that's what I told myself.

She interrogated me. One question after the other: Why was I going to L.A? Where had I been? Was I looking for a wife and children? The usual questions you ask a complete stranger. I gave false answers. I was Jimmy and going to L.A to meet my wife and three kids, all of whom were no longer wearing nappies. I tried to ignore her by gazing into the darkness and counting the streetlights, but she kept rabbiting on.

The way she pushed her left breast into my ribs and rubbed her leg against mine gave me the creeps. I was relieved when we arrived in Atlanta.

"Hey, here's my number in case things don't work out with your wife and kids," she said as she tried to kiss my cheek.

"Great," I said, pulling back. "Gotta dash, need the loo, see ya then." I jogged into the mens, which smelt like a rose garden.

Thankfully, when I came out the nappy stinker had gone. I bought a plastic looking hotdog, covered it in ketchup and mustard and sat wondering what I'd missed by sleeping all day. I'd just travelled up through Florida and Georgia and didn't have a clue what the country looked like. Did it matter? I was a day closer to L.A and the next bus had to smell fresher.

There were more free seats as we set off for Dallas, almost twenty hours away. Overnight I managed to doze all the way through Birmingham and Jackson, and even missed the Mississippi River. When we pulled in at Monroe, a ton of people piled on the bus, moaning that there were too few seats.

"Hey buddy, can I sit here?" said a tall chubby lad in his early twenties. Other passengers glanced at him, surprised at his deep booming voice. His wispy blonde hair came down to his shoulders. He seemed normal and, more importantly, only smelt of stale cigarettes.

"Yeah go for it," I said. After the usual questions, Chad asked me if I'd been to see a baseball game.

"What? You haven't." He clenched my shoulder, shaking me slightly.

"I've only been here three days, and one and a half of those I've spent sitting on a bus," I said, knowing I was never going to pay to watch men play rounders with tight trousers on while spitting out tobacco. He let go.

"Ah man! You have to go man; it's the greatest, what are you, a soccer fan?" He sounded disappointed.

"Yeah, soccer, we say football though."

"Yeah I know, that's stupid, ain't it?" Did he realize he was insulting me? "We play football too, but the guys wear like protection and that, to protect their balls, man. Who's your team anyway?"

"Oh, you probably won't know them, Tottenham." He slapped his forehead as if trying to jog his memory. "Their nickname is Spurs."

"Spurs?" he said, grinning. "What you mean like the basketball Spurs in San Antonio? So not only you steal our name for games but the teams too?" He laughed, and so did I, but I had to clarify a few things.

"I think you'll find that we invented football, man."

"Really, are you sure?" He looked genuinely surprised.

"Very."

"Oh well, if you say so. I didn't know that, you learn something new every day." His phone rang. "Excuse me."

I enjoyed the sun on my face as we drove passed wispy clumps of trees in green open fields. I listened to Chad, as did everyone else within a five metres radius thanks to his profound voice. His mate had been in a fight so he was moving to Kansas to set up a new bar. He was trying to persuade Chad to go.

"How am I gonna get to Kansas, man?" he asked me.

"Why don't you just follow the yellow brick road?"

"The what?"

"The yellow brick road, you know, Dorothy, Wizard of Oz?"

"Oh yeah," he said, laughing in a sarcastic way. I thought it was funny.

Chad was the only normalish guy I met on the Greyhound trip, and it was shame we parted at Marshal.

"I'm gonna go find that yellow brick road now, you watch after yourself, and get down to see some baseball man; you'll love it."

Dallas was a major let down. It was the only place I'd really heard of on my road trip and since Dallas, the corny American series, had been such an influence on my athletic abilities in my youth (I used to bounced up and down to the theme tune in my cot) I was gutted the place was such a dive.

As soon as I left the bus, I noted a change in character of the Greyhound passengers. People barged into me as I stared at the departure notice board. I had a four-hour wait. The restaurant queue looked more like a prison canteen's queue, and the food looked tasteless.

I chanced a wander outside. Three blocks later, two blokes had asked me for money and one asked if I wanted to sell my rucksack for a gram of coke. I went back to the food queue.

After some rubbery steak, watery mash, and mushy peas, I still had three hours to kill. I entertained myself by watching chubby Americans stuff their faces, argue about their bus queue place, and throw all their spare change into the arcade machines. It was the slowest part of the journey, and possibly my life.

Just when I thought I'd made the wait, a dappy, high-pitched voice announced over the speakers there would be an extra hour delay. I felt annoyed, but nothing compared to several obese American women who started shouting in the air.

"Why you come down here and say that to my fucking face."

"Yeah, why I bin waiting for fucking ages already, now get that driver off his fat fucking ass now."

"Good saying girl, I say when he come we beat his puny fucking ass." I won't even type what their kids said.

I felt sorry for the skinny, geeky driver that turned up. Apart from the three weighty women and their kids laying into him, half a basketball team let rip.

"Bout time you jerk," shouted one. The lads towered over the driver and threaten to shoot some hoops with him if he didn't make up the hour.

"Man, this is a disgrace, I paid my money, I pay my taxes," said one as we settled on the bus.

"Yeah, this service is shit, we should all be getting refunds," said another.

"We should have them shut down, maybe we can rob the driver," said a teenage son.

The worst was still to come.

At the next stop, an extra fifty pissed off passengers were waiting. The bus was overbooked and the driver had to decide who could get on and who had to wait for the emergency bus. Rather him than me: those picked still moaned and swore, and the others were close to thumping the jittery man.

As we set off, everyone cheered and took the piss out of the driver. Then the situation got extremely out of hand. About a mile down the road, the bus broke down.

"Hey what you doing jerk?" shouted one bloke.

"He's asking to have his butt kicked, man," shouted another. Everyone went mental, hurling abuse at the driver. I felt tense and frustrated about the delay too because I wanted to arrive in L.A at a reasonable hour to catch the metro, and not pay for a taxi, the money I could have used to stay with Gigi.

I couldn't have been stranded with a worst bunch of morons while waiting for a new bus. Most passengers got off to smoke and bitch with each other. I stayed on, away from the insults and tension. We finally got going, four hours behind schedule.

The rest of the night was uneventful. My travelling companion until El Paso was a Mexican lad who hated baseball. Speaking in Spanish made me feel nostalgic. What would I do with my time in Australia with no language to learn? I missed Latin America.

The fidgeting Mexican kept me awake and I felt relieved when he got off at El Paso. I slept on and off until we got to Pheonix, a few hours from L.A. I was glad to be close: my knees ached from all the sitting, I craved some decent food, and I needed a shower. Even though we were almost six hours behind schedule, and I'd probably have to get a cab in L.A, I didn't care; I just wanted to get off the damn Greyhound Bus.

Then I met the biggest weirdo of all.

Yet again, a crowd of moping passengers waited to get on at Phoenix. I pretended to be asleep and ignored the tap on my shoulder until it turned to a firm shake.

"Hello, can I sit here," said the feminine voice. Her perfume reminded me of my Nan. I kept my eyes shut. "Hello, please, sir, there're no more seats." Oh well, I thought, maybe it was another Gigi. I opened my eyes.

"Hi," said the tall black man in a camp voice. His afro wobbled as he went to sit down. "Do ya mind if I sit here?"

"No, it's fine." Just my luck.

"What's your name?" he said in his squeaky voice, holding out his hand. "I'm Daisy." It was Jimmy time. As he shook my hand like a withering old lady on her death bed, his purple fingernails scrapped my palm. If you hadn't guessed, Daisy was a transvestite.

"So," he said, "where are you fraamm?" When I told him I was from London, he almost screamed. "London? Wow, that's so exciting. What are ya doing all the way out heeerreeee?" As he took off his high heels, his skin-tight purple trousers sparkled with glitter.

"I'm going to L.A to see family, and then getting a plane to Australia."

"Wow, you're going on a plane, how brave," he said, patting my shoulder. He offered me some grapes. The goodness popped in my mouth as I bit into the first one. Fruit at last.

I turned the attention to him, which he loved. Daisy was going to see his "mama" in L.A and maybe work in some bars.

"Between you and me, let's just say some dancing will be involved," he said, winking. Daisy was a bit of a laugh and helped make the last stint of the journey pass by quickly. He was happy chatting about his family in L.A.; he was obviously desperate to see them. He couldn't believe that I'd been away from mine for so long and that I didn't know when I'd see them again.

"You're a courageous young man being so far away from home," he said. "Your mama must miss you."

"Yeah, I guess she does." For the first time in a while, I thought of home. I'd been away for a while and the fear of returning wasn't as mortifying. I still wasn't ready though, there was still more to see.

As we arrived to L.A, brightly lit motels, bars, casinos, and cheesy welcome signs dotted the side of the road. I let Daisy sit by the window for the last hour; after all, he hadn't seen his home town for almost two weeks.

I'd survived, and my auntie had been right, the Greyhound *was* full of weirdoes.

My legs rebelled after being stuck on a bus for so long and I walked round L.A for two days. My time there would have been better if I'd had more money, but I was fine strolling about. I loved the lively atmosphere on Hollywood Boulevard where my hostel was, checking out Star Street, taking photos of the Hollywood sign, and wandering round Beverly Hills famous people house spotting.

Apart from a huge bookshop (I hadn't been in one for nine months, remember) my favourite part was Santa Monica and Venice Beach. A buzzing Blues and Jazz festival on Santa Monica Pier had Americans jumping about making fools of themselves just as much as the British do. I felt at home.

Along Venice Beach, where Gigi had her flat (No I didn't call her mate by the way), everyone was active: riding bikes, running, skate boarding, and generally keeping fit. On muscle beach, huge blokes and toned up women were beefing up their pumped bodies.

I walked along the beachfront, passed the tacky markets, bars, and amusements, until my feet could no more. I would have stopped for some beers and food but I had to save my money, prices had rocketed since Brazil, so I caught the bus back and stopped off at a supermarket for a tin of beans and some bread, which I ate back at the hostel.

The next day I saw one of the worst places for me in America; Downtown L.A. Litter caked the streets and the area had a funny rotting smell. Tramps wandered about, shouting at nothing while pushing their possessions in shopping trolleys. I felt sad seeing such desperate people, not only in Latin America had poverty struck victims. Witnessing the clean and well-kept business district just round the corner made it worse. Rich suited men and women were going out for lunch, or grabbing a sandwich to take back to their luxurious offices high up in the skyscrapers.

L.A was a remarkable place, but I was ready to go. The short adventure, or holiday, was over. Sydney was next and I needed to get a job quickly. After that, I had no plan, no connecting flight, and no idea where I'd be heading.

# 14 Australia: Get Me Out of Here

I'd been looking forward to living Down Under. Maybe if I'd gone direct from England then Sydney would have been a novelty. However, after nine months in Latin America learning languages, experiencing different cultures, and living on the edge, my fear of returning home early became a reality.

I felt as though I'd time warped back to London. Sydney was bustling with Europeans, Australians, and Asians charging about. Eating out was just as expensive, gloomy grey clouds blocked the sun, and chavs stood on corners chomping greasy smelling MacDonald's. Even the street names were strangely familiar: Oxford Street, Bond Street, Elizabeth Street.

I found it difficult to get on with the other travellers in my hostel. Most were full of energy and excited about Sydney, but my first instincts were that I had to find a job, save some money, and go somewhere more interesting.

After two days I got an interview with a language academy in the centre. The director felt that my level of grammar was too low for the Korean and Chinese students but she gave me a trial. Compared to the Latin American's relaxed manner, Asians demanded a more detailed explanation of *everything*. They questioned me and I started to question myself. Explaining grammar and vocabulary without knowing some of their language seemed impossible. I was out of my depth and the director noticed. I only lasted two days.

I dropped my CV off at every academy in Sydney and waited. Meanwhile, desperate for money, I got a job cold calling for the Sheraton Hotel premier member package. After two weeks I was going mad; craving to get back in the classroom.

Eventually, I got a break with an English academy for Koreans in Belmore, a few stops from central station.

"Your CV seems to be in order," said the director, Mr Kim, as he tapped it twice on the table next to a wooden bowl full of oranges. He was a well to do chap, dressed in a navy suit, and spoke in a posh English accent. "Tell me, how is your grammar?" He picked up one of the oranges, threw it to his other hand, and began to peel.

"It's improving, I know that Korean students can be very demanding and I'm always prepared."

"That's good," he said. "I wouldn't want a teacher who was bad at grammar now, you understand?" He popped a segment in his mouth and stared at my CV for a while before grinning. Luckily, he didn't give me a test and I got the job, but with much more work than I'd bargained for.

There were no textbooks so I had to create and type up lessons from scratch. All Mr Kim gave me was a grammar book and a few sample lessons. For someone who was crap at grammar, the learning curve was massive. I spent about two hours a day typing away in the internet cafe to plan a three-hour class. After, I sent a copy to Mr Kim so he could check the content. The process was long, but I began to understand how to construct a lesson.

My Brazilian and Ecuadorian students would have eaten the Korean ones for breakfast. I only had four female students, and they were shyer than a bunch of squirrels. Conversation classes revolved around me asking questions, and then me answering my questions. They loved the grammar exercises though; I'd never seen such a group of eager scribblers. The classes were less entertaining than in Latin America, but they did the work and were grateful of my help.

A benefit of working for Mr Kim was that he paid well, compared to the $2 an hour I'd been earning in Ecuador, I was on nearly $300 a week, tax free. I quit my sales job and moved into a flat, sharing of course.

Compared to my prison cell in Salvador, the new pad was a palace. The owners were a middle aged Chinese couple. Chris was a happy man and always up for a quick chat, but his wife was a misery guts. She never smiled and always tutted if I was in the kitchen when she wanted to cook. I wasn't bothered and felt happy to be in a comfy flat with a lounge, TV, and sofa, even if I did have to share my bedroom with a weird lad from Hong Kong.

Franco was an extremely skinny, softly spoken chap, and seemed embarrassed every time we had a chat. He always wore pyjamas in the house and carried a jingling yellow teddy bear. The bedroom was only big enough for one, but Chris had cramped in two mattresses at right angles to each other to get double rent. Apart from a desk, which Franco used because he was at university studying art, all we had was a mirrored wardrobe.

"Must be quite sexy sharing a room with those mirrors," said Nish after I'd shown him round. He was in Sydney for a bit before travelling up the East Coast.

"Yeah, shame you're not in there too, eh?"

"Why does he carry that bell?"

"I dunno. It's connected to his teddy."

"Maybe it's to warn you when he's coming back so you can stop wanking."

"Yeah, it helps actually."

I was glad Nish was in Sydney, partly because we could go out for my 25th birthday, but mainly because of the wake-up call he gave me. I'd been feeling low and confused about my direction.

I spent my birthday alone, wandering round my favourite spot, Darling Harbour, and then chilled out on Bondi Beach. I enjoyed the time to myself, and was looking forward to celebrating in the evening with Nish. However, he had another party and couldn't meet me until later so I went out on my own.

By the time he'd arrived, the bouncers were throwing me out for being too drunk (something I'll never understand about Sydney). We went for another drink, but deep down I was unhappy and miserable.

The next day I returned to Darling Harbour to rack my brains about why I felt sad. I sat on some wooden steps and gazed out at the boats; seagulls squawked as they flew about the yachts, couples strolled along sharing ice-creams, and the sun warmed up my face. Financially I was unable to leave Sydney, my teaching job was too much work, the students were dull, and I missed learning and practising a language. I still wanted to travel Australia, but I needed a more challenging and exciting country to live in. In part, I felt as though my adventure had ended.

I spent three weeks moping about until Nish got back from his trip up the East Coast of Australia.

"If you're idea of a good time is getting pissed and chasing girls, then go; it's beautiful, but easy," he said. "I need adventure and a challenge. I preferred South America, mate."

"I might as well do it while I'm here," I said. "When will we see each other again?"

"Who knows, after New Zealand I'll be in Thailand. Why don't you go and teach there? I've heard it's amazing."

"I hadn't thought of that."

I began reading up about Thailand and got back my motivation. The culture and way of life seemed much more exotic than Australia. Images of tuk tuks whizzing about the chaotic streets of Bangkok, smoky food stalls, and the party islands induced adrenaline round my veins. My heart raced when I read about romantic Chang Mai and trips to Laos, Cambodia, and Vietnam. I could even pop up to China. The Trans-Mongolian Railway had always been a distant dream too.

The main drawback was the working conditions. I read several articles warning teachers about cruddy schools and agencies that treated staff like slaves, piling on the work load, and restricting their freedom. Also, most of the schools wanted teachers for one year but I preferred not to make such a long commitment. I applied for a couple of jobs in Bangkok saying I could work on a six months contract to begin with, and waited.

One Monday I went to work, but only one student turned up.
"Only one today," I said to Mr Kim on my way out.
"Yes I see," he said. I'd never seen his face so tense.
"Not too good, is it?"
"Not really."
In the afternoon, once I'd finished planning my lessons for the next day, he sent me an email.

*Dear Barry,*
   *Regarding the classes, I am sorry but I will have to stop them with immediate effect as from tomorrow. Can you please return all material to me?*
*Mr Kim.*

My first thought was; what material? My second was; thanks for the notice, Mr Kim.

Luckily, I had another email from Mae, the director of Maewill, asking me to come in for an interview. The academy was near Manly and when I entered, I thought back to all the plush language academies that had turned me down in Latin America. The school looked modern with newly smelling blue carpeted floors and white painted walls.

Finally I had some luck. Mae, wife of Will, the other director, was much more down to earth than the other directors I'd met in Sydney.

"So, I guess you must be raring to go after such a dull class?" she said after I'd explained to her about Mr Kim's students. "Well, you won't have that problem here; our students are first class and great fun. They can be demanding, but it's all about learning how to deal with them on the spot." She offered me a part time job starting the next day on a two-week trial.

The classes were tough. My first lesson set the tone for the trial period. I had a mixed class of fifteen Korean, Brazilian, Slovakian, and Chinese students. I was teaching the difference between present perfect and present simple, still confused about the rules.

"But how do you know if the action is finished or not?" asked Petal, a thin Chinese girl with a black bob haircut. Her name might suggest she was innocent, but she had a wicked streak. "You have not explained it very well." She thumped her fists on the desk and shouted in Chinese. Other students grunted in approval.

"That's a good question," I said, laughing. "You are a bright student." She tightened her lips and stared.

"Well?"

"I'll have to tell you after the break, let me check first." The teenagers left, muttering and shaking their heads. I didn't want bad vibes getting back to Mae, so in the staff room I asked around.

A couple of teachers showed me that if the action was completed, using words such as 'yesterday' 'last week' 'last month', then it was past simple, and if the action began in the past and hadn't finished or was relevant now, using words such as 'yet' 'already' or 'since', then it was present perfect.

After the break I explained the rules with more examples.

"How's that, Petal?"

"Better," she muttered, tapping away on her electronic dictionary.

The trial period was hard graft. I'd never taught such keen students before and explaining rules and vocabulary to a mixed class was difficult. The students had different needs: the Chinese and Korean students were there to get a high enough level of English to get in the Australian public school system, whereas the Brazilians and Europeans wanted to improve their English on more of a holiday.

I was nervous about keeping my job and worked hard. I spent ages planning and took grammar books home and studied so I could explain the rules. No matter how prepared I was with the vocabulary and grammar, someone always had a question I hadn't prepared for; normally Petal.

"But why, why is it like that?" she would say, scrunching her fists. The Brazilian students would laugh, which infuriated her more. "You guys don't care; you are only here for fun. My parents will kill me if I don't get into the Australian school."

When the end of the two weeks arrived, I was certain that Mae was going to let me go.

"So Barry, how do you fancy working here full time for two months?" she said.

"Yes," said Will. "The Chinese students seem to like you."

"You're joking?" I said, "I thought they thought I was useless at grammar."

"Some have said that you were rusty to start with," said Mae. "But you're better now, plus they like the way you handle Petal."

I was stunned. I had a full time job and with my new, higher, wage packet, I'd be able to save up for a trip up the East Coast of Australia, and maybe even a flight to Thailand.

Teaching at Maewill was better than anywhere I'd taught before. I learnt loads, Mae and Will were top directors, and I had a good crack with the other teachers. My favourite day was Friday because there would be some type of excursion, maybe to Sydney Harbour, karaoke in the common room, or table tennis tournaments, which the Chinese lads always won.

There was a rotary system so we changed classes every two weeks. The Brazilians were a cool bunch, always happy and smiling. Some funny lads from Slovakia were always bantering with each other and trying to chat up the Japanese students.

Mae would also lumber me with three young Korean brothers because no one else wanted to teach the 'hyperactive ones'. Tommy, eleven, Johnny, nine, and June, six, were my first younger learner students. At first I felt as though I was babysitting, but after the initial shock of their boisterous ways, I was able to teach some English. They were in awe of my rubbish card tricks and hang man games. The problem was their attention span, after ten minutes of one activity they got bored. It was hard work but rewarding and Mae was appreciative, as were the other teachers.

After a month, one of the teachers left so Mae moved me back with a class mainly of Chinese students.

"What's wrong?" I asked the snivelling teenagers.

"We no want new teacher."

"We miss our teacher."

"When can we get her back?" said Petal.

It took me ages to win them over. For about a week they failed to participate, constantly questioned my grammar explanations and some even bunked off.

When I told them I'd travelled and taught in South America they seemed to listen more.

"But you travelled alone?" asked Petal.

"Yeah, I had no choice." The class wooed.

"And you live here alone?" asked Petal.

"I live with a Chinese family, but mine are in England." They whispered to each other. "Why, don't you lot travel around Sydney on your own?" I joked. They all shook their heads.

"We are too scared," said Petal. "A lot of us don't like Sydney, we are afraid of the Australian people, they look at us funny."

"So what do you all do at the weekend?"

"Stay at home and study," said one lad.

"We want to go back to China," said another.

I felt sorry for the poor little foreigners. Suddenly they looked younger and more vulnerable. I tried to motivate them to get out and explore the local surroundings at the weekend, but the next Monday they'd stayed in studying. After a while we had more fun in class and I enjoyed teaching them as much as they enjoyed coming, I think.

Outside work, I had a dull social life. Most of the teachers at Maewill had their own busy schedules and Franco, was, well, Franco. He was a shy lad, rarely left the room, and when I tried to speak about girls he went quiet. We got on all right; he would study at his desk every night while I read on my bed; the perfect married couple.

Besides, I was happy saving money for my next adventure. I ate simple food such as pasta and rice with chicken, gave up drinking for almost a month, and spent my weekends walking round Sydney. My favourite spots remained Darling Harbour and Bondi. I used to walk to the beach from the centre in just over an hour, walk round the paths along the coast, and then go home and read. I kept motivated by thinking of the money I was saving for Thailand.

After just over two months at Maewill, I received an email from a man called Siriluck offering a six months teaching contract in Bangkok. Actually having the contract made me question whether I wanted to go. I had to leave Maewill soon anyway because my Australian work visa only allowed me three months with one company. I felt concerned about the cowboy schools in Thailand. What if they made me work slave hours for little pay?

I emailed Siriluck several times about the working conditions and visas and he said they would provide accommodation and a comfortable salary. Everything *seemed* in order. I accepted the job and started planning a three-week trip up the East Coast, into Ayers Rock, and then back to Sydney for a flight to Bangkok.

Mae and Will were excellent when I told them, but warned me not to tell the Chinese students until a couple of days before.

"They tend to get emotional," Mae said.

On my last day at Maewill we went on a harbour bridge cruise as a final goodbye with teachers and students. It was a great end to an excellent part of my trip. As Mae had mentioned, the Chinese students were particularly sad, some were even crying, weeping like lost kittens. I hadn't expected that kind of a send off.

One wrote me a touching letter. The letter explained how Chinese parents frowned on their children for wasting their time travelling or walking about aimlessly in places they didn't know when they should be studying. Her parents were particularly strict. She said that my travel stories had inspired her to explore Sydney, to get out and see the world and be a free spirit:

*'I know now that it's not all about studying, and there is a whole world to see. Thank you for pushing me to get out and inspiring me to explore. Good Luck, from Petal.'*

She also gave me a yellow teddy, which didn't have a jingling bell like Franco's, but the thought was there.

That act of kindness made my time in Sydney worthwhile. I may not have enjoyed the city as I'd hoped, but I was learning more about how to become a teacher and experience the delights of helping others to achieve their dreams. I guess it's not only about teaching English.

Unlike other countries, my mini trip in Australia was more about the adventure than the people. To start with I was in a relaxed holiday mode. I travelled by bus up to Byron Bay, a surfing town, where I just chilled on the beach for a day. I got bored strolling round the shops and museums in Brisbane so I shot up to Hervey Bay.

On a three day 4WD trip around Fraser Island, the world's biggest sand island, I met a decent bunch of British lads and girls. We had a laugh getting lost, drunk, and seeing the wild dingoes. Roughing it on the island was amazing and seeing deadly sharks darting about from a cliff called Indian Head was the highlight. However, my adventure really got started when I learnt how to dive on the Whitsundays.

Ever since my parents took me on a glass bottom boat in Majorca, I'd been fascinated about the underwater world. I caught an overnight bus from Hervey Bay to Airlie Beach, a small town catered mainly for divers, to explore the Great Barrier Reef. Airlie was blessed with beauty. On my first day I strolled round the grass area by the beach and gazed out at the dark green islands, wandering where the sailing trip would go. I chilled out by a pool on the sea front and waited for my medical so I could get on a PADI diving course.

"So you're ready to learn about the underwater world?" asked Matt, the Kiwi instructor. Two Taiwanese girls, Tara and Kim, sat next to me in the tiny classroom. We nodded in agreement. "Choice," he said, extending his thumbs and pinkie fingers while shaking his wrists. "You're gonna love it. I've been diving twenty years and still get a buzz every time I float around under water. It's an alternative to travelling in space; I was never very good at flying."

Matt taught us about the equipment. I had to wear a 'BCD' jacket for buoyancy, check my 'regulator' for breathing, and I had an extra 'O' ring I was unaware of. He demonstrated various underwater sign language symbols. My favourite was holding my hand over my head and waggling the tips of my fingers like a fin.

"Yeah but we won't need that one, right?" I asked, chuckling.

"There is almost no chance of seeing sharks on this part of Australia, but best you remember the sign. Moving on...'

Getting dressed in the tight swimsuits and breathing in the air while the gas canisters hissed felt strange. I'd seen plenty of diving footage on the telly, but watching Matt swim below in the deep practise pool was exhilarating. The sensation of floating mid water was incredible. At first I was shooting about like a bubble in a lava lamp, but I gained control of my buoyancy levels and copied Matt's 'choice' sign.

On the second day we passed the theory and practical tests. While under water we took off our BCD's, filled up and emptied the mask with water, and helped each other to the surface. We were ready for the two-day sailing trip around the Whitsundays to learn to dive for real.

Matt walked us up the wooden pier to the pirate style boat, wished us luck, and gave us a big 'choice' wave. On the deck were ten other divers, our instructor Mick; a German lad with a shaved head apart from a pony tail, and Skip; a playdough faced Australian.

"Now listen here, and listen good," Skip said, chewing on some straw from his hat as he stood facing everyone. "This is my boat, what I say goes. I don't want any drunken behaviour. We're here to have some fun, but control your booze. The plan is to sail until the evening where we'll drop anchor by a dive site for an early start. Now sit back and relax."

My new colleagues were a bunch of gormless bores. I tried to mingle while we ate a pasta dinner but everyone stayed in their cliquey groups and no one was up for a beer, apart from a red faced Australian man already stumbling about the deck.

My cabin buddy Han, a Dutch lad in his early twenties, who paraded around in his Speedos, boasted about all the amazing dives he'd done. He might have been interesting if he hadn't been so smarmy.

As I sipped a beer on my own on the deck watching the sun set, I knew the excursion was not going to be about the people, or the party, but the diving. I went to bed.

"Emergency," shouted Han, waking me up, my bed was vibrating and a loud whirling sound was coming from outside, "all on deck, all on deck." He darted out the cabin. I rushed on some clothes and raced upstairs. The boat was lodged in the sand and tipping at an angle with the shore only thirty metres away.

"What the fuck's going on?" slurred the red faced Australian. His breath stank of booze. The Skip snarled while revving the engine and fought with the huge wooden steering wheel.

"We're fucked," said Han. "What about my dives?"

The Skip continued heaving.

"Is the boat stuck?" said an Australian woman.

"To fucking right it is," said Redface. "The Skip's gone and anchored right next to the sodding beach."

Everyone had gathered on deck and was moaning. How had the skip managed to anchor so far away from the dive site? What were we doing right next to the beach? And how were we going to get our dives in to pass the course? I was worried.

The Skip ordered Mick to take everyone on shore in the dingy because the tide was going out and the boat could topple. When we got on the beach it was still only 7am and most of us slept. Within a couple of hours everyone apart from Redface was playing touch rugby. The Skip and Mick ran rings round everyone.

"Maybe if you anchored boats as well as you played rugby we wouldn't be sitting here," shouted Redface as he sipped a beer from the touchline.

After a while the sun began to scorch and everyone bombarded the Skip with complaints. I kept quiet, not wanting to stir, and watched the boat sway. Six hours later, everyone was relieved when Skip fired up the engine.

We stopped near a rocky island where other boats were anchored and divers bobbed on the surface. We still had time to dive.

I know we'd practised in the pool, but clipping on the gear and watching the experienced divers jump off the boat made me nervous. When they came back they were ecstatic.

"I'll let the bastard off," said Redface. The Skip was lying in the sun on the deck sipping a beer, content that he'd rescued the day.

Mick ordered me to stand with my flippers half hanging off the edge of the boat. The yellow tank pulled me back slightly. After three, I jumped and splashed in the cold water. Bubbles drifted round as I surfaced and did the 'OKAY' sign for Mick. I breathed louder, my mouth clenched on the mouthpiece, my fillings tingled. Dunking my head in the clear water and gazing towards the deep coral increased my breathing.

Once the Taiwanese girls were in, we swam behind Mick.

"You need to go and wait for me down there," he said, pointing to a sandy clearing under water. "And remember, don't touch the coral."

I went first while Mick watched. I'd love to say I drifted down like an octopus, but I bummed around, trying to control the air in my BCD, and plummeted like an ogre with weights attached to its arse. I found the sandy patch and swayed about as the surface glistened above. I felt a rush of adrenaline, as if in an underwater documentary.

Tara appeared, but Kim remained on the surface. I did the 'choice' sign and Tara copied. We helped each other to kneel on the sand until Mick returned alone; Kim had freaked out.

We performed the safety tasks and followed Mick on a tour round the coral. He glided along like a water baby while we bumbled about like a couple of Mr Blobbys. Mick demonstrated front and back spins, and then guided us. Flipping about was easy with the heavy tank, and the water stayed out of my nose. As Matt had said, I felt like I was floating around in space. When we had to drift up I felt sad, like when the teachers used to ring the bell after break.

On board everyone was buzzing and had forgotten about the disastrous start. Chatting with the others was easier now that I'd experienced diving; even Han seemed less of a twat.

After some more pasta, I thanked Mick.

"You're very welcome, it's my job. Tomorrow's site is better, and you can see Elvis."

"What's Elvis doing in Australia?"

"He's a fish. Hopefully you'll see him tomorrow."

By the next morning we'd sailed beside a new rocky island, but because of regulations we had to use the dingy to get near the coral. Kim bottled out, so just Tara and I waited as Mick yanked the motor's cord. The engine made a whirling sound and we skimmed along the surface.

I enjoyed the backwards drop into the sea, but gasped as the cold water froze my body. Tara and I kept our buoyancy levels better and completed the tasks. While we were on the seabed, Mick pointed behind me, at first I thought he'd made the shark sign, but there was no need to panic; Elvis, a blue Napolean Rasse fish, was bumbling over. As Elvis circled above, his green and blue gills flickered and his giant lips opened and closed as if he was saying hello. He glided over our heads and drifted between our bodies. How something so heavy moved with such grace was fascinating; the mysteries of the sea.

After Elvis fled, a shoal of fifty black and yellow fish whizzed over. Mick opened a bag of bread and they went crazy, darting all over the place. I'd fed fish in aquariums, but never been surrounded by so many.

Once on the surface we'd become Open Water Divers.

"Congratulations guys, you've both passed," Mick said, shaking ours hands.

As we returned to Airlie beach, listening to David Gray's Sail away, I watched the sea bob up and down, content I'd come closer to the underwater world and had experienced the marvel of the Great Barrier Reef.

Before I left Airlie, I had to get a birthday present for my mum.

"How many times have you jumped then?" I asked Chad, my lofty tandem skydiving mentor. I was hanging in an elastic pouch in some sexy yellow overalls. Chad was showing me what to expect from the eight-thousand foot jump.

"Just over three-thousand."

"And no accidents, right?"

"Yeah, sound as a pound, mate."

When the propellers cranked up and the tiny white plane took off, my legs began to shake and my stomach knotted up. What was I doing?

The plane shook as we rose. The Whitsunday Islands looked like tiny green splodges of jelly in giant bowl of blueberry ice cream. After ten minutes, Chad clipped on to my reigns as I sat facing the door.

"Get ready; when I open the door, the wind is going to smack you in the face." As the door flew open, the wind crashed against my ears and gushed down my throat. My legs trembled as we edged forwards. The cameraman scurried along the wing and positioned himself so he could film when we jumped.

"Ready?" shouted Chad.

"Yeah," I shouted.

"Cross your arms." He tugged my back. I crossed my arms. The air pushed me sideways. "On three: one...two...three."

My head jolted back and the wind raced against my face as we dived out the plane. We span around and flashes of blue and green flickered before my eyes. When Chad tapped me on the shoulder I straightened my arms and we stabilised. We were falling flat, plummeting through the air. When the cameraman popped in front, I did the 'choice' sign and tried to shout but the air blocked my speech.

"Ready?" Chad shouted. I stuck up my thumb. Chad tugged something and we shot up, the elastic pulled on my chest and groin. The parachute opened and flapped in the wind. As we glided down there was pure silence.

"How about that, mate?" Chad said as he steered us down.

"Amazing, I'm buzzing man." My legs were still shaking but I was relieved the jump was over as we drifted towards the runway.

When we landed the cameraman was waiting.
"Happy Birthday Mum," I said, panting.
"Where's the best place to skydive, mate?" asked Chad.
"Whitsundays."
Within ten minutes they'd made the video of my sky dive so I could send it home for my mum's birthday.

The final excursion was over two thousand kilometres away in Alice Springs. From Airlie Beach, I shot up to Townsvillle, the dullest place I went to in Australia, and then hopped on a bus for twenty-four hours through the outback to Alice Springs.

Alice was a dry, unpleasant town in the middle of nowhere. For the first time since Brazil, I felt uneasy walking about. Apart from the intense heat and constant flies buzzing round my face, some aboriginal lads on a street corner, drinking from a box of wine, confronted me as I left a supermarket.

"Hey mate," said one, blocking my path. "Can't spare any food?"

"Sorry, all I've got." I shrugged and paced past. They called after me but I kept on. They hadn't done anything, but memories of Brazil came flooding back. The confrontation spooked me; I'd forgotten what a luxury feeling safe had been in Australia. I spent the rest of the day chilling by the pool in the hostel complex, protected from the outside world.

I'd been hoping for a party clan on the three-day trip to see Ayers Rock, or Uluru as the aboriginals say, but I was lumbered with another sensible bunch.

"Hey, are you with this group?" I asked a skinny lad with a black crew cut, as he tapped his watch.

"Yes, I am. Where is ze bus?" He glanced at his watch twice and huffed.

"I dunno. Maybe we missed it."

"I hope not. I am so excited about ze trip. Ayers Rock will be marvellous." He tapped his watch again and held it close to his ear.

"You're not from Germany, are you?" I said in as much a positive way as I could muster at 7am.

"Yes." He raised his eyebrows and spoke to me in German.

"I'm English," I said, waiting for the usual silence.

"Great, I like English people. I am David. Good to meet you."

When the minibus turned up, 'twelve minutes late' according to David, we sat at the back. Eight Japanese girls entered, giggling and pushing each other, and a blonde chick sat in front of David.

"Okay troopers," said our guide through the microphone. "Let's get cracking, shall we?" He wore a light brown, linen outback suit and a beige hat with corks hanging. "I'm Steve, and I'll be your chauffer, cook, guide, and mother for the next couple of days, I don't do dirty nappies though," he said, cackling. "We're gonna do about four-hours driving before we reach our first site. Get comfortable and leave me in peace, okay?" He cackled again. "Only joking, feel free to ask me any questions." As we pulled away, the group of Japanese girls cheered and soon Steve was whizzing us along a dusty road in the outback.

"That is why they call it the outback," David said as we stared out the window. The ground was dry and flat with a few weepy bushes scattered about.

"Why's that?"

"Because there is nothing here, we are a long way from anything, as they say we are 'out the back of beyond'"

"Is that right?" said the blonde chick. She was American.

"Of course," said David, opening his guide book. "Everyone knows that."

"Well, I'm not everyone, I'm Chloe."

"Well Chloe, now you know why the outback is called the outback."

"Fascinating," she said, rolling her eyes. David failed to pick up her sarcastic tone and read the outback section out loud.

"I just wanna see why this rock is supposed to be so amazing," said Chloe.

"Oh, but it *will* be amazing. It's almost ten kilometres in circumference and one kilometre above sea level." David held up a picture of Uluru from his guidebook.

"You certainly know your facts," Chloe said, her voice trailing off. David read again, but we fell into a daze and stared into the outback.

We stopped for lunch near some canyons and Steve guided us round. We followed him along a dry clay path above a deep ravine. The air smelt musky.

"Now be careful you don't fall over the edge," he said to the Japanese girls posing for photos in front of a sheer drop. "We don't want any accidents until you've at least seen Uluru. After that you can do what you want."

Steve led us round the canyon and down some spiral stairs until we reached a small lake hidden in a rocky cove. The water looked refreshing after the sweaty walk.

"Watch out for the crocs," said Steve.

"He's joking," said David.

"Am I?" Steve tip toed along the black rocky surface towards the edge of the lake. "Last guy to swim in there came out with one leg." Chloe scrunched her face and shrugged.

"I'm going in," she said. She stripped down to her bikini, tottered along, and dived in.

"How is it?" I shouted.

"Awesome," she said, ducking under again. When I got near the edge I slipped on the slimy surface and splashed in, almost colliding with a huge boulder under the water. It felt good to wash off the grime and wake up a bit after the lethargic lunch.

Steve drove us a couple of hours to a campsite with bedded wooden huts and a barn with a stove and long oak table.

"It's not quite the outback, eh?" I said to David as we explored our hut.

"No, these beds are better than the hostel's," he said, squeaking the mattress.

Steve cooked up a massive feast of vegetable soup to start, meatballs and pasta for main, and cake made by his wife for dessert. After, we sat round a crackling campfire and Steve taught us a few outback songs, until light rain began to fall.

"Who's gonna sleep under the stars then?" said Steve as everyone grabbed their things and headed for the huts.

"How, it's going to rain?" said David.

"It won't last long," said Steve. "Plus, we've got some waterproofs."

When the rain died down, Steve, David, Chloe and I got in our sleeping bags covered by the protective pouches and fell asleep gazing at the thousands of stars.

Most slept as Steve drove the next morning. I kept an eye out the window, hoping to be the first to catch a glimpse of Uluru.

"Okay boys and girls," Steve said on his microphone, waking everyone up. "Keep a look out on the left; we should see her any minute now." David shot up.

"There it is," shouted Chloe.

"Where?" said David.

"Oh yeah, look," I said, pointing to what seemed like a huge mammoth slugging through the outback; an enormous mound in the middle of nowhere. David shrilled with delight.

Steve said that thousands of years ago Australia was under the sea and over time erosion broke off bits from the ground, until this giant monolith remained.

"It's mysterious," Steve said. "Wait until you get up close; there's something spooky about Uluru. It's sacred to the Aboriginals; they believe the rock is god like because of its formation. They don't like tourists climbing up and claim that it's theirs, but the government has declared it an official tourist site."

As we approached, the size of Uluru stunned everyone, especially David.

"It's fucking massive," he said, clapping as we stood at the base. Tourists were climbing up a path by holding onto a metal rail.

"David," said Chloe in a surprised tone. "That's not like you."

"But look, it's a fucking massive rock, glorious." He threw his hands in the air and jumped slightly.

"Okay mate, don't have an orgasm," I said, patting him on the shoulder.

"Right guys," said Steve. "Those who want to climb, can. Those who want to respect the aboriginal people's wishes can come with me round the sides."

"What you're not climbing up?' David asked Steve.

"No, I prefer to respect the aboriginals; I've been up a few times anyway."

"What happens if we go up?" I said.

"It's a sacred place; imagine walking over a church or a synagogue. Many people do walk up Uluru so I wouldn't worry. I just have to inform you."

David and I went first, while Chloe went with a couple of the Japanese girls round the side, the rest of the Japanese girls waited at the base, plucking up their courage.

I felt guilty about going up, but I'd come so far and wanted to see the views. The climb was steep. Most other hikers suffered in the scorching heat, stopping for breathers and sips of water.

As we reached the first peak, I felt a touch of vertigo; I knew the rock was solid enough not to collapse, but the wind blew strong. I remembered when my father taught me to fly a kite, the wind gushed so hard that I thought the kite was going to whisk me away, I was only four, but since I've had a thing about high windy places.

Once over the main peak, the rest of the walk was flatter. We followed the white arrows and jumped over boulders and cracks until we got to the top. Tourists ambled about, taking photos and congratulating each other.

We sat on the floor looking into the wilderness. As expected the landscape was dry and flat, but in the distance were random bunches of huge boulders and rocks. The wind blew harder, but I couldn't see directly below so I felt safe.

"This is marvellous," said David, wiping the sweat from his brow.

"Yeah, not bad, I can see the pub from 'ere."

"Which pub is that?"

"Just over there behind that tree, can't you see it?"

"No I can't. Hang on a moment and let me put on my glasses." The joke was lost.

A couple of Japanese girls turned up and we posed for photos. In the centre was a placard that read we were 866 metres above sea level and gave the distances to various mountains in the Northern Territory.

"How come we're still in the Northern territory when we're supposed to be smack bang in the middle of Australia?" I asked David.

"That is a good point. Maybe the Australian government have a problem reading compasses," he said, laughing. "You see, northern territory, problem with compasses, oh my, this is a marvellous rock." He giggled to himself. I guess you had to be there.

Steve popped open a couple of bottles of champagne once we'd joined the masses and driven a couple of kilometres away to watch Uluru change colour at sunset.

"That was an amazing experience," said David as we sipped the bubbly. "How was the tour round the side?" he asked Chloe.

"Eerie,' she said, shivering. "Steve told a few tales about people who'd gone missing in the ancient times and how people used to travel to Uluru from all over Australia to heal diseases. Some were magically cured. It was definitely worth coming on the trip though, awesome."

Even from a distance, Uluru emitted a strange spooky force. We gazed in silence as the brown rock slowly turned orange, then red, and, finally purple.

"It's a beautiful rock," David said, wiping the corner of his eye.

"Don't cry mate, this isn't a World Cup Semi-Final, you know."

"No, it is far more important."

As Steve drove us away from the giant purple mammoth towards our camp for the night, I felt ready to leave Australia. The trip up the East Coast had been fun and Australia had a lot of 'marvellous' sights, but I craved a different culture, one that hopefully Thailand could offer.

# 15 Thailand: Meet the Sister

"Now you have interview with sister," said Siriluck, the hamster faced Thai woman I'd been liaising with from Australia. Siriluck was an agent who found teachers for schools. I know, I thought she was a man, but that was just the first surprise when I arrived in Bangkok.

"What, your sister works in the school?" I asked. Siriluck giggled as she drove on. For 10am the traffic was horrendous. A gang of motorbikes whizzed past my open window and petrol fumes shot up my nose.

"Not *my* sister, *the* Sister." She cackled, put her foot down, and darted in the right-hand lane.

"What do you mean *the* Sister?" I hoped she'd made a grammatical mistake. What if there *was* a Sister and I was working in a religious environment?

"Sister Leonora," she said, as if everyone in Thailand knew Sister Leonora. "You may get a bit scared."

"A bit scared?"

"Yes, I only want help you, this my job and I want you work for school, but prefer honest." She smiled. What was the Sister going to do, force me to confess my sins? "Some teachers come out interview and shocked, but don't worry, she no as bad as everyone say."

"Great, thanks for the warning." I wondered what I was letting myself in for. Would I be working in a monastery and need to pretend I was religious? Surely you had to be religious to work for a nun.

As we swerved in and out the cars, slim Thai women and skinny Thai men walking on the pavements glared at me. Siriluck steered left at a Seven Eleven on the corner and we cruised down a quieter road with detached houses protected by white walls.

"Here we are," Siriluck said as a security guard let us pull into a car park big enough to fit fifty cars.

"What *this* is the school?" I peered through the gaps in the trees at the three storey building. There must have been six or seven classes on each floor.

"Yes, pretty, you like?"

"It's not bad," I said in a sarcastic tone. As we strolled across the concrete playground, which had four basketball courts, I noticed the air smelt fresher. Perhaps the high trees kept out the pollution. I felt intimidated by the size; it was a real school, twenty times larger than the academy I'd started at in Quito.

We turned past the gigantic dining hall and stopped outside a bungalow surrounded by hanging trees and a flowery garden.

"Are you ready to meet the Sister?"

"Ready as I'll ever be." Siriluck rang the bell on the gate and we waited. A door slammed shut. My stomach tensed. I didn't know, but I was about to meet someone who would have a major impact on my life.

"You made it then?" a sharp voice called out. Siriluck replied in Thai. From a distance the Sister seemed tall but by the time she'd reached the gate, which came up to my chest, she could barely see over. She smiled as she swung it back. Her white habit was tight, hiding her ears and showing the lines on her patchy, wrinkled face. Her rectangular black framed glasses rested on her button nose.

"This is Sister Leonora," Siriluck said, placing her hands flat together under her chin and bending forward. I tried to copy but felt silly attempting a *wai*.

"Oh, that isn't necessary," said the Sister, almost cross. Her accent sounded Spanish. "A simple handshake will do." She clasped my hand and winked. "Well, you are a handsome man. Come now." I relaxed slightly, but not for long.

We followed in silence as she clonked in her tiny black shoes along an echoed hall and up three flights of marbled stairs. I was sure I'd heard a quote about not trusting women with small feet, or those that hid their ears in a white habit. She slid open her tinted windowed door and propped herself on a swivelled chair behind her desk, which was covered with piles of papers and black folders. Several pictures of Jesus hung on the wall. Siriluck sat next to me.

"So, you are ready to work for Our Lady of Perpetual Health School?" She smiled as she clasped her chubby fingers together.

"I'd like to; it's a lovely school."

"Lovely, yes, but work is to be done," she snapped.

We chatted about my work experience and agreed that, if chosen, I could work on a six-month contract, even though she wanted me to stay longer.

"So, are you catholic?"

"Of course,' I said, hesitantly, eyeing a picture of Jesus. "My father is religious."

"That is good, we like healthy minded teachers. Siriluck would have told you that we do things a little differently here."

"Yes, she did," I said, smiling at Siriluck, who smiled back. She hadn't told me a thing.

"Here at Our lady of Perpetual Health we have an English program for children who are taught through English rather than English directly."

"Sounds interesting, so I'd be teaching maths and science and things?"

"Yes, can you swim?"

"Swim?"

"I will put you down as the swim teacher too." She scribbled in her pad. "Okay," she said slowly, moving closer. Something serious was coming. "About living in Thailand; I can see you are a handsome man and well presented, but new teachers need to appreciate our culture. I am from the Philippines, so some things were new to me too."

"Sure, that's fine."

"First we need to make you presentable." She glanced at my, almost, shoulder length hair.

"You want me to cut my hair," I said in a low tone.

"Certainly, all the children have short crew cuts and our teachers need to be respected."

"Okay," I said, reluctantly. After she'd told me about the free accommodation next to the school she put on her serious voice again.

"There are conditions."

"You don't say." She pretended not to hear me.

"The female Thai teachers here will find you exotic. They may even speak to you." That was a bonus, wasn't it? "Some Thai women find that selling their bodies is a good way of making a living." I nodded. "We had a problem with our last teacher, Mr Stuart, who was dismissed because of his uncontrollable sexual urges." I tried not to laugh.

"Don't worry, I can control mine." She gazed to see if I was joking.

"Very well, do you drink or smoke?"

"It's a bit early in the day for me." She frowned. "Yeah, I like the occasional beer on a Saturday night with friends."

"There will be no drinking on school premises, and no hangovers; we have had problems in the past. You must not leave during school hours either, you will be needed."

This seemed a bit much, but the worst was next. I knew I had to leave Thailand to sort out a Non Immigrant B visa, but I'd hoped to see some of Thailand before term started.

"When you get your visa you must come back and do your lesson plans."

"What lesson plans?"

"We must have lessons planned two months in advance." Normally planning for a week was tricky enough. I hadn't even met the students yet. I had to stand my ground.

"I see Sister, but I was planning a trip round Thailand after getting the visa."

"Why do you people always want to travel, don't you know it is dangerous? Are you here to work or play?" Her voice became sterner.

"A bit of both." We sat in silence while she scanned her Jesus calendar.

"You can have a couple of days. Don't forget you have Christmas and Easter to travel. You are needed *here* now." She stubbed the table with her index finger, and then smiled.

I felt annoyed but I needed the job and without permission from a school I'd never get a long term visa. She gave me details on how to get to Penang in Malaysia and warned me of the problems between the Muslims and Buddhists in the south.

"Well, I'm neither so I should be okay."

"This is not a laughing matter Mr Barry, you need to take care; this is a dangerous world." She wagged her finger.

"Yes sister," I said. "Why did you call me *Mr* Barry?"

"It's a Thai custom. The students call teachers, *Kun*, by their first name, so you will be Mr Barry." She stood up, which made her lower down, to put an end to the meeting.

"So I got the job?"

"Yes Mr Barry, now get to Malaysia, we must get prepared for the next term, it will be a tough one. God bless you."

As Siriluck drove out the school grounds, I tried to comprehend what had happened. I blamed myself. I was the one who wanted to leave an easy going environment in Australia to experience a different culture. I thought of home and still felt a pang of fear about returning. I desperately wanted my adventure to continue and learn more about the world. I felt frustrated that I only had a couple of days to travel and had to spend a week writing lesson plans for a class I'd never met. Siriluck sensed my disappointment and treated me to lunch.

"Why is everyone staring at us?" I said as pairs of surprised Thai eyes gazed while we sat on red plastic chairs by a metal table. We were in a small restaurant along a main road near the school. Several waitresses gossiped around the buffet style spread and the smell of chillies sizzling in a pan filled the air.

"Not us, you. You are *farang* now, people love stare at *farang*." A *farang* meant foreigner, and I'd never felt more so. Siriluck ordered and we waited.

"What's the Sister all about? Sounds more like a prison than a school."

"I know, many teacher say same, but some enjoy. The Sister hard, but you have to respect wishes." A waitress plonked two plates of rice on the table and the steam blew in my face.

"What's this?" I said, poking at the meat.

"*Khao Phat Moo*- egg fried rice with pork, you like?" I took a mouthful.

"Yeah, not bad." She sprinkled some dark orange flakes on hers.

"You want? Is spicy?" My spice taste buds had been in hibernation since Mexico and I should have known better than to cover my plate and shove a heap in my mouth. The burning sensation made me splutter rice over the table.

"Here drink," Siriluck said, handing a metal beaker with an ice-cold sugary tea drink. Once I'd got my breath back, I continued the meal. With every spoonful I began to enjoy the taste of Thailand, and by the time Siriluck had paid the bill (about £2) she had persuaded me to take a different view.

"I know my job make you stay, but I honest. Some teachers leave, but others say is great person. She like order and discipline, only want best of people, with time you see."

I had no choice; most schools wanted a year's commitment and term was about to start. Perhaps something positive would come out of working for a hard-nosed nun. As long as I broadened my experience teaching and got the time off I'd been promised to travel then I could deal with a few lesson plans and silly rules.

Siriluck took me round the shopping precinct in Bangkapi (the district where I'd be living) so I could buy some plain white, and blue, shirts. Monday, Wednesday, and Friday were white days, the others blue. As we strolled round the mall I felt out of place. I'd never been stared at so intensely. The looks were unlike Salvador where people were checking out what they could nick. The Thais seemed genuinely surprised to see a Western man walking about their neighbourhood. We walked passed a mobile phone stand and a group of young lads, who looked feminine, pointed and giggled. Surely there were other *farang* living in Bangkapi. I'd have to get used to it.

Despite Siriluck's help, the visa run was a disaster. I flew down to Hat Yai, where I stayed the night in a cockroach infested hostel, and in the morning caught a bus over to George Town, in Penang. When I finally got to the immigration office it was a Friday so I had to wait all weekend to get my visa, which meant I lost the days I had to travel. If there hadn't been torrential rain then I might have been able to see some of the island, but I ended up returning to Bangkok extremely wet and pissed off. So much for travelling before term started.

"I miss badminton," said the Thai teacher back at school when I asked about the keys to my flat.

"I wouldn't mind a game either," I said. "But I haven't brought a raquet."

"No, no," she said, pointing at herself. "I Miss Badminton."

"Nice to meet you Miss Badminton."

"No," she said in her high pitched voice, swinging for my upper arm while grinning. "No Badminton, Badinton. You come."

Miss Badinton was different from the slim pretty Thai women I'd seen. Her rigid frame and crooked teeth made her look like something out of the Munsters. She smelt like a crumpled up wet towel left to dry in a damp room and kept grinning in a seductive way as we walked through the deserted school grounds.

"Today quiet, soon many children, much noise," she said, tapping her ears.

About forty seconds outside the gates, we stopped and she pointed towards a huge white house.

"This you." she said.

"What?" I gazed at the mansion. It couldn't possibly be for me.

"Not all you; only one room."

I chose the spacious bedroom at the top on the third floor. I had my own blue bathroom, an area for a kitchen (not that I cooked), and a bedroom big enough to fit four double beds. There was even a decent view over the trees surrounding the school and other houses. After living with so many different people on my travels, I felt relieved to have my own flat.

As I settled the deposit with Miss Badinton, she gave me the keys and stroked my hand. I was grateful for her help, but her suggestive grin freaked me out.

When Sister Leonora gave me her first orders, six months seemed like a lifetime away.

"Right Mr Barry, I can see you've cut your hair, much better." She sounded calm. "I hope you enjoyed your time gallivanting around the country, now it is time to work." Her voice became stern.

"Sure Sister, I had a good…"

"It's not of interest to me what was good, or even bad, the fact is we need lesson plans done for the next two months, now this is how it shall be done." She grabbed a wad of blank lesson plans and slammed them on the desk.

After she'd shown me what to do, she warned me that the lesson plans had to be neat and tidy.

"Take pride in your work." She wagged her chubby finger and I wondered how it would look caught in her door.

"Of course, Sister," I said, smiling. I was determined to remain calm, "just one doubt, Sister."

"It better be valid."

"It's just that I don't know anything about the class, the number of students, age, level, how can I plan for a bunch of kids I don't know?"

"At least you seem interested." She smiled. I had a class of twenty-three students, all of varying levels, shapes, and sizes. If I had any doubts I could ask Mr Geoff or Miss Lucy who were 'busying planning their lessons' in the staffroom.

The staff room was stuffy with five teachers gathered round a long table. On the walls were glass cabinets full of games, books, stationary, and a few puppets.

"Now laddy,' said Miss Lucy in her Irish tone as she slapped a metal ruler in the palm of her beefy hand, "I wouldn't get your knickers in a twist about the lesson plans." She broadened her wide shoulders and ran her hand through her short blonde wavy hair. "Everyone knows that the *Witch* doesn't even look at them, rumour has it she can't even read; the blind old bat." Mr Geoff chuckled and two Latin looking female teachers, who were busy scribbling, sniggered.

"Don't listen to Miss Lucy, mate," said Mr Geoff in his Australian twang as he stroked his dark goatee. "Get them done. If you cross the Sister, she'll have ya."

"Christ the Lord, will you look at him," said Miss Lucy. "Mr Geoff appears a bit scared of the old battle axe. Don't mind him; the Sister won't bite, much." She giggled and her large breasts shook under her light green shirt. All the female staff had to wear green shirts, and grey skirts which came just below the knee.

"Listen," said Mr Geoff, whispering as he edged over the table. "The only reason Miss Lucy can speak like that is because the Sister is scared of her."

"She is not," said Miss Lucy, pointing the ruler at Mr Geoff. "I might have brought her to tears a few times, but no one could scare that giant monster. She knows I'm a shit hot teacher. Everyone should stand up to her."

"I would but I need my job," said Mr Geoff. "The only reason I stay is because my kid can learn here for free. It might be run by a bunch of crazy nuns, but the education system is excellent."

"So how come they let you teach here?" Miss Lucy cackled as she punched Mr Geoff playfully on the arm.

"That's enough Miss Lucy, or do you want me to go and tell the Sister that you aren't doing your lesson plans?" The Latin teachers whispered to each other and put their heads down. Silence followed as the Sister stomped down the hallway. The door slid open.

"Are you taking good care of Mr Barry?" The Sister smiled smugly.

"Yes Sister," said Mr Geoff, smiling. "We're just showing him how to do the lesson plans."

"He'll be grand, so he will," said Miss Lucy, grinning. The Sister nodded, slid the door shut, and clunked down the stairs.

Mr Geoff and Miss Lucy made it clear that if you got on the wrong side of the Sister, then she'd make your life a misery. During Miss Lucy's two years, ten different teachers had left, most in tears.

"What are the students like?" I asked.

"Brilliant," said Miss Lucy. "You'll never teach a nicer bunch of kids, isn't that right Mr Geoff?"

"First class, I just feel sorry for the little uns."

"Why's that?"

"Why else?" said Miss Lucy. "The Sister controls them."

"When she's around," laughed Mr Geoff.

"Yeah, you'll see. If she, or your assistant Thai teacher, isn't there, then watch the buggers cause mayhem."

I got off to a bad start with my Thai assistant, Miss Nittaya. When I walked into our classroom, she was making some posters. White metal chairs were stacked on top of the wooden tables. The walls were a bare blue.

"I prepare for class, Sister want good things, many work, many work," she said with a croaky voice. Her flabby double chin shook and her thick black hair wobbled.

"Do you have a sore throat?" She gazed blankly. I clasped my throat. "Have you got a sore throat?" I said, just as croakily. She nodded, ducked her head, and wandered into the corner of the class. I presumed she was just busy, but Mr Geoff told me she had a problem with her voice.

"You mean you copied her?" Miss Lucy said, gasping.

"Yeah, I didn't know."

"Let's just hope she doesn't report you to the Sister for abusive behaviour," Mr Geoff said. I tried to make up with Miss Nittaya by offering to help, but she gave me the cold shoulder; not the best of moves for a new work colleague.

Despite the constant bitching about the Sister, the banter in the staffroom was fun. Mr Geoff and Miss Lucy were decent company and I got my lesson plans done in a couple of days. The work was tedious, but not as bad as they made out.

Occasionally Miss Badinton would pop in and check on her files and cabinets. She was the only Thai teacher who spoke to me, the others *waied* and smiled, but never introduced themselves.

On the Friday, two farang teachers arrived: Miss Liz from Hull, and Miss Marissa from San Diego. They were part of a program that arranged jobs for farang teachers in Thailand. They'd been on a training scheme for a week and were annoyed about the lesson plans.

"I just can't believe I've gotta spend all weekend preparing these crappy lessons, everyone on the course is going out for a beer," said Miss Liz.

"Yeah, it's like, so much work to do," said Miss Marissa. "I'm like so tired after the last week, I need a break already."

"I've been here nearly two years, get used to it," said Miss Lucy. "She'll drive you to your grave, so she will."

I joined in with Miss Lucy and Mr Geoff's informing session about the Sister.

"Yeah, and she made me get my hair cut when I arrived."

"You're joking?" said Miss Liz.

"That's incredible," said Miss Marissa. The Sister slid back the door.

"Are you ready," she snapped.

"What for?" said Miss Lucy.

"Not you. Mr Barry, Miss Elizabeth and Miss Marissa, come on now, it's time to meet everyone."

We jumped up and followed her downstairs into a giant hall where about three hundred Thai teachers, ninety percent female, stopped nattering and gazed as we ambled in. I felt nervous; no one had mentioned we were going to meet anyone. The Sister sat us next to a few of the Thai teachers who I'd seen wandering about. I sat next to the only male teacher.

"I Mr Sirichild welcome Thailand," he said, winking as he squeezed my right bicep. He was in his late forties, wore thick black glasses, and looked more Chinese than Thai. His smile made me feel at ease.

The noise of the chattering became louder until a Priest waltzed in with three nuns and the Sister. Everyone stood up and waied. I tried but I still felt silly.

While the Priest did his welcome back speech, I was surprised that most of the teachers started talking again, at least until the oldest nun, who I nicknamed the Empress, took the stage. She could have been in her early one hundreds with the amount of wrinkles on her face. As she babbled on in Thai, I wondered why we were in the meeting.

"What's the point in us being here?" I whispered to Liz.

"I don't know. I think we have to stand up in a minute."

"You what?" My stomach tensed and legs tingled. "Are you gonna do a wai thing?"

"I guess so, oh, I don't know." Mr Sirichild overheard and told us just to stand up and wave if we were unsure.

The Sister came on stage and introduced the farang one by one. When I stood up and turned to face the audience, I attempted a wai. I felt strange and out of place, but I think I earned some respect. We were then told we could go back to our lesson planning.

Mr Kevin, the sixth and last, farang teacher, was in the staff room. He'd been in England with his Thai girlfriend and seemed calmer and more relaxed than the others.

"How's the sister?" he asked Mr Geoff.

"Same as ever, you done your lesson plans?"

"Yeah, course I have," he said, sarcastically. "I'm thinking about copying last terms ones, not as if she's gonna know." I hit it off with Kevin straight away; he'd travelled a lot and liked footy (if you can call football from Nottingham 'footy'). He didn't seem bothered about the Sister.

The six of us had one thing in common; the Sister was there to control our lives. Some would put up with her, others not, which was why working there was so dramatic.

## 16 Christmas Plans with Uncle Gary

After the week of lesson plans I was lucky enough to catch up with my uncle Gary. He had a telecoms business and home in Phuket, but also a house ten kilometres from my flat in Bangkapi. Gary had been living in Thailand for five years and had just had a baby with Pom, his Thai wife. The last time I'd seen him was when he showed me his disappearing thumb trick.

"You still remember that?" he said as he emptied a bottle of Chang into my glass. Pom sat next to him, spoon feeding rice to Nicky.

"Of course, I use it on all my students, they love it. This is a great spot." I gazed left towards the sun glistening over the lake. Mosquitoes buzzed about my head.

"Yeah, we love this restaurant. It's one of the nicer parts of Bangkok, once you get out of the craziness of the centre it's a pleasant place to live."

As we downed bottles of Chang and munched bowls of *Khao Phat Moo*, a gorgeous noodle dish called *Pad Thai*, and Thai green curry, I began to realise how much more myself I felt among family.

"So you've been away from your parents for how long?" Gary asked.

"Fourteen months."

"Your mum must be missing you."

"Yeah, they all do I guess. I miss them too."

"Don't you wanna go back?"

"Not yet. I've still got a lot to see. Besides, why would I want to go back to England?"

"I know what you mean. I love it here."

Once we'd cleaned the plates, and half the fridge of Chang, we went back to Gary's plush pad. He had all the mod cons, wide screen TV, plenty of DVD's, stacks of CD's, and a really comfy leather sofa. We chatted about family, the old times, and how he'd made his fortune in Thailand and fallen in love with Pom.

"I'm settled here now. My business is booming in Phuket, it's been a hard graft, but I wouldn't have it any other way now."

Uncle Gary had travelled all over South East Asia and listening to him was inspiring. One of the main reasons I'd chosen Thailand, and Bangkok, was to travel. When I told him the Sister spoiled my plans he suggested staying with him in Phuket at Christmas.

"Really, what I can stay with you guys?"

"Yeah sure, I know what it's like at Christmas without family, you're more than welcome. We've got a house near the beach and you can stay with us, no worries."

"That would be brilliant. I've got two weeks off at Christmas."

"Let's do that then, it'll be perfect. You'll just be lonely back here without family, unless you meet a wife."

"No chance of that, mate."

When we shook hands and made a pact, we were none the wiser to what was coming that Christmas. Like most people in Thailand, and fourteen other countries, we weren't to know that over 230,000 people were going to lose their lives because of history's deadliest Tsunami.

## 17 Teaching English was Superior than the Sister

During my first day at school I had serious doubts about whether I could work under the rules of the Sister and teach young learners. The morning started well. The noise of three thousand students was deafening after a week of silence, but seeing kids of all ages darting about the playground with huge smiles on their innocent faces was uplifting. I'd never seen such a happy bunch on their first day at school. Random boys shouted 'hello' and waved while some ran up and asked my name.

Miss Nittaya seemed to have forgotten about my foolish impersonation and introduced me to our class as they sat on the floor nattering in the playground. She made them stand up and most only came up to my hip. They looked tired, but had cute smiles.

"Gday, Mr Barry. Ready for ya first day, mate?" said Mr Geoff.

"Sure am, where's everyone else?"

"Dunno, maybe they're still doing lesson plans, or the Sister has exterminated them already."

Once everyone had turned up and the kids got in line, the farang teachers stood at the back and the Thai teachers at the front. At 7.30am, the playground was like a military camp. Three thousand students lined up in neat rows while the national anthem played out from speakers hidden in the trees. The chants of the songs and prayers gave me goose bumps.

After a couple of speeches by the nuns we marched the students in; the younger ones held hands. Once they'd placed their shoes on the blue stacks in the corridor and the boys and girls lined up separately, the Sister stormed down.

"They are naughty boys in this class Mr Barry," she said as she inspected the shoes. "You," she snapped, pointing to one. "Why are the shoes so messy?" The lad darted towards the stack, tidied the shoes, and raced back in line.

"You will need to keep them in order," she said as she patrolled past. Miss Nittaya had a go at the boys, but they were already sniggering. Once everyone had waied each other, Miss Nittaya ordered them to wai me as they shuffled into class. Most seemed nervous and kept their head down, apart from one kid with dark bushy eyebrows.

"What you name?" Before I had the chance to answer, Miss Nittaya clipped him round the back of the head and he sprinted in. I followed and sat at my desk at the back while Miss Nittaya sorted out the class. A couple of the boys were messing about and Miss Nittaya drew a black line next to their names on the board. They hushed up.

The glass door slid open and in walked the Sister.

"Well?"

"PLEASE STAND UP," shouted one of the girls at the front. Everyone shot up.

"GOOOOODDD MOORRRRRRNNIIING SISSTERRRR." She inspected the children's blue and white uniforms and piles of books.

"You have a noisy class Mr Barry," she said, loudly. "They like to play, so you need to be hard." She glared at the ones who had been chatting.

"Of course, Sister," I said, as if in trance.

One girl with bunches was blinking and fidgeting; as if she was going to wet herself.

"What is it?" the Sister blurted. The girl stood still. "Okay Mr Barry, we will be in the grand hall now, you can bring your children, quietly." The door closed and everyone sighed with relief.

"What is she like if they're misbehaving?" I asked Miss Nittaya, who smiled and said something to the class. The kids laughed. There was a bond between everyone, and a rebellious pact against the Sister.

No one had told me about the meeting so my first lesson plan had already changed. No wonder everyone said the lesson plans were a joke. This was a sign of the lack of communication to come.

Once Mr Sirichild had organised the six classes into neat rows, the Sister waltzed in and everyone stood in silence. She welcomed the kids in English and introduced the new farang. Each class cheered their teacher. Then she spoke in Thai, the longer she spoke, the more irate she became. The fear in the Thai teacher's faces showed that she was lecturing the kids.

I was thrown by the tense atmosphere and my first lesson was a disaster. I felt nervous in front of the twenty-three nine-year olds. I'd never taught such a young group before. Miss Nittaya watched from the back while I introduced myself and showed pictures of London, but when she nipped out, the kid with the dark bushy eyebrows shouted something and two of the boys started running around. The whole class laughed as I chased round and tried to get them to sit down.

I was just about to lose my cool when Miss Nittaya stormed in, grabbed two by their collar, and marched them up the corridor telling them off in Thai.

The class settled down after that, but I felt frustrated not being able to understand their language.

"How was your first class then?" said Mr Geoff.

"It could have been better."

"That class can get out of hand."

"Miss Nittaya had to drag two of them out."

"Ah, yes. She must have taken them to Mr Sirichild. He's the chief punisher, if any of your kids are playing up, just send them to him, he'll sort them out."

I was knackered after my first morning; I hadn't expected kids to be so energetic. Lunchtime was crazy too. I helped Miss Nittaya escort our class down to the dining room where there was space for five hundred noisy monkeys. We towered over while they gobbled down their meat and rice dishes, making sure they all finished, and then we ate.

"This is my favourite," I said to Mr Sirichild as I took a mouthful of Khao Pat Moo.

"Good, good," he said, squeezing my arm. On the other side of the dining table sat a line of five female Thai teachers, none of the farang had come down yet. Every time I looked up someone else was staring, some with evil glares.

"Don't worry about them,' said Mr Sirichild, sensing my tension. "It take time to feel at home here." It was the first time I witnessed the coldness of some of the Thai teachers. After lunch I tried to get some peace in the staffroom.

"She's a real bitch sometimes," said Miss Lucy, slamming the staffroom door.

"What now?" said Mr Geoff, "Lesson plans?" We'd handed the lessons in to the Sister for inspection.

"How did you guess?" she said, throwing her folder on the table. "She wants me to do them again, God Jesus."

"I hope she doesn't say that about mine," said Miss Marissa. "I've taken like ages."

"Me too," said Miss Liz.

"That's bollocks," said Mr Geoff, reading Miss Lucy's legible writing. "How can she make you do them again?"

"She's got it in for me, I tell ya. I'm paying for that extra holiday I had. Once you get on her bad side that's it, you're in for; I've seen it too many times before." She stormed out.

Everyone else's lesson plans passed the Sister's ruthless inspection. Mine had a few ticks in pencil by the side, but, as Kevin said, I doubt she'd read them in detail.

I was relieved to get home that evening. The first day had whizzed by, but my mind was racing. The Sister's abrupt way with the students and teachers was harsh and I wondered why she acted like a mean cold woman. I was determined not to let her get to me and try to teach my class some English.

During the first week, the Sister patrolled the corridor and randomly entered everyone's class. Her snooping bothered the farang.

"She's a wicked, wicked woman," said Miss Lucy. "Earlier she came in my class and made one of the girls cry because she had been looking at her walking past. She deserves to be struck down."

Each morning the Sister made sure the children were in straight lines in the playground and the shoes were stacked tidily. At the end of the day the students had to put their chairs on the tables and sweep the floors before they could leave. For Thais, a clean floor was vital for positive energy.

I saw several students leaving her tinted office in tears with their heads hung low. The Sister certainly made her authority clear to everyone in our department and most of the Thai teachers seemed scared.

The conversation in the staffroom normally revolved around the Sister. Everyone would bitch or take the mick. I joined in, of course, but tried to concentrate on my teaching and let the politics go over my head.

After teaching, and learning, in liberal environments, I felt sorry for the students. They had a long day; 8am to 4pm, and most of them had extra-curricular activities. When I saw how mean the Sister was, I cringed inside, why was she always so cruel?

I was determined to give my class entertaining lessons and let them have some fun while learning English. I took note of how Miss Nittaya controlled the naughty ones with a points system and extra homework. To start with she stayed in my class while I taught, but over time I began to handle the manic group.

"They are good kids," Mr Sirichild said, "but you need show who boss, use game at end as reward, and they listen."

I kept the lessons fun with guessing activities and team games and by the second week everyone cheered whenever I entered the class. My three favourites were Bee, Batman, and Nam.

Bee was a whiz kid at maths and finished most of the exercises before some had sharpened their pencils. It was impossible to keep him at the same stage in the book as everyone else so I just let him run ahead. Looking back, that was one of my biggest problems, keeping the whole class on the same page. At break Bee would always offer the other kids strips of seaweed or dried worms. The seaweed was salty and tangy, and the dried worms were like mouldy mud.

Batman, who I nicknamed because of his batman key ring, would pick up vocabulary the quickest. For a nine-year old his pronunciation was excellent too, his father had worked in the States and helped him a lot.

My favourite was Nam; my class translator, helper, pet, and all round genius. He was a funny kid and loved drawing pictures of lemmings. Every art lesson he'd beg me to let him draw a picture of the class, but in lemmings format.

"What's that then Nam?" I would ask, pointing at his latest drawing.

"He is the bad man, like Panu,' he said, referring to one of the naughty kids. "He try to kill the other students with cannon, you see?"

"And what's he going to do?"

"What he do? You see, you see,' he said, running off laughing.

The girls were a funny bunch. Miam was the class representative who ordered the class to stand up when a teacher or the Sister came in. She was a bright kid and always had a smile on her face. Beam was a proper little madam, even though she was only eight. She'd get her make-up out in class and start checking her hair in her pocket mirror.

The only problem I had teaching the girls was that they were obsessed with drawing cartoon pictures of girls. Even during maths, they tried to draw pictures in their notebooks and when I stopped them they cried.

As with most classes there were the trouble makers: Kevin, Panu, and Neung. Kevin was half-Thai and half-Chinese and a lot paler than the others. His level of English was so low that he could barely say how old he was. I tried to help him but he was a rascal. When he didn't want to work, which was most of the time, he'd wander about swapping everyone's pens and pencils and run back to his seat before I could catch him.

Panu was even more impossible to control. He was a darker kid with deep black eyes and a rustled haircut. He would get up in the middle of the lesson, run about screaming until I told him off, and then lay on the floor.

"Get up Panu," I'd say, but he'd refuse. By this stage most of the other kids were out of their seats, and Kevin had a new collection of pens. Panu knew what he was doing; I had to leave him on the floor to control the rest of the class, and he would get out of doing much of the work.

Kevin and Panu had a bladder problem.

"Toilet," was their favourite word (and the only one they wanted to remember). I normally let them go because if not they'd distract the class.

After a while I found out that the real reason they wanted to leave was because they were on guard duty. After a couple of weeks, I noticed that every time the Sister sneaked past, the class were behaved. When she drifted out of sight, they would look up and smile, even Miss Nittaya looked pleased.

Panu and Kevin went to the 'toilet' to check on the Sister. Sometimes their loo journey would only last three seconds before they'd run back in shouting. The Sister would walk past, hunting for naughty students, or slack teachers. We had an 'off the record' agreement; they'd watch my back, and I'd let them have a couple of toilet breaks. The Sister was none the wiser.

The naughtiest student was Neung. He used to go into a sulk, scream the class down, or hit the others boys for no reason. Miss Nittaya had a lot of patience, but took him to Mr Sirichild on several occasions.

One day Miss Nittaya was on her break when Neung hit Batman on the ear.

"I've had enough of you Neung; you can't hit people's ears," I said, almost dragging him to Mr Sirichild, who I'd never seen in action before.

"Thank you Mr Barry, I'll take it from here." Mr Sirichild smiled gracefully.

On my way out, I turned. Neung stood at the front of the class and Mr Sirichild had a large wooden cane in his hand. Several loud whacks echoed down the corridor as I entered my class. Neung found it difficult to sit down for a while after that, but funnily enough he was quieter in my lessons. That was the last time I took anyone to see Mr Sirichild. Fair enough, Neung had been a naughty boy, but it was slightly over the top.

Friday was Swimming Day and the kids loved the session.

"Are we doing swimming this Friday, Mr Barry?' Nam would ask on Monday morning.

"No, not this Friday." When word got around the kids would moan until I admitted there was swimming. It was a great way to threaten the class if they were playing up.

The Sister made me responsible for three swimming sessions in a row. The first was with Mr Kevin, the second with Mr Geoff, and the last with all of us and Miss Liz. We normally tried to get the kids to swim, but the session always turned into a giant game of water polo, a huge pretend ninja fight, or the kids jumping on, and trying to drown, the teachers.

Swimming was the highlight of the week, partly because the kids could let off some steam, but mainly because the Sister never came down. I liked to think she was watching from a far, secretly allowing us to have fun at the end of a hard week.

Over a couple of weeks, I really enjoyed teaching. Miss Nittaya said they were improving and I was happy to be able to give them some fun in their restricted education.

Apart from the constant moaning about the Sister, there was also tension between the farang and Thai teachers. Miss Rancha, Miss Liz's assistant, was the liaison between the Sister and everyone, but her English was appalling and sometimes she failed to tell us about meetings, timetable changes, and orders from the Sister. We normally found out from Mr Sirichild; the most helpful of the Thai teachers.

There were often mini bitching sessions and I got the feeling that the Thai teachers were always gossiping about the farang, normally while on their breaks eating strong fish smelling snacks.

Miss Badinton was problematic. She was the main librarian and key holder for all the glass cabinets in the staff room. If we wanted some props, puppets, or videos, then we had to run it by her, but she was particular about her keys. She was all right with me, but the female farang teachers hated her.

"I don't trust her," said Miss Marissa. "She always gives me evil glances."

"Yeah, I know what you mean, I don't get on with her at all," Miss Liz said.

"She's all right with me," I said.

"That's cos you're a guy, she's alright with the men," Miss Lucy said.

"Be careful Mr Barry," said Mr Geoff. "She probably gets horny when you ask her for a key."

There was an even bigger divide between the Thai and Philippine teachers: Miss Karen and Miss Gigi. From what Miss Lucy told me, the Thai's hated them.

"There're a lot of Philippines over here, and I think the Thais feel threatened. Miss Karen and Miss Gigi work harder than anyone else; but that's because they owe the Sister for saving them from their country, it's a shame because they are both lovely girls."

I was unsure why some of the Thai teachers seemed so anti-farang, but I found out later.

## 18 Trying to Learn Thai

Despite the Sister's warnings, I decided the best way to immerse myself in Thai culture and learn the language (while having some fun) was with the Thai women. I wanted to keep my social life separate from school, so when I struck up a conversation with a young lady called Naam, while waiting for a bus to go to Bangkapi, I was delighted.

We arranged to meet downtown on a Sunday; coincidentally an old travelling buddy from Salvador was in town on the Saturday.

"So where are you meeting this *chica* then?" asked Nish, who was in Bangkok for a couple of days before heading off to India. He'd been travelling round Laos, Cambodia, and Vietnam.

"Tomorrow morning outside McDonalds," I said, sipping a Chang. Nish and I sat on high stools while a group of rowdy English lads were smacking pool balls in the corner of Gullivers, a smoky Irish bar on Khao San Road. It was my first time down backpacker's alley and I felt rattled after the stuffy three-hour bus journey, especially as I'd only travelled fifteen kilometres.

"Sounds romantic, does she speak English?"

"Not really, that's why I'm meeting her, so we can teach each other."

"What else are you going to teach her?" he said, winking.

"We'll see, won't we?"

"I still can't get over your new shit haircut."

"No choice mate, it's one of the Sister's rules."

"The Sister," he said, almost spitting out his orange juice. "Don't tell me you've gone all religious on me?" I filled in Nish on the Sister's ludicrous ways.

"Sounds a lot stricter than the schools in Brazil," he said.

"Tell me about it, the students are great though and I'm working in a real school."

"Ah, aren't you lucky, come on, I'm hungry."

"You're always hungry."

As we left Gullivers, the evening's heat whacked us in the face. We dodged through the manic crowd of beered up travellers, ignored the haggling Thai tuk tuk drivers revving their clacking engines, past the steamy noodle stalls, and into a restaurant style bar.

Seeing Nish again was great; we remembered our time in Brazil and Sydney and he told me a few stories about Southeast Asia.

"I loved every second," he said, beaming. "Travelling here is more of an adventure, like South America. Aren't you glad you left Australia?"

"Definitely, I might be working for a crazy nun, but Thailand is far more exciting."

"You're gonna love it when you get going again. Just be careful of the stray dogs in Cambodia, one of the bastards bit me on the leg."

Listening to his enthusiasm got my travelling taste buds flowing, my journey was a long way off, but when Nish spoke highly of a place, I knew I'd like it too.

As Nish slurped on his green curry and I shovelled down Khao Phat Moo, a Thai lady wearing a short red dress pulled up a chair by the table opposite.

"Hello men," she said with a strange high-pitched voice while pouting her red lips. We looked at each other and raised our eyebrows.

"Hello woman," Nish said.

"You two are English?"

"He is," Nish said, pointing to me. "I'm from India."

"Oh, India, I like India." She clapped several times as she grinned. "And you two are with your girlfriends?"

"No, he has just finished with his wife,' Nish said, patting my shoulder.

"Oh really," she said, moving closer to me. "You look fun time Bangkok?"

"Yes I do, but I like men," I joked.

"Oh," she said. "You know, I man and woman, you want man you have me?" She, or he, leaned over and stroked my head.

"No thanks."

"Why you say you like man?"

"He like man," Nish said. "But only big man; you too small."

"I big man, I show you, I big man." He stood up and went to lift up his dress.

"NO, NO, NO," Nish shouted. A few people glanced over and the lady boy stormed off.

Strolling down Khao San gave a different dimension to Bangkok. It was a special street tailored for travellers and tourists. You could get a ticket to anywhere in Southeast Asia and buy all the latest films, music albums, and counterfeited clothes. The noise and commotion could be intimidating, but being among so many different nationalities was exciting. Nish and I spent the evening in various bars, watching Premiership football, trying to steer clear of the Thai lady boys, and generally having a laugh.

The next morning Khao San was much quieter and the streets were littered with empty glass bottles and polystyrene trays covered in dried noodles. Most travellers stumbled about holding their heads and hiding behind their dark sunglasses.

"So where's the next exotic location I'll see you?" I said to Nish.

"Well, we've done Rio, Sydney, and Bangkok. I guess the next time will be in good old Watford."

"Yeah, you're trip's almost over." As I patted Nish on the shoulder he grimaced and nodded. India was his last adventure and he was reluctant to move a step closer to England.

"Yeah, good luck with the Thai *chica*, sort your bloody hair out though, mate."

As the familiar smell of McDonalds filled my nostrils, I felt nervous about meeting Naam. We kept our distance, no kiss on the cheek or even a wai, just a quick hello and we stood in silence.

"So where are we going?" I said. She grinned and her cheeks puffed out. She gazed at the floor, stroking her jet black hair.

"No understand," she said, frowning. I pulled out my map, repeated the question, and pointed to Khao San. She blurted in Thai and looked in her dictionary.

"Not know Grand Palace?" she said.

"I've heard of it."

"We go?"

Conversation was limited as we strolled over Sanamluang Park. Kites flapped in the sky as Thai parents helped their children. Naam stopped to watch.

"So, the Grand Palace," I asked, pointing towards the golden domes in the distance.

"Yes, Grand Palace."

"How do you say that in Thai?"

"*Phra Borom Maha Ratcha Wang.*" The lost look on my face made her giggle.

"Maybe we should start with the basics, how do you say 'hot'?"

As we past the clothes markets towards the end of the park, Thai men lingered round the palace entrance offering to be guides.

"Bad people," Naam said, pulling me away. She dragged me past the queue of farang and insisted on paying.

"You guest," she said, smiling after looking in her dictionary.

I loved strolling round the huge golden domes and observing the detailed drawings of Buddhas and dragons. We meandered round the sacred grounds, in and out of the various white, gold, and red temples, and admired the golden half-woman half-bird statues.

"Come, see Emerald Buddha," said Naam, almost pulling my hand. We entered *Wat Phra Kaew*, and Naam waied at the Emerald Buddha and lit a candle.

"No feet Buddha, no feet Buddha," she whispered, pointing at the jade Buddha high on a glistening tower of golden treasure. The crowd of Thais and farang were kneeling on the floor with their feet pointing away from Thailand's most sacred symbol. Some bent right over, almost touching their heads on the cool ground.

"Is important place, much energy," Naam said, wiping her teary eyes.

After about three hours walking round, I treated Naam to lunch. She led me to a row of restaurants a few streets away and all the waitresses greeted her.

"You're popular here," I said.

"Yes. You have girlfriend?" I was stunned by her bluntness.

"Me? No, no girlfriend. What about you?"

"Yes, yes I have girlfriend." She seemed pleased with herself. Either she'd made a mistake and had a boyfriend, or she was a lesbian. I was unsure which I'd prefer.

"You have a GIRLfriend?"

"Yes, yes," she said. I drew a stickwoman picture of Naam holding hands with another woman.

"No no, no," she said, blushing. She stumbled around in her dictionary. "Girlfriend no, boyfriend yes, but he bad man."

But the time we'd finished eating, Naam had interrogated me about ex-girlfriends and what I thought about Thai women. I felt confused; she seemed like a sweet and innocent girl, not the type to cheat on her boyfriend. I wasn't up for getting in trouble with a jealous Thai boyfriend chasing me around Bangkok, what if he was a kick boxer?

"When see?" she said after I'd flagged down a cab.

"I'm not sure."

"You like me?"

"I better go."

"I like you."

"Right, I'll call you then," I said, slamming the cab door.

She called four or five times, a day, for the following week, most of the time I was in lesson; that was my excuse anyway. After a week, just as I was getting into bed, she rang again.

"Where you are?" she said.

"I'm in bed."

"Bed, okay, why no call me?"

"Sorry, I've been busy."

"Busy?"
"Yes, teaching, you know."
"No understand, you like me?"
"Yes, but you have a boyfriend."
"Yes, boyfriend, you me boyfriend."
"What? No, no boyfriend."
"My boyfriend," she said, slowly, "he kill." I went silent. Did that mean she'd killed him or he wanted to kill me?
"What is, he kill?"
"Yes, yes he kill, my boyfriend."
"Right, okay, see you then, I've got to sleep now, bye bye."
"Barry, boyfriend you me." I hung up. She called again. I switched off the phone.

After Naam's crazy antics, I became wary of learning the language by chatting with Thai women. When Mr Geoff told me stories about 'friends' who had dated Thai women only to find they were after money or a visa out of the country, or worse, they used to be men, I got paranoid.

I started to notice just how many of the men looked feminine, but it wasn't until after a night down Patpong that I believed anyone could make the common 'Transvestite' mistake.

One of my best mates from home, Chris, was visiting Thailand with his friend Mark and they only had one night in Bangkok.

"Take them to Patpong," said Mr Geoff when I asked about places near Sukhumvit where they were staying.

"What's there?"

"You wanna see pussy show?" he said in a funny Thai accent.

I'd heard about the famous shows in Bangkok, but, like many places when you're travelling the world, you have to see the marvels with your own eyes.

"What's the plan then?" Chris said, rubbing his hands together. He hadn't changed; he still had short black hair and stocky build, but looked whiter than normal. We were on Sukhumvit road having dinner before the evening's shenanigans. "We've got one night."

"Well, a mate said that the place to be is Patpong."

"I've heard about that," Chris replied, smirking.

"What is it?' Mark said, inspecting his spoonful of rice. Mark had a puny frame, which perhaps explains what happened to him that night.

"I haven't been so I can't say for sure, but apparently it's supposed to be a laugh." I winked at Chris, who nodded back.

We finished up and made our way over to Patpong (named after the family Patponpanit who own most of the area's property, not because of the ping pong shows).

"Oh look, a market," said Mark as we turned down Silom market. He led the way.

"Hey you," said a Thai man with a patch over his eye as he shoved a white card in Mark's face. "You want PUSSY SHOW?"

"Sorry?" said Mark, frowning.

"*Mai dai kap* - no thanks," I said, pushing Mark on.

"What *is* this place?" Mark said, twitching his eyes from left to right as we walked past the Go-go bars. Music blasted out as Thai women danced on the tables dressed in fluorescent bikinis. We shuffled round the markets and the bar promoters pestered us.

"I suppose it wouldn't do any harm," Chris said as we entered a quiet bar, (when I say quiet I mean there weren't many people, the trashy Thai pop music was deafening).

"This is madness," I said, grinning at Chris to show him my new UV lit up teeth. A Thai woman wearing an aluminous pink bikini led us to some bar stools.

"You want dance?' she said, squeezing my thigh as she gazed through her green contact lenses.

"*Mai dai kap*." She moved on to Mark. Soon two women were stroking his hair as he squirmed on his seat.

"He's loving it," Chris said.

"No he isn't," I replied, laughing.

Luckily for Mark, an overweight European bloke came in and the two women ran over. Within ten minutes they'd left together.

"You bastards just let them hound me," said Mark, doing up his top shirt button.

That was just the beginning. The next bar made the first look like the Sister's tame front lounge. It was kicking with loud music, lots of farang (male and female), and on a long stage in the middle a handful of half-naked Thai women were gyrating round metal poles.

"There's something different about the women here," said Chris as we plonked by the bar.

"Do you think they're blokes?"

"He blatantly is," I said, pointing my beer bottle towards a lady boy wearing a long blue dress and a funny peacock style head band. His chin was wider and firmer than the women's chins in the previous bar, and his back seemed squarer.

After a short while, a group of 'women' surrounded us.

"You want dance?" said one, stroking my shoulder. Her voice had a strange deep tone.

"You want good time?" said another.

"I show you fun lucky, lucky," said a third.

"You big boy, I show you my body," said the fourth as she went to lift her top. We pointed them in Mark's direction.

One of the women perched on Mark's knee and rubbed her (or his) breasts in Mark's face.

"Some people get all the luck," Chris said as we waved. Mark was trying to elbow her away, but she was feisty.

By the time we'd finished our beers and left, we realised that all the Thai women in the bar were actually men; but at different stages of their transformation. Their female likeliness was frightening.

I next went to Patpong with two female friends, Helen, a tall brunette, and Em, a slim blonde, who I had met in Australia.

"So are you going to take us to Patpong's?" Helen said as we sat down Khao San sharing a bucket of Samsung whisky.

"What, are you serious?" Em said.

"Yeah, why not? I wanna see what all the fuss is about," Helen said.

When we met up the following Monday, I explained the two options: go to the same type of bar I'd been to before and risk being hounded by Thai lady boys, or go see a ping pong show.

"Classy," Em said as we walked up the red stairs past the mirrored walls. We were nervous about what to expect and I felt weird going with girlfriends. As we entered the burgundy doors, the familiar trashy pop music boomed out. Inside smelt musky and the lights were dim. About ten blokes were waiting on sofa style benches and three completely naked Thai women (and these ones *were* women, I think), danced on a stage.

"This place is awful," Helen said.

"They look so miserable," Em said as we plonked in the corner. The dancer's smiles were drearier than the enthusiastic lady boys in the other bars. A chubby Western man was propped up against the bar while four naked Thai women stroked his long greasy hair and plied him with drinks.

The famous show began. Another five unclothed women lined up on the stage. I was expecting an erotic show, but the stunts couldn't have been more soul destroying. One woman stepped forward as the others jingled their bits. She pulled a banana from behind her back.

"What is she going to do with that?" Em asked.

"What do you think?" Helen replied. I won't go into details, but the pop the banana made as it flew across the bar was quite impressive.

"This is madness," Em said.

"Yeah, how did you get us to come to this," Helen said as the next one stepped forward with a smoking cigarette. We watched women perform with darts and ping pongs balls, but left when one came out with a line of razor blades.

"I've seen everything now, thanks for that Barry," Em said, hitting me on the arm when we got outside.

"Don't blame me, it was Helen's idea,' I said.

Despite feeling awkward, by the end of the night they were glad they'd witnessed the madness of Bangkok.

After a couple of weeks, my attempt at learning Thai was going poorly and I began to crave British company. At the weekends I started hanging around with Miss Liz and Miss Marissa and the group of farang teachers they knew.

A job agency had stitched some up. They were only being paid about 10,000 baht (just over £200) a month, taught six different lessons a day with fifty students in each class, and were working in small, urban villages outside Bangkok. Some felt they were entertaining rather than teaching; something to bear in mind if you are thinking about teaching in Thailand.

The group were cliquey at first, but after a few crazy nights down Khao San and Sukhumvit, and a mental weekend on Koh Samet, one of the islands in the East, I made a few friends but the bloke I got on most with was Den, a lanky lad from Manchester.

"Never thought I'd get on with a Londoner," said Den, as we chinked pint glasses while on a bar down Sukhumvit.

"Guess you wouldn't understand real English being all the way up there."

"Wanker!"

I still wanted to learn the language, but finding Thai people to hang around with was difficult. Then I had some luck. I found out about a local sports centre where a massive group of Thai lads played five-a-side football every night.

As usual in Bangkapi, the locals stared when I turned up. I'd only been watching for ten minutes when a lad with spiky hair wearing a Manchester United shirt came over.

"Hello, I Chuck, you play football?"

"Yeah, but I haven't played in a while."

"Okay, you practise with us, we need team."

About ten guys gathered round to watch as I played kick ups with Chuck and his mates. They were better than me, but I made an impression.

"We play now, if you good, then you in team," he said, leading me on to the pitch. Word got around that a farang was playing and spectators of all ages lined up along the side to watch. Every time I got the ball or made a decent pass, everyone cheered, as if I was some sort of celebrity. We stayed on for four games and I set up two goals.

"You good player," Chuck said. 'You practise with us; we play every night, from seven o'clock, league start in three week." The other players shook my hand; they seemed pleased having a farang on their side.

During the first week at football, random blokes greeted me as I turned up to play. The word had spread and even more lined up to cheer me on. I felt embarrassed at times; especially when I played crap, but I could understand the novelty.

Between the games, I chatted to Chuck and Bee, the only other one who spoke English, about English expressions and the Premiership. They were keen Manchester United fans and knew more about the current state of the English league than I did. I picked up a few Thai expressions, numbers, and swear words, but my pronunciation needed a lot of work.

In the second week, when I scored my first goal, about twenty blokes came up and shook my hand. Even though it was only a practise game, they were so excited that I was part of their group. One lad who turned into a good friend was Rooney. He was a first class finisher with an aggressive attitude. His level of English was as bad as my Thai, but we got on all right. His mum owned one of the local restaurants and I'd often eat there after the games. Most of the lads would drink whisky until the early hours of the morning. I normally refused though as I had work the next day.

"What you think Madrid?" Chuck asked one evening.

"They're good, why?"

"Because we Madrid. You Beckham," he said, holding up the latest Real Madrid shirt. "I have you kit next week; you pay one hundred baht, okay?"

The league meant everything to the lads and when it kicked off over one hundred fanatics were there to play or support. We were up first against Chelsea. My teammates were a lot more serious than normal as we warmed up. They even decided to drop the farang for the first half. Initially I was disappointed, but when I saw the level and pace they were playing at, I could understand their tactical decision (save the best player till last).

The first half was tense, but thanks to Rooney we were one nil up at half time. When he scored, the crowd went wild and I ran on the pitch to pat him on the back.

"Good, Rooney good," he said to me at half time.

"Okay Barry, you play now," Bee said, wiping his brow.

I managed to keep up with the pace of the game and even set Rooney up for a second goal. Unfortunately, Chelsea got one back and then I gave the ball away in the last minute, which led to the equaliser.

"Can you tell everyone I'm sorry," I said to Chuck. Everyone shook my hand; at least we got a point.

The next evening I started and scored the winning goal. The crowd went mental and a massive group swarmed around me after the game. We went for food to celebrate and I stayed for a couple of whiskys.

"Rooney want know how feel when score goal?" Chuck asked.

"Amazing," I replied. "Like when England score in the World Cup." Everyone toasted to Beckham.

After a month with the lads I felt like one of the crew. My Thai was still rubbish, but I felt welcomed. I couldn't understand why it had been so easy to settle in with the football lads and not with the Thai teachers at school. Then I discovered the truth.

# 19 The Harsh Truth and the End of Miss Lucy

"You go for pay now," said Miss Badinton in a snappy tone to the farang in the staffroom. She stood like a soldier as we piled out the staffroom.

"Finally, the only good part about working in this hell hole," said Miss Lucy. We rushed down the stairs and queued up outside the Empress's office. A few Thai teachers waiting tensed up and looked away.

"Why do they always turn their backs on us on pay day?" I asked Mr Geoff. The Empress called out my name.

"I'll tell you after."

The Empress was standing as I walked into her stuffy office and waied. She nodded her wrinkled face and smiled as she slid a chunky white envelope over the table.

"Count," she murmured. I licked my thumb and counted the thirty 1,000 baht notes, stuffed the wad in my pocket, signed my wage slip, and waied. As I went past the line of Thai teachers, some turned up their noses.

"I don't get it, mate," I said to Mr Geoff as we walked back to the staff room.

"It's pretty obvious. Why do you think most of the Thai teachers are so cold towards us?"

"I dunno, because we're weird farang invading their school."

"Yeah, that and their wages."

"What dya mean?"

"It's supposed to be hush, but the Sisters pay more for native English speakers."

"Yeah, but it can't be that much more."

"We're on at least four times the amount of the Thai teachers."

I was stunned. I could understand that the parents paid more to have their kids taught by native English speakers, but not by such a drastic amount. Considering how many extra hours the Thai teachers did, I thought they'd have earned more. The Philippine teachers were on even less. Most of the Thai teachers had families and homes to pay for, how did they survive? I was appalled at the Sister's unjust ways and felt guilty for earning more.

Miss Lucy told me not to be so hard on myself.

"I know it seems harsh, but the Thai teachers live like kings compared to the average Thai."

I tried to be more understanding and interact with the Thai teachers, but I only really got on with Mr Sirichild and Miss Nittaya. I appreciated how they felt towards farang; I'd have been angry and perhaps jealous too. They should have blamed the Sister's daft system rather than us though.

Not only was the wages system a farce though, often the organisation in the school was a shambles.

"As you all know," said the Sister, after calling an urgent meeting with everyone in the main hall, "in two weeks we will have a Maths and Science day." I glanced at Mr Geoff. He shrugged. "Is there a problem, Mr Geoff?" snapped the Sister.

"No Sister."

"Mr Barry?"

"Well," I said, feeling the eyes of the Thai teachers staring at me. "You said, 'as you know' but no one has mentioned anything about a Maths and Science Day."

"I see," she said, glaring at Miss Rancha, who squirmed in her chair. The Sister explained that we had to prepare some 'displays', in English, for when the parents visited. "The parents are paying a lot of money for their children's education and we must provide them with a satisfactory service."

"Sorry Sister," said Miss Lucy. The Sister's face tensed. "But what exactly do we have to do?"

"It should be in English, only English, with each class a different theme," she said, banging her pen on the desk after every syllable.

"But what exactly?"

"Is it not clear, Miss Lucy?"

"Obviously not," she muttered.

"What was that?"

"I said it's *not* very clear."

Mr Sirichild stepped in to explain. The idea was simple. Each class had to prepare a display, which could include games, maths puzzles, or science experiments, along with some presentations in English.

Despite the constant hounding from the Sister, Miss Nittaya and I got things moving with our class. The kids loved the change from the usual lessons (as did we), and when the big day finally arrived, unbelievably, everyone was ready.

To make the parents feel at home, the farang had to dress up in traditional Thai clothes.

"I can't see how this is related to maths and science," said Mr Geoff, as we compared our patterned red, blue, and gold silk shirts in the corridor. Panu and Kevin ran past sniggering.

"Me neither," said Mr Kevin, scrunching his teeth.

"Keeps the Sister sweet though, doesn't it?" I said.

"I look pathetic," said Miss Lucy. "This dress is for a slim Thai woman, not a chubby Irish one." No one said anything. She did look a tad uncomfortable, especially around the chest area.

"Hold up, speak of the devil, look lively" said Mr Geoff as we started talking to the students.

"Very smart gentlemen, very smart," said the Sister, who, strangely enough, had a weird grin on her face.

"What's got into her?" I said.

"Parents," said Mr Geoff.

"She's always like this on open day; you'll see a different Sister today," said Mr Kevin.

"She's as false as they come," said Miss Lucy.

The Sister's menacing stares turned into enthusiastic glances and her stern, rigid manner became relaxed.

"Mr Barry is a good teacher," she said to Nam's father. "And his class is wonderful."

What amazed me was that if she told any of the kids off, she would joke afterwards.

"How does she do it?" Miss Lucy said as group of parents surrounded the Sister. "She's the devil in disguise."

Miss Karen and Gigi won the prize for the best display and the Sister presented them with some flowers in the grand hall in front of the parents. She also gave out sweets to the students and a thank you gift to the teachers. I got a mug (not that I ever drank tea in Thailand). The parents left, delighted with the performance.

Despite the show for the parents, part of me wondered about the Sister. Perhaps that was the real her and she was a kind woman putting on an act for the children's discipline. At times she could be pleasant, but only when she was alone. I tried to imagine she was a better person than she made out, but Miss Lucy made that tricky.

Everyone knew that Miss Lucy liked a drink, or five, and often she'd turn up reeking of Thai Samsung whisky from the night before. On a couple of occasions the Sister shouted at Miss Lucy about her messy lesson plans and requests for extra holiday, but one week the tension pinged.

"She's a bloody fraud," said Miss Lucy, stumbling into the staffroom one Thursday morning. The room had been silent. "Blooming Wicked Witch of the East," she added, with a slur.

"What're you saying Miss Lucy?" asked Mr Geoff. He looked concerned.

"I've had enough of the old bat; all she's interested in is shipping the parent's donations in to her own private bank account in the Phillipines. She'll drag us all down with her. It's time to jump ship before it's too late." She stormed out.

"The shit is going to hit the nun," said Mr Geoff.

After half an hour we realised Miss Lucy was not coming back so we took turns to cover her lesson so the Sister wouldn't find out, but you know what she's like.

"Mr Barry," she snapped as I was at the front of Miss Lucy's class. Where were Panu and Kevin when I needed them? "You are *not* Miss Lucy, where is she?"

"Oh, hello Sister, Miss Lucy, well…"

"Yes, come on, where is she?"

"I'm not sure Sister." I wanted to stay out of the catfight. The Sister stormed down the corridor, shouting Miss Lucy's name and demanding to know where she was. When she stomped past my class a few minutes later, her habit was about to ping off.

The next morning was an ugly scene. Miss Lucy turned up, stumbling about in the playground for the morning songs, obviously still Samsunged up to her eyeballs. Mr Geoff tried to explain to her that the Sister was on the rampage, but she wanted to go out with a bang.

Once everyone was upstairs, Miss Lucy went in to her class (some claim it was to warn her class that the Sister was a wicked witch). I was in the staffroom waiting for the action.

"Miss Lucy?" the Sister said, poking her head in. "She's supposed to be in here." I shrugged. A minute later, they stomped down the corridor, screaming and shouting at each other.

"Where have you been?"

"That's none of your business."

"It is my business, I am the Sister."

"I couldn't give a flying fuck *who* you are." They continued the argument in the Sister's office until the door slammed and Miss Lucy clonked back down the corridor.

"I'm gone, all the best now," said Miss Lucy, popping her head in the door. Tears were running down her cheeks. "I told you now; she'll drive you out so she will, watch out for that bitch."

And that was the end of Miss Lucy.

"Miss Lucy has decided to end her time here as she has psychological problems," said the Sister in a meeting the day after. "She was a good teacher, and the children loved her, but she wasn't right in the head. Now, moving on, there is a new issue to be discussed, leaving dirty cups in the staffroom…"

The farang knew Miss Lucy's patience had been coming to an end, but the Sister's comments shocked us.

"She wasn't right in the head?" said Mr Geoff. "That's rich coming from a dwarf whose new obsession is dirty cups."

"The Sister's obviously trying to cover the truth," Mr Kevin said.

"I don't know, maybe the Sister's right," said Miss Marissa. "Miss Lucy was going a bit nuts."

Once the dust had settled, the Sister seemed perkier than normal. I'd go as far to say it was mildly pleasant working for her. She was cheerful every morning, greeted us with a smile, and spoke highly of the students. Maybe I had been right and the Sister did have a caring side.

The new teacher, Miss Laura, wasn't up to Miss Lucy's standards. She was a forty-year old woman who didn't want to teach children and her class, who were on study strike because Miss Lucy had gone, were unwelcoming.

Miss Lucy's final words of wisdom got round and most students were convinced the Sister was a witch, some even thought the Sister had made Miss Lucy disappear (I didn't start that rumour, promise).

"Mr Barry," Nam said one lunch. "Why is Sister smiling more?"

"I guess she's having a good moment in her life, maybe she wants to be nicer to everyone."

"I think not. We know she is witch, we see change in time."

Most teachers waited for the bitter streak to return. In the mean time, we made the most of the peace and quiet. Personally, I was enjoying teaching more than ever and was getting positive results out of the class. They were picking up vocabulary more easily and I had more control over the naughty ones.

"Your class are improving," said the Sister. "Keep up the work." I was pleased to be in her good books; I wanted her on my side so I had no problems spending my Christmas holidays in Phuket with Uncle Gary.

# 20 How the Sister Saved my Life

Everyone was looking forward to the Christmas break; at least we thought we were.

"Christmas is coming and children love Christmas," said the Sister in another emergency meeting. "Each class will perform a show to the parents." That sounded bearable. "Our teachers will perform in a show with the Thai teachers afterwards." That sounded interesting. "And this will be on the day before Christmas Eve." That sounded bloody awful.

"But Sister," I said. "I thought we had holidays that week, some of us have planned to go away."

"Yes Mr Barry, I thought you would say that," she said, sternly. "No, we have an external visit shortly afterwards and everyone must work, the students will benefit." The Thai teachers nodded while the farang let rip.

"What do you mean? My parents are coming out," said Miss Marissa, pulling on her hair.

"I'm visiting my girlfriend's family in Chang Mai," said Mr Kevin, slapping his knee in rage.

"I'm going to see my uncle in Phuket," I said. My pulse was racing, how could she be so cruel?

"But why do you want to go to Phuket anyway?" said the Sister. "It is dangerous and you never know what is going to happen."

Maybe she knew something, but everyone was furious. Instead of the two weeks she had promised, we had Christmas Eve, Christmas Day and Boxing Day, and then four days over New Years.

I was mad and went to see her the next day.

"But Sister, I trusted you."

"Look Mr Barry, things change. Surely you can see that the children need more lessons this year, especially your noisy class."

"A couple of weeks ago you said they'd improved."

"What nonsense."

"What, don't you remember?" She looked away.

"Maybe, that is not the point. We have people coming in and everything must be ready."

"Well, if I can't have days off at Christmas, I want some extra time at New Years when I get my visa extension."

Eventually she gave in, but I was gutted about not being able to go to Phuket with Gary. Miss Liz and Miss Marissa invited me to their organisation's Christmas Eve party and Christmas Day lunch, and about fifteen of us booked tickets down to Koh Phangan for an all night party on the beach to celebrate New Year's Eve, so we had *something* to look forward to.

The farang respected the Sister even less and the atmosphere became tense; lots of slamming doors, petty arguments, and students running riot. I was surprised at the lack of parents who came in to dispute the Sister decision, but maybe they were glad of the extra peace and quiet.

Despite feeling annoyed with the new decision, I stayed out of the politics and concentrated on preparing the Christmas show for my class. They loved dancing and performing so I was happy to help.

Miss Nittaya helped me get the boys ready for Slade: 'I wish it could be Christmas' and the girls ready for 'Rockin' Robin' by the Jackson Five. We practised most lunch times and in between lessons, but they normally got overly excited and forgot to sing.

"They are dancing well, but they need to sing, this is English, not a Dance Academy," said the Sister after a rehearsal.

"Whatever you old bag," I said under my breath.

"Sorry Mr Barry?"

"I said 'of course Sister'," smiling. "Three bags full Sister."

Miss Rancha asked me to pick a song for the teachers to perform. I rewrote 'a Partridge in a Pear Tree', but she said it was 'too conflicting'.

"I don't see the problem," I said to Mr Geoff.

"Maybe it's the two wicked Sisters' line?"

"Yeah but that was only a bit of a joke."

"What about the six pissed off teachers or the five grumpy students bit?"

"They won't understand anyway." I changed the lyrics to more 'christmassy' ones, but getting the farang and Thai teachers to practise was a nightmare. The farang were up for a laugh, but the Thai teachers felt embarrassed dancing to a routine.

The 23rd of December came round and I was proud of our class when they performed in front of the parents. They needed a lot of encouragement to get going, but did a great job.

"Well done everyone, I have some prizes for you," I said back in the classroom as I dished out a load of sweets. Surprisingly, in return, most gave me a Christmas present. The other teachers received gifts too; a sign of Thai generosity.

Once we'd seen the kids off, the teachers got ready. A giant stage had been set up in the grand hall and each table was neatly decorated with silver cutlery and a red table cloth. The farang were dressed in

Christmas hats and Mr Geoff had the full Santa outfit. Some of the Thai women wore their traditional dresses and the men the typical silk shirts.

After we'd tucked in to the 'special Christmas meal', which was just the same rice dishes as normal, the Sister and Empress went on stage.

"What song do you think they're gonna sing?" I asked Mr Kevin.

"Oh I dunno, We Wish You a Nunny Christmas?"

"Yeah or maybe, Joy to the Nuns," said Mr Geoff. They chose not to sing, but opened the show after a few holy words.

Each act before ours was a traditional Thai dance accompanied by soft music, and compared to our ridiculous Christmas routine we stood no chance of winning. The audience seemed to appreciate our classy dance moves, but the highlight was when Mr Geoff gave presents to the Sisters from his huge red sack.

We came fourth, and the evening was funnier than I'd expected. On the way out the Sister wished everyone a happy Christmas.

"Don't go far from the school though," she said, squeezing my shoulder and winking as I walked past.

Someone must have sent her a sign. If only she'd been able to warn the whole country.

The Sister's decision turned out to be a blessing in disguise. I was feeling emotional about being away from home and as it was my second year away, I was thinking even more about my family, especially now that I would be away from Uncle Gary in Phuket.

The Christmas Eve get together with the farang teachers was like being back in England, apart from the humidity and sticky weather. After a free food and booze buffet in the Siam district, we gate crashed a bar down Soi 4 Sukhumvit, took over their Karaoke machine and sang our way into Christmas.

We had a decent night, but waking up alone with a hangover on Christmas morning was unpleasant. I was fine until I opened the package my family had sent. I felt lonely and missed everyone at home more than ever. I tried to play the guitar I'd bought with money that my parents had sent over, but I wasn't in the mood.

I was glad when I met up with the farang teachers for Christmas lunch in a smoky English pub. The smell of stale beer wafted through my nose as I entered. Christmas tunes were playing in the background and the bar was full of British laughter, blokes with pot bellies stood at the bar telling jokes and enjoying the day.

"What you having?" asked Den, handing me a Christmas cracker.

"It's gotta be the turkey."

After my first roast in almost a year and a half, and several pints of cider, I called home.

"We have a little present to give you Barry," said my Mum over the phone.

"What's that then?"

"Me and Dad are coming out."

"What, over here, when?"

"In February; as long as I can get the time off work." It was great news.

I spent the rest of the day with farang in various bars down Sukhumvit. At about midnight we caught a tuk tuk to Khao San road where we stayed in a bar until Boxing Day morning. The last five of us crashed out in a hostel down Khao San at about 8am.

When we woke up at mid-day on Boxing Day and strolled down Khao San to find some lunch, everything seemed normal. Even as we tucked into lunch and someone mentioned a storm had hit the islands in the south, no one flinched. We chatted about the great Christmas day we'd had and our plans for New Years.

No one knew what had actually happened.

I got home and charged up my mobile phone.

*ARE YOU OK?* Mum

*GET IN TOUCH PLEASE. JUST LET US KNOW YOU ARE OK!* Dad

I thought they were overreacting; I'd spoken to them the day before. Then I had a message from a mate.

*ARE YOU ALIVE?*

Alive, why wouldn't I be? I turned on the TV. Even though the news commentary was in Thai, I could see that disaster had struck.

I called home.

"Dad, I'm okay. What's going on?"

"Jesus Barry, we were all so worried; there's been a huge Tsunami in Thailand and other countries."

"Where exactly in Thailand?" I said.

"In the South, near Phuket."

"That's where I was going to see Gary."

"Yeah we know; we hoped you hadn't got a last minute flight or something daft." I tried to call Gary, but it went straight to voicemail. I hoped he was safe.

The severity of the Tsunami hit me the next morning. You often hear about natural disasters on the news, but when you're in the country, or could have been right where thousands had died, the effect hits you harder.

The playground was less jubilant than normal and many of the young ones were weeping.

"Have you seen what happened, Mr Barry?" Mr Geoff asked.

"Yeah sort of, I couldn't understand the details though."

"Thousands have died man. They say it's one of the worst natural disasters of all time."

The Thai teachers were in shock and we all tried to console the children.

"Big wave, Mr Barry, big wave," Nam said as he made the motion of the Tsunami with his hands.

After an extended ceremony, everyone bumbled up the stairs. At the top was the Sister. She smiled and held my hands.

"God has saved you Mr Barry, God wants you to live," she said, softly. The bags under her eyes were dark, as if she'd been up praying all night. I felt guilty for having moaned about travelling and wanting to see the country.

"And your Uncle?"

"I don't know; I can't get through."

"Keep trying, I'm sure he'll be fine," she said.

After a few more attempts, I got through.

"Mate, are you all right?"

"Yeah we're fine; my business has been smashed to bits though."

"I'm so glad you're safe."

"Me too, Phuket is not a pretty place at the moment. Everything is destroyed. It's heart breaking. We're getting out of here quick. We were lucky though, we'd planned on going to the beach that morning, but I was in bed with a hangover. God knows what could have happened. Maybe that old dragon saved your arse."

"The thought had crossed my mind."

Uncle Gary and I were lucky, as were Chris, Mark, Helen, and Em, who had all been in Phuket a few weeks before.

At around 10am on the 26th of December 2004, when the Tsunami hit, I was asleep down Khao San. 800 kilometres south others were fighting for their lives. Thousands died in a couple of hours and millions of pounds worth of damage was done, not only in Thailand, but India, Indonesia, Malaysia, The Maldives, Myanmar, Somalia and Sri Lanka.

The Tsunami affected millions, if not through lost loved ones, then by flattened homes, destroyed businesses, and ruined livelihoods. Being in the country had a big effect on us. Most of the teachers were too distraught to teach on that first morning, but the Sister insisted we kept busy.

"There has been a terrible disaster, but it will help you to continue working, think of those unfortunate ones if you need motivation," she said in a soft manner.

Luckily, none of the school's children or families was affected directly. The initial shock got easier, and overtime we got on with our normal lives, but what took me longest to comprehend was why such a beautiful, harmless country was being punished.

I like to imagine the bottle of Chang is normally half-full so I took something positive from the Tsunami. I began to appreciate how fortunate I was to be able to travel the world and teach English. Whether or not the Sister, or God, saved me from the Tsunami I'll never know, but since then I've tried to live my life to the max.

## 21 A Full Moon Party Lights the Way

Everyone was in two minds about whether to go to Koh Phangan to celebrate New Year.

"What we gonna do?" I asked Liz a couple of days before.

"I dunno; we've bought tickets now, what else can we do? I can't stay in Bangkok."

"Yeah me neither, it'll be strange though; knowing we're on one side of Thailand having a party, while on the other they're searching for bodies."

Some toyed with the idea of going down to Phuket to help. Some argued that we only had a short break off work and there wasn't much we could do in a couple of days. Others said we had to continue with our plan to Koh Phangan for their local business. Thais were worried that the number of tourists would decrease, so we had to do our part to keep businesses flowing. In the end, none of us went to help, but instead we made donations to registered charities and also to our schools.

Like most of the other farang teachers, I wanted to escape from reality and take a break from work and forget about the disaster. I wasn't overly proud of going to enjoy myself while the country was in mourning, but I'm glad I experienced a New Year's party on the beach.

The mood was sombre when ten of us met up down Khao San to catch the overnight bus. To start with we spoke about the Tsunami, but once we'd headed south, everyone perked up and left the tragic memories behind. By the time we'd reached the ferry crossing to Koh Phangan the next morning, no one mentioned the 'T' word and the attention was on the party ahead.

"This is going to be a mental party," said Den as we watched a group of British lads drinking beer at 8am. The ferry was full of Europeans, Americans, and Australians. Most seemed mashed already, as if they'd been partying hard since Christmas.

As the wind blew through my hair while we cruised past lush green islands, I felt relieved that I was out of smoggy Bangkok. The ferry docked and everyone piled off along the wooden pier. Our group jumped in a taxi van and shortly we pulled up alongside cabanas by the sea.

"This is perfect," said Liz. We were in a quiet area about thirty minutes from the main full moon party beach at Haad Rin. Most of the group chilled in the squeaky hammocks or had a nap until mid afternoon.

I had a moment to myself and gazed over the horizon. Coverage of the Tsunami flashed through my mind. I was glad to be alive.

Before we set off for the night party, we lined our stomachs with stodgy rice and Phad Thai, and a couple of cheeky beers. Once everyone was spruced up, we jumped in a taxi van and sped up and down the hilly roads until we arrived at the madness.

We strolled down the row of bars pumping out house music, past women in dresses, sarongs, or bikinis, and blokes in slack Thai pants, or normal jeans and shirts. Some had luminous paint on their faces and arms and carried glow sticks, and others wore glow headbands.

We met up with more teachers (twenty in total) from Bangkok and the drink began to flow. After a short bar crawl on the main street, we headed to the beach where the real party started.

"This is gonna be a mad night," Den said as we stood staring along the beach as hundreds of party goers raved on the sand. The moon glistened off the sea as farang danced about, juggled balls, or did stunts by swinging ropes with balls of fire. No one would have guessed what had happened a few days before.

"TO MUSHROOM HILL," shouted Den as he pointed towards a bar on a hill at the end of the bay. The bar was the perfect place to see in New Years. The view from the terrace was back over the raving beach. The funky house music electrified the atmosphere, as did the drinks menu.

*Passion Fruit, Lemon, and Chocolate MUSHROOM SHAKES*

I thought back to what various colleagues had told me about the lethal drinks.

"You'll be laughing all night."

"You won't be able to move."

"It was one of the funniest things I've ever done."

"It was the worst night of my life." I decided to wait when I saw a bloke dressed up as a Dalmatian with a crazy grin on his face.

At midnight, we were on the dance floor giving it large to Auld Lang's Syne with house music thumping in the background. I thought about my family and mates back home and flashes of the Tsunami entered my mind again. I was grateful to be with people I knew.

After the usual New Years greetings, Den persuaded me to try a chocolate shake.

"This should be an experience," I said as we sipped the thick substance through the pink luminous curly straws.

"Yeah, a couple of the others had some yesterday; they were buzzing all night."

"Crikey," I said, nervously. I'd never drunk a mushroom shake.

The effect only lasted an hour for me. My legs became light and everything slowed down a little, but, unlike others who were mashed and even hallucinated for a couple of hours, I was soon in a normal, beered up, state. We spent the rest of the night dancing from one bar or spot on the beach to the other.

As light came, I sobered up and noticed how many drunk farang had collapsed on the beach. Most had sweaty messy hair, bulging eyes, and luminous paint smudged all over their faces and bodies. Part of me felt ashamed to see farang so out of their brains and I was glad when we got back to the cabana.

By lunchtime the next day, everyone was up and chatting about the previous night. Everyone had enjoyed the party and, despite the hangovers, we agreed to go back for some more and make the most of our time on the island.

On the third day, the hangover kicked in and we came back to reality. We went on a brief tour round the island but most were on a downer and the 'T' word crept up a few times. We went to a couple of beaches, but the mood was sombre; we were paying for having such a good time.

In a silent moment as we gathered at the top of a hill looking over the south part of the island, I imagined a giant wave wiping out everything in sight and felt terrified. I thought about the Sister. Had she really saved my life?

The next day everyone headed back to Bangkok while I went on a visa run to Penang. After catching the ferry to the main land, I caught a bus to Hat Yai and then a cramped minibus to Malaysia. The journey was long and arduous, but I was glad for the time to reflect on the last week. I'd enjoyed the break from Bangkok and spending time with other farang. My original plan of emerging myself in the Thai culture and learning the language had faded away. Teaching had become my main focus, and after the Tsunami I missed my family more. I was glad my parents were coming to visit and that I could show them I was doing something worthwhile.

On the trip from Hat Yai, an English couple constantly moaned about the traffic and stops we made.

"This is ridiculous, why is it taking so long?" said the young lad, thumping the roof.

"Yes, we've paid our money," said the girlfriend. "We shouldn't be stopping so much, and these seats are uncomfortable." Their petty comments annoyed me; life was too short for moaning.

The following day, once I'd filled out the forms for my visa in Georgetown, I caught a bus to Batu Ferringgi, a beach resort in the north of the island. After the madness of Koh Phangan I was pleased with the quietness of the village. I followed a thin sandy path which led to a hostel, checked in, and went for a stroll.

A strange negative energy was floating about Batu. The restaurants were empty, the locals had glum faces, and the beach was deserted apart from a few stray dogs, which fought for a spot by a knocked down tree. The sand was harsh and covered in bits of broken bark. During my afternoon on the beach, only about five farang came out of the cabanas and no one swam.

The restaurants were busier in the evening, but a subdued atmosphere floated around. I enjoyed the peace though, and after I scoffed down some delicious fat noodles with prawns and squid covered in thick gravy, I caught an early night.

The food might have been tasty, but something was off. I dreamt that I was vomiting and when I woke up at three in the morning my stomach was gurgling and the room was spinning. My bowels rumbled and I ran for the toilet. I won't go into the details, but the night was horrific. I coped with the trips to the loo, but the sweating and shivering freaked me out.

In the morning I thought I was in serious trouble. I had to get back to George Town, get my visa, and then catch a flight, but I could barely stand. Maybe I was paying for being selfish and going to the New Year's party rather than helping out in Phuket.

Despite my blurred vision and dizzy spells, I stumbled over to a pharmacy on the main street and bought some medicine to block my stomach. After, I stocked up from a Seven Eleven next door on orange Fanta and chocolate biscuits.

On the bus back to Georgetown it was touch and go but I made it to the visa office and jumped in a cab to the airport.

"Oh wow; an English man," said the hairy armed driver in a chirpy English accent. "You don't look so good."

"I feel pretty rough; I got food poisoning."

"Yeah, a lot of people have after the Tsunami."

"Did it come here? That would explain the state of the beach and long faces."

"Of course," he said, smacking his forehead. "Batu Ferringgi got hit and a poor family, who lived in a cave in the bay, drowned."

"Wow, I'm sorry to hear that."

"It could have been worse, but the whole island is sad now. It's a tragic time for Penang and the world; it's always the poor who come off worse."

The trip away from Bangkok gave me a chance to appreciate a few things. Farangs had it easy; we'd got together, booked a ticket down to the islands, and more or less forgotten about the Tsunami. Some had given to charity, but, as far as I know, none of the Koh Phangan group volunteered to help in Phuket, but why? Perhaps because staying in a safe environment at work, away from danger, and continue teaching was easier.

Some felt that by teaching we *were* giving back to society. I certainly did. Having come from a sales job in London, where I was just another number and money was the main motivating factor, I'd learnt that teaching was a worthy job. I had the skills to educate people to improve their lives, which was more beneficial than making money to survive in a superficial world.

I spent more time thinking about my lessons and tried to improve my teaching. I still had fun but I took my lessons more seriously and saw improvements in the kids' English. Even Panu and Kevin learnt to say more than 'toilet.'

The external visit which had caused the Sister to cancel Christmas got called off because of the Tsunami and after a month, no one spoke about the disaster. I'm sure others thought about it as much as I did, but we just got on with our lives and the school became normal again. The Thai teachers were still off the farang, the farang still moaned and made sarcastic comments about the Sister, and the kids still thought the Sister was a witch.

Someone *had* changed though.

"I have some news," said the Sister in a dull voice. We had gathered in the giant hall. The Sister seemed weaker than normal, her eyes tired. "I won't be here much longer." A couple of the Thai teachers gasped. I felt remorse; was she ill? "I am leaving the school." The Thai teachers muttered, and Miss Rancha's eyes welled up as she sobbed.

"Why?" said Mr Geoff, who a few weeks back might have been tap dancing on the table. He seemed sad too.

"After the disaster I have been in contact with helpers in Phuket. I have decided to go down and help." Everyone stared in silence. "There is a lot of work to be done in the South and I must be there to ensure peace is brought on those who have suffered." When she smiled weakly, I felt for her; I'd never seen her vulnerable side.

"I have been praying every night for those who have suffered, but it's not enough. I am sorry to leave, but I have a new mission now."

"What about the school?" said Mr Sirichild.

"Don't worry; I'll be back at some point. You can take care of things between you. I have to do my part."

Everyone left the meeting speechless. The Sister was going to the South.

My opinion of the Sister had fluctuated, but she won back my respect in that meeting. After thinking about going to help in Phuket before New Year's and deciding to enjoy myself, I admired the Sister's courage. She'd always come across as a hard-nosed woman, but I know now that she just wanted to discipline and educate the children.

I saw her mission clearer; she was just a lonely old lady who wanted to do some good in the world. If that meant people had to hate her, then so be it. She became an inspiration to me. I respected her decision to leave her precious school that she tried hard to keep in order and go down to try to give peace to people whose lives had shattered.

## 22 Bye Bye Bangkok

The school ran just as well, if not better, without the Sister. The farang were more relaxed not writing so many lesson plans and the Thai teachers came out of their shells and seemed more comfortable. At the end of the day, instead of preparing and tidying, they'd natter and snack on packets of seaweed and spicy papaya salad.

I continued as I had been; with or without the Sister, I still wanted to teach English.

My parents coming to visit was one of my trip's highlights. They'd been worried after the Tsunami and I'd begun to realize the importance of family.

They normally went caravanning round England or beached on one of the Balearic Islands, so I was proud that they ventured out to experience a different culture.

"It's quite high, isn't it?" said Dad as we looked out over the smoggy capital from the 53$^{rd}$ floor of the Baiyoke Sky Hotel; the tallest building in Bangkok.

"Yeah, but don't you just love the view," said Mum.

"It would be better closer to the floor. But never mind, one of these beers will settle my nerves," he said, hissing open a Chang.

Dad was still his wide backed burly size, perhaps with a few more grey hairs, and Mum was slimmer with blonde tints. After eighteen months, seeing my parents laugh and smile made me feel at ease and safe. Mum kept hold of my hand as we talked. I'd forgotten how well we got on and having them near was emotional.

On the first night, I took them to a swanky restaurant down Sukhumvit. On the way, as we were leaving the metro, Mum startled.

"Is it normal to see elephants walking in the street?"

"Depends where you are, why?"

"Cos I can see one over there," she said, pointing towards a short Thai man leading his bumbling elephant through a crowded side street.

"Blimey, my favourite," Dad said, switching on his video camera. "That was a bit of luck," he chuckled.

"A bit of luck," I said, sarcastically. "I've only seen one elephant in five months, and you've already seen one in five minutes."

They loved whizzing along on the Klong taxi, despite the sewage stench, and catching a tuk tuk to the Golden Palace. They even liked Khao San road.

"I could sit here all day and people watch," said Dad as we sipped beers while farang strolled about the market stalls. Mum was unimpressed with the toilets though.

"It's not like back home, is it?"

When Mum realized she could haggle at Chatuchak market, one of the largest outdoor markets in the world, she did with everyone, even in the restaurants.

"You did say I could haggle, didn't you?" she said after the waiter stormed off.

"Not with food and drink, that's a fixed price."

They were impressed by the size and commotion at Chatuchak, but stunned by the poverty.

"That's so sad," said Mum as a man with only half a leg squirmed on the floor, scraping a green plastic cup with his arm.

"I've seen him a couple of times," I said. "That's Bangkok; one moment you can be in a luxury hotel and the next helping poor people on the street with nothing. I've never seen somewhere with so much inequality."

"I noticed the shacks along the canal. It's terrible," said Dad.

On the days I was working, my parents got up to a few mini adventures. One day they went on a mad tuk tuk ride round the backstreets of Bangkok, and on another they were on a guided tour of Wat Po and almost got ripped off by the tailors.

"It was ridiculous, after the tour they took us to see some clothes shops," said Mum.

"Your mother said she was up for it."

"Well I didn't know, did I?"

"Yeah anyway, these people took us to a flashy tailor shop."

"Yeah, and they insisted we look round. Some tourists were going mental. Your father was getting annoyed."

"Of course I bloody was. They were trying to stitch us up."

"Yeah, I don't blame you," I said, trying not to laugh.

"So where are we going tonight?' Mum asked.

"It's a surprise, you'll see," I said, not wanting to spoil the delights of Patpong.

"No, No, I've seen it all before," said Mum, blanking the haggler shoving the 'Pussy Show' board in her face as she browsed the market.

"That woman just pinched me on the bum," said Dad.

We stayed out of the Go-go bars, but went down Soi 4 for some food and drinks.

"Here, what's up with these waiters?" Dad asked.

"Why?" I said.

"They keep looking at me a bit funny."

"Well, this is a gay street," I said.

"You what?" Mum said, almost spitting out her Phad Thai.

"Yeah look about; that bar over there's a gay bar and most of the waiters are gay."

"Blimey, oh yeah," Dad said. "Why do you come down here then?"

"I dunno we just do; it's different to back home."

"Yeah I can see that," he said.

Like any son or daughter, I was proud to be able to show my parents how I'd created a new life and career. Showing them round Our Lady of Perpetual Health was a special moment. I only wish they could have been able to meet the Sister.

I was nervous about their visit, but not as much as the kids.

"I have butterflies Mr Barry," said Nam before they arrived. "I think Kevin too."

"Why do you say that?"

"He vomit in classroom."

"Lovely."

Kevin had puked over his uniform and the only spare clothes Miss Nitayya had were blue striped pyjamas.

"You found it all right then?" I said as I met Mum and Dad at the entrance.

"Yeah, this place is huge,' said Dad.

"Yeah, tell me about it."

"But Barry, it's beautiful. It's a proper school," said Mum, patting me on the head. Some things never change.

As we strolled round the grounds I could tell my parents were in awe.

"This place is amazing," said Mum. "I'd love to work out here."

I left them in the staff room chatting with the teachers and checked the class were ready and behaved. Poor Kevin's face was a pale shade of green, but the rest were eager to meet my parents. Their faces were beaming as I slid back the door. The kids were just as quiet and angel looking as they had been on my first morning.

"Oh, this is nice," Mum said, gazing around the room. Miss Nittaya came forward and they shook hands.

"Okay Nam,' I said, winking at him to initiate the greeting.

"PLEASE STAND UP," he shouted.

"Good afternoon Mr and Mrs Barry's Mum and Dad,' said the class. Panu presented a welcome card.

"That's lovely, thank you little boy," said Mum.

"Right then, who's got a question?" I said. Everyone shot their hand up. My parents were still grinning.

"Go on then, Bee."

"What is your name?"

"My name is Sean, and this is Jackie, my wife." Everyone wooed.
"Nam."
"What is your job?" he asked Mum.
"Well, I work in a school, like here, but not so beautiful, and I work in reception so it's not like the class, you see." The kid's faces were blank.
"Not so complicated," I whispered.
"Okay, sorry, yes, I work in a school and Sean is an engineer." Everyone wooed again.
"Next question?"
"You love Miss Jackie?" Neung asked. Everyone started laughing.
"That's a good question," said Dad. "Yes, of course I do." Everyone cheered.

After a bombardment of questions, Dad took over and played noughts and crosses against the class. Mum had a go too, but kept getting beat. They were naturals with the kids, and watching them interacting put a lump in my throat; I couldn't believe they were in Bangkok, in my class.

At the end, they presented my parents with their welcome cards and Miss Nittaya gave Mum a big bunch of yellow and white marigolds.

"Wow that was wonderful Barry," said Mum as we walked over the playground towards my flat. "It brought a tear to my eye."

"No wonder you like this teaching lark," said Dad.

In the evening we met up with all the teachers in a buffet style restaurant. It was the first time that the farang and Thai teachers in our department had gone out for a social event.

Outside school the Thai teachers were actually a good laugh. They had lots of questions for my parents and Mr Sirichild showed them how to cook their own food on the special mini cooker. I was grateful the Thai teachers made an effort and were welcoming. Perhaps we should have gone out more often.

My parent's holiday had been their best ever, and they left drained and emotional after a crazy week in Bangkok. Showing them what it was like living and teaching in another country made me feel as though the previous year and a half had been worthwhile. Being on my own had been difficult at times, but I'd got through the challenging moments and had become a teacher.

When you're living away you tend to forget the importance of certain things, like family. I missed everyone back home. When my parents left I realized I had grown up (well, a bit) since leaving England. We had more in common and I felt more like an adult. Travelling alone had changed my life. I'd developed the confidence that I never had while living in London. My fear of returning home was beginning to fade. Perhaps it was time to head to England, but the question was how?

March approached and I got a TEFL summer job offer to teach in London in July. I could have flown straight from Bangkok, but would have been too easy. I wanted an adventure, a challenge, a mammoth trip home.

"What about the Trans-Mongolian?" Den said one Saturday night while down Khao San.

"That's always been on my list, perhaps I could go back that way."

"It's a bloody long route, plus you'd have to get a move on with the visas, there's loads of paperwork involved."

I had the travel buzz again, but would I be able to travel overland back to England? The problem was the time. My contract finished at the end of April so I only had about four weeks to get from Bangkok to Beijing to catch the Trans-Mongolian to Moscow.

After researching the internet, the trip was possible, but tight. The tricky visas were for China, Mongolia, and, especially, Russia. I had to book accommodation in Moscow and also my Trans-Mongolian rail ticket before I could get the Russian visa. It was a rush, but I managed it.

"You're going back via China and Russia?" asked Mr Geoff. "What an end to your journey."

"Yeah, I'm all geared up for it now."

"Blimey, watch out for those Babushkas on the Russian trains, I've heard they're feisty ones," he said, winking. I was sad to leave my students and friends, but excited about ending my journey on a high.

When the Sister returned briefly to Bangkok, at first the atmosphere was tense, but once we saw she was calmer, everyone continued as normal.

"I hear your parents were here, Mr Barry," she said on the first morning. Her eyes were tired, but the friendly way she spoke suggested she'd been revitalised.

"Yeah they were. How do you know that?"

"I know things Mr Barry, I know things," she said, grinning.

"Yeah I can see; how was Phuket?"

"Sad, very sad." Her eyebrows dropped and she forced a smile. "There are many volunteers and soon the local people will be able to get on with their lives."

In a strange way, having her back was comforting. We feared her less and the students respected her more. Within a week she'd mustered up a new event for the parents.

"The International and Culture Event will be our best performance yet," she said with a twinkle in her eye. The classes were put into new groups and each farang teacher, along with two Thai teachers, had to prepare a dance to represent a country. I chose Spain because I thought I could persuade them to dance salsa. Getting them to hold hands and learn a routine took ages though.

"Mr Barry, I hope they are ready, they are a very noisy group," she said as the boys and girls got in separate lines on stage for the first dress rehearsal. The boys wore black tuxedoes, red waistcoats, and black bow ties, and the girls had a white flower clipped in their hair and wore red, yellow, or green flamenco dresses that the Thai teachers had made.

"Don't worry they're just a bit nervous."

"Well come on, get them ready," she said, clapping her hands. I whacked on the funky salsa music. The girls began their solo dance while the boys stomped their feet, then the boys did a routine while the girls clapped and twirled. Once they'd formed couples and did individual dances, they gathered in a large circle for a group dance.

The Sister seemed shocked they were holding hands and dancing so close, but by the end she was smiling.

"Well done Mr Barry. Well done children, very good," said the Sister, winking at me.

The main event was huge. External media organisers came in to set up a fifteen metre stage in the playground with professional lights and video cameras. Not only was the English department performing, but forty other groups as well.

On the night, the students were hyperactive and running about like crazy. The teachers were nervous after all the effort we'd put in. When it was our departments turn, everyone lined up in the corridor and followed the Sister towards the playground.

As we waited behind the stage, the energy was overwhelming. Hundreds of parents were in front while red, green and blue lights flashed in rhythm to the Thai pop music.

"It's time to go on," Miss Liz said, running over to everyone. The first group marched on. I had to help hold up the background scenes we'd made, so I had a decent view of the performance. My group looked nervous on stage but they did an excellent job and moved to perfection. Watching them strut their stuff in front of a massive audience gave me goose bumps. We'd worked hard, but seeing the kids' happy faces as they bounced off stage made it worthwhile. I'd miss the little buggers.

The countdown to the end of term meant exams and the last week was the most stressful. The kids seem unfazed by the revision classes and exams, but the teachers ran about like headless Buddhas. Everyone in my class passed apart from Panu and Kevin. Well, unofficially. Miss Nittaya bumped them up; Mummy and Daddy would have been angry.

End of term also meant the end of football. I'd been playing occasionally with the lads and we were less close than at the start, but when I told them I was leaving they organised a mini whisky party round Rooney's Mum's restaurant. The day after I felt sure of my decision to leave; I'd had a fun night, but my level of Thai was still poor and I couldn't hold a conversation. If I stayed, I'd always be a farang.

I agreed to teach a new, younger class in the intensive summer course in April, which meant I had to say goodbye to my students. The majority were going away for the summer because Bangkok was too hot; some days reaching over fifty degrees.

"You must wait until the last day to tell them you are leaving or they will get emotional and become rebels," the Sister said.

"But that doesn't give much time to say goodbye."

"Yes, it is better that way. They are children. They have grown attached."

On the last day, after we played a few games and ate loads of sugary sweets, I announced I was leaving. They seemed surprised, but Miss Nittaya explained that I was going back to my family. She asked me to draw a map of how I was getting there. Once I'd drawn a map of my route overland from Bangkok to Moscow, I felt daunted.

"But how are you going all that way without an aeroplane?" asked Nam, tugging on my sleeve.

"I might catch one plane, but it's going to be an adventure."

I gave the girls a little doll and the boys a ninja headscarf. The boys jumped out of their chairs and whooped as they pretended to fight. The girls sobbed.

"What's up with them?' I asked Miss Nittaya.

"Don't worry; not you, some change school now, very sad for them,' she said.

Nam was the only lad who seemed upset.

"But why you no teach us in summer school?" he said, pushing his glasses back on the bridge of his nose.

"I have to teach a younger class now," I explained. "Mr Geoff is teaching you, he's great fun," I said, but he dropped his shoulders and ambled away. By the end of the day, everyone had shed a tear or two; even Miss Nittaya used a hanky to wipe her eyes.

"We miss you Mr Barry," she said just before they left waving.

I was privileged to have taught such a generous and appreciative class. Since then, eight years later, I've still never taught a better bunch.

The Sister kept her promise of giving us a week's holiday at the end of March and my sister Sarah came out to visit. The mini adventure to Koh Chang was a great taster before going travelling again.

Unlike my parents, Sarah had changed loads in eighteen months.

"The last time I saw you, you were a spotty teenager, now you're almost a woman." Her blonde hair had grown down to her lower back and she looked more like a female version of me, only prettier.

"Easy tiger," she said, punching me in the arm. "I'm still only seventeen."

Sarah wanted to get a feel for travelling because she'd planned on taking a year out before starting university. She got off to a bad start though.

"What do you mean you can't move?" I asked after our first night out on the beers down Khao San.

"I just can't," she grumbled.

"But we've got a pool in the hotel, come on."

"Sorry, I just can't," she groaned. The mix of jet lag and drinking beer on an empty stomach had hit her hard.

Koh Chang was a paradise island. We found a cheap (500baht, £3.50) cabana on White Sand Beach and soaked up the sun, drank plenty of booze, and caught up with each other for a week.

Time flew as we swam in the warm sea, messed about with the dogs, Buster and Rhymes from the restaurant, and spent the evenings watching fire jugglers, listening to live music, and singing karaoke.

The highlight of the trip was meeting Mr Chad, our jungle trekking guide.

"Be careful now, follow me, can die," he said as we followed along a dry mud track into the jungle. Sarah raised her eyebrows.

"What do you mean?" asked Sarah.

"You will see," said Mr Chad, whistling as he bounced along. Mr Chad had dark skin, black hair, and was skinny with brown stained teeth. On the trip down his van had stunk of ganga.

Even though the air was muggy, the shade from the scorching sun was refreshing. The dirt path became narrower and we had to push away branches.

"There aren't many animals about," I said to Mr Chad.

"No, animals no much, sometimes monkeys, but insects, big ants, they dangerous, can die." Sarah was walking with her arms folded to avoid contact with the trees, luckily she hadn't heard.

A bit further, Mr Chad jumped in the air.

"OKAY STOP," he shouted. "Here big ants, no touch, can die."

"Stay back; or you'll die,' I said to Sarah, jokingly.

"No joke, can die, man die last week."

I peeked down. A line of black chunky ants were carrying leaves and twigs about ten times their size.

"Just jump over," I said from the other side of the line.

"But what if I land on them?" Sarah said, hopping on the spot.

"Jump, high," Mr Chad said as he did his highest jump.

"Okay, here I come," she said, squealing as she jumped over.

"She no die!" said Mr Chad, in surprise.

We continued cautiously, deeper into the jungle. After Mr Chad had pointed out some rubber trees and a great view over the island near a waterfall, we stopped to cool down in a river. Mr Chad sat on a rock and lit up a spliff.

"Sit here, very cool, sit, sit," he said, pointing to a small natural rock pool.

"Fuck it's freezing Mr Chad," I said as I laid back. "Have you got a beer?" I joked.

"No, I have ganga. You want ganga?"

"Nah, not for me," I said, looking at Sarah.

"Oh, no I'm okay," she said.

"If you want I have, no problem, no problem," Mr Chad said, taking a five-second drag. "You see this tree?" he asked, pointing to a bamboo tree. "Bamboo make good bong, good bong, you know," he said, sniggering.

We made it back to the van and on the way to our cabana Mr Chad invited us out on his boat the following day.

"We go snorkel, if you want, you come. Maybe bamboo bong, but you no die."

Mr Chad's boat trip was mental. Other tourists were on the boat but we got special treatment. Once we'd set sail, Mr Chad invited us in the captain's compartment. Four other Thai lads, including the driver, were sitting on a mattress listening to Bob Marley tracks while passing round a spliff.

"Don't worry, I make bamboo bong later," Mr Chad said, seeing I was left out.

We reached a dive site and everyone jumped in to snorkel from the top deck.

"Watch me," shouted Gai, Mr Chad's cousin, as he dived off the boat with a harpoon. He returned a couple of minutes later with a fish flapping about at the end of his spear.

After a quick snorkel and a tasty fish and salad lunch, we stopped off on a tiny island's beach. Within thirty minutes the rain began to fall and Mr Chad summoned us back on the boat.

"Need go quick, weather bad; no want die," he said, pointing to the massive grey clouds looming. We set off towards the mainland, but soon the rain was lashing down. Mr Chad invited us back in the Bob Marley cabin while the other tourists got wet.

"Can you see Koh Chang?" Sarah asked as she passed me the bamboo bong again. "It was there a second ago."

"Nope, it's gotta be there somewhere," I said, taking a drag. Having not sampled the Thai ganga before, the effect was strong, and lasting.

"I still can't see Koh Chang," I said to Sarah, laughing a couple of minutes later.

"Me neither," she said, giggling back.

"No Koh Chang, Koh Chang gone," Mr Chad said, clapping.

"No problem, I good captain," Gai said.

Despite the clouds getting thicker and darker, and being swayed by the bamboo bong, I had absolute confidence in Gai. If he could jump off the top of the boat with a harpoon and catch lunch, then he could get us home. Bob Marley helped; we didn't worry, and we were extremely happy.

When good old Koh Chang came into view, we let out a massive cheer, which the people below, who were suitably soaked, must have heard. They seemed narked off when we appeared, giggling and dry.

The rest of our time on the island, we spent chilling on the beach and generally not doing much. Sarah was definitely up for travelling after our mini adventure.

"It's just so different to back home; the thought of college gives me the blues."

"Yeah, I feel the same about Bangkok at the moment."

"Yeah, but you're going travelling again in about a month. I've got to wait almost a year," she said, which cheered me up, even if it didn't her.

When Sarah left she was hooked on the idea of travelling. Who can blame her; it can happen to the best of us.

The Sister returned to Phuket and teaching during the summer school was much more relaxed. We finished earlier every day, there were no exams, and my new class of six year olds were, surprisingly, less rowdy. After the trip to Koh Chang, I had the taste for adventure and spent most of my time researching about my trip and counting down the days.

The last big event was Songkran.

"What is it though?" I asked Mr Sirichild.

"It is Thai New Year, end of dry season. Before lot respect, but now all country have crazy water fights." He shook his head and tutted.

"Sounds like fun," I said.

"Yes fun for farang, all country crazy, water fight in all places, you go Khao San road, have good time."

Mr Geoff was a fan of Songkran.

"So what's the plan Mr Barry?" he said, rubbing his hands together.

"I'm heading to Khao San with a few mates."

"Ah yeah, I was there a couple of years back, it's a ball. You'll have a great time, all those women running about in wet T-Shirts, you'll love it."

The Thai teachers celebrated by setting up an inflatable swimming pool in the main hall. They placed floating candles and flowers on top which filled the room with a sweet fragrance. Some students did a special Thai dance while Mr Sirichild blessed the farang with holy water and gave us a red and white flowered necklace. Then we danced round the pool while the kids sat in hysterics.

"Don't tell anyone about this," I whispered to Kevin as I twirled my wrists round.

"As long as you don't," he said, spinning on the spot.

Songkran meant we had five days off. The Thai teachers warned me about strangers drenching me in the street, especially being a farang. On the first morning, I walked to the end of the road to get some beers because we were meeting round Mr Geoff's house for a barbeque. As I got towards the end, a few kids were messing about throwing water. One spotted me.

"FARANG," he shouted as five kids screamed as they charged up and poured bottles of ice cold water on my head and down my neck. I had no ammunition, but I got a couple back after I'd stocked up in the Seven Eleven.

The carnage continued at Mr Geoff's house. He had a six-year old son, who had water guns about the same length as him. We spent the day eating, drinking, and throwing water at each other. Compared to the following day down Khao San, it was just a teaser.

The bus into town took ages, but watching the Thais go mental was fun. Random people were throwing buckets of water at whoever was nearest. Kids threw water at old people, old people at kids, anyone was a target. The constant tooting horns and smoky traffic by Khao San was worse than normal. Street stalls sold water pistols, water bombs, and even flour. I bought a water gun the size of my arm for about two quid.

Khao San was busier than ever, but the great thing was that everyone was smiling, not that Thais were usually miserable, but everyone seemed extra happy.

It was a bizarre set up. Where else in the world can you sit and have a beer and get involved in a massive water fight with people from all over the world. Such an event could only have happened in Thailand, anywhere else then real fights would have broken out.

As the day went on, more farang I knew turned up and Khao San became busier. Beers and whisky buckets were flying, everyone was drinking and throwing water all day and most of the night.

Thais and farang mingled in harmony for three days solid. I'd never experienced such a peaceful, but manic festival; a great way to end my time in Bangkok.

The summer school was over in a flash. I had my Russia visa, and was excited about the trip overland.

On my last night out with the remaining farang mates, we had a few too many tequilas and I did a 'Miss Lucy' on my final morning.

"Hey Mr Barry, have you heard?" said Mr Kevin. "We're getting paid this morning?"

"What? But we normally get paid in the afternoon. Shit, can you smell alcohol?" I said, breathing gently. I needed that last pay packet to get to China.

"Crikey, yeah, where did you go last night?"

"Out with some mates, you got any mints?"

"You'll need more than that."

I panicked. I'd presumed the Empress would pay us in the afternoon as normal. I managed to scrounge a few mints off Miss Gigi before we went to get our envelopes.

"Just don't breathe on her," said Mr Geoff.

"Hmm, hmm," I said, clenching my mouth tight. The Empress called me. I took a deep breath.

"So Mr Barry, is today your last day?" She must have had some English lessons; she'd never spoken to me before.

"Yes, Yes," I said, quickly.

"Are you okay?"

"Yes, yes."

"Okay, do you want to say something?" she said after giving me the envelope.

"No, no, it's okay," I said.

"Thank you," she said.

"Thank you," I said, bowing as I darted out.

The rest of the day was sad. I'd enjoyed my time at Our Lady of Perpetual Health and would miss the students.

"Will you come back Mr Barry?" Nam said at lunchtime as I sat talking to him and Batman for the last time.

"Maybe, if you continue your English."

"Yes, I will, I like thanks to you," he said, giving me a hug. Batman laughed nervously and we slapped a high five.

I said goodbye to the Thai teachers and thanked Miss Nittaya and Mr Sirichild for their help and hospitality. Then I said goodbye to the farang.

"Watch out for those Russian women," said Mr Geoff.

"Yeah, especially the Babushkas," Mr Kevin added.

After almost seven months, it was time to go. I still had to say goodbye to one person though.

"Mr Barry," Mr Sirichild said as I was walking towards the gate. "The Sister is in her house, you can see her?"

"I thought she was still in Phuket?"

"She came back early." I turned round and walked towards her house.

"You are leaving now?" she said, surprised. She was wearing her normal white habit, her ears tucked neatly away.

"Yeah, I need to catch my bus."

"Where are you going?"

"I'm off to North Thailand, Laos, Cambodia, Vietnam, China, Russia, and then home."

"Oh, that will be dangerous. You must take care."

"Yeah, I will Sister."

"Will you be back?"

"I doubt it; I need to be closer to my family now." She smiled and squeezed my hand. Hers were cold.

"You will be missed, thank you for helping our children. I wish your family well."

"Thanks for all your help, I know we didn't always see eye to eye, but you're not a bad boss, sometimes."

"Oh, oh," she said, hushing me away. "I am not here to be liked, only to help others," she said, winking.

## 23 Laos: Drifting and Dodgy Shakes

"I'm gonna miss the fucking boat," I said to Rich, the blonde scuba diving lad I'd been travelling with from Chang Mai. We'd met on an overnight bus from Bangkok and had spent four days touring north Thailand, mainly in the bars. We were in a hostel in Chiang Khong, a quiet town on the border of Laos.

"Shit, I knew we shouldn't have had those last shots," he said, jumping off the higher bunk and thumping on the wooden floor.

The long boat to Luang Prabang left every three days and I only had four weeks to get to Beijing to catch the Trans-Mongolian. Getting stuck in dull Chiang Khong would severely damage my plans. We rushed on our clothes, packed up our stuff, I grabbed my guitar, and we ran down the hill to immigration.

"I've gotta get that long boat," I said as we skimmed over the Mekong River to the Laos border in a thin motored barge. I imagined the Sister and my class waving goodbye from the dry bank. Thailand was drifting away.

"You'll make it," said Rich, slurring. He still seemed drunk. Rich had been fun to travel with, despite his gore stories about the bodies he helped to dig up after the Tsunami. "I'm gonna hitchhike northern Laos," he added, rubbing his head.

Within a couple of minutes we'd pulled up on the river bank and had sprinted up to the Laos immigration point. Once I'd collected my stamp, I asked where the long boat left from.

"You run, run with me," said a Laotian woman, pacing off down a dry mud track. I wished Rich good luck and darted off.

I followed along a thin path until we came to a grassy bank. Floating on the river was a dark red long boat, which looked like a giant Dutch man's clog. The Laos woman shouted as the driver cranked up the engine.

"There's always one," said an English lad as I panted down the thin aisle, knocking into various farang. I handed my rucksack and guitar to a young Laotian lad, who lugged it on top of a pile next to the engine room, and I plonked down on the last free seat at the back.

I could have had a better start to the two day boat trip to Luang Prabang. I had to rest my skinny backside on a hard splintery wooden bench. I'd missed out on the wafer thin cushions that the other fifty farang had. The space between my knobbly knees and the bench in front was just big enough to fit my pinkie finger, and that was sitting at a seventy-degree angle.

As we drifted down the chocolaty Mekong, the rocky motion and strong farang body odour made my gusty hangover worse. From my sitting position the surface of the water was only a couple of feet below my eye level. My mouth was dry and head pounded. I only had half a litre of water.

The surroundings were much more important than my comfort though. I was travelling along with nature. The backdrop of green mountains, fluttering birds, and splashing water on the side of the boat eased the pain. Each bend that we turned, or straight that we flowed along, reminded me of why I loved travelling so much; the freedom to drift was a gift.

I was uninterested in starting conversations with other travellers about where they'd come from or where they were going. I made no eye contact and leant on the glassless windowsill and gazed at Laos' beauty.

"Mate, where you heading?" asked the chavy bloke in front.

"*Que?*" I said.

"What're you a foreigner?" I wanted to explain that we were both foreigners, and that he was a twat, but instead I said.

"Solly? I am froma de Spain, me no Englishy."

"Don't even speak our language," he said to his girlfriend. The nonce failed to notice the copy of 'The Great Train Robbery' by Michael Crichton on my lap.

We entered a faster stretch as a speedboat passed and waves collided with the side. A couple of fools hanging out of the windows to top up their tans were rocking the boat and water crept over the windowsills.

"Please, sit now, this no fun ride, you passenger make piss with river," said the driver. A few sniggered, including yours truly. The lads calmed down and we cruised on.

We stopped for a toilet break and stocked up on essentials. A few people with tents got off and disappeared into the hills so I nicked their wider seats. The one-inch cushion made a massive difference to my bony bum, and I even picked up a new travelling companion, a Laotian woman.

She had the same physical appearance as some Thai women; jet-black hair and slightly tanned skin, but her eyes were more rounded and puffier.

"Where go?" she asked.

"Luang Prabang, and you?" (I know I said I was uninterested in conversation, but she was exotic).

"Pak Beng, my village." She pointed ahead. "You need bed?" Hello, I thought. "My father have hostel, you stay?" She seemed harmless and cute, so I agreed.

Thanks to my dictionary, we had fun communicating in our pigeon Thai and English. Laya smiled constantly and when I got out my Discman she clapped and squeezed my arm. I kept changing songs to see if she knew the next track. When she did, she yelped, bobbed her head, and hummed in tune.

When I gazed towards the mountains, Laya would tap my leg or pinch the back of my arm for attention. I didn't mind because she was fun and her positive energy was contagious. She made the journey fly by, and soon we were approaching Pak Beng, a small village built high on the mud banks. The journey had taken almost eight-hours.

We moored and twenty local lads came sprinting down a hill, whooping and cheering. I'd never seen locals get so excited about strangers arriving; as if we'd come from Burma with crates of gold. Farang climbed off the boat, stretching their stiff backs and legs, and the bundle swarmed round.

The lads were keen to help everyone, and no doubt make a few bob from the hostel owners, but they kept snatching farang's bags and pulling their arms. Many farang got flustered and a couple of rows broke out. I was glad I'd met Laya as we scarpered up the mud bank towards the village.

Local kids waved and wolf whistled at Laya as we strolled past. Her Dad greeted us with open arms, well Laya anyway; he shook my hand but was more interested in my wallet.

"I very happy you stay here," he said as I handed him the money. He tucked the cash in his pocket and disappeared out the back. I never saw him again.

"Come see terrace," said Laya, pulling me by the arm through the lounge towards the wooden floored outdoor restaurant.

"Wow," I said. We were high up the bank with a clear view over the mountains. The sun was beginning to drift down and rays of light shone through the evening mist.

"Look, funny," she said, pointing to the farang still arguing with the lads by the river. Laya showed me to my room.

"Shower there," she said, pointing down the narrow corridor. "Good stay." I wanted to ask her if she fancied a coffee, but what looked like her sister appeared and they went off laughing.

I still felt hung over and tired and was glad to have some personal space. After a long hot shower someone knocked at the door. Perhaps Laya was inviting me out, I thought, foolishly.

"Who is it?" I asked through the paper-thin door.

"Hello, hello," said a manly voice. "You have guitar?"

"Eh?" I said, opening the door. A topless chubby Laotian bloke in his early twenties stood grinning.

"Guitar?" he said, peaking in.

"Yes I have a guitar," I said coldly.

"I play good, I play? Show you?" he asked, jigging about. I had to block him entering. I might have said yes, but I was knackered and not in the mood for him to show me up on my guitar.

"Maybe tomorrow, sorry," I said, closing the door. He stuck his foot in.

"You want chocolate? Hash?" he whispered. He took a massive sniff as he pulled out a handful of puff.

"No thanks, I'm tired, sorry."

"Okay, but later I play guitar and you have chocolate, okay?" he said, waving the strong smelling hash in my face.

"Probably not," I said firmly, shutting the door. "Cheeky fucker," I muttered.

"I no fucker, only want play guitar," he said. The door really was paper-thin.

During the night, someone knocked on my door. I was half-asleep and thought Laya could have been asking if she could listen to my Discman.

"Yes?" I said, hopefully.

"Chocolate?" whispered the pest. I considered getting up and giving him what for, but I was snug. I ignored him and eventually he left me in peace.

The next morning he was lurking in the corridor like a guitar-deprived vulture.

"Breakfast?" he said. I barged past with half-open eyes. "You go today? I buy guitar, lots of chocolate." He followed me towards the bathroom but I slammed the door in his face.

After I'd checked out and thanked Laya for helping me, he was waiting outside the hostel.

"I'll be back tomorrow, you can have my guitar then," I said, shaking his hand. I felt sorry for him, but sometimes it's necessary to be nasty.

The second day's drift along the Mekong was more pleasurable without a hangover and I even had a thicker cushion for my achy arse. Some farang must have stayed in Pak Beng, (I can't think why) as the boat was less claustrophobic and less rocky.

I remained in an unsociable mood and preferred to finish my book while floating down the river in a Dutch man's clog, now a light blue colour. The journey flew by and I was disappointed when Luang Prabang floated past.

Luang was about thirty times larger than Pak Beng, but even so, within half an hour of walking down a street market, wondering how clothes, postcards, and replica Buddhas could be cheaper than in Bangkok, I'd bumped into someone I knew.

"So where's your funny sidekick gone?" asked a familiar whiny voice. Emma, a friend of Joe, who'd been part of the farang group in Bangkok, was grinning as she squinted her blue eyes.

"What, Rich?" I said, remembering that Rich had chatted her up in Chang Mai. They'd suited each other as they were about the same height; just over five foot. "Somewhere in north Laos, why, have you missed him?"

"Not as much as I've missed you."

"Look at you, a couple of days on a long boat and you pick up a sense of humour."

I was glad to see Joe and Emma after some time in my shell. I'd hung around with Joe a few times, but never really got to know her. Emma was over for a trip through Laos, Cambodia, and Vietnam.

They'd been more sociable than me on the boat and had met two northern lasses. They'd also got to know a group of lads who they'd planned on meeting that evening.

"Fancy coming to watch the sunset up on a hill?" Emma asked.

"Sounds romantic."

"Not just with me; all of us you idiot."

"Well if you put it like that, how can I refuse?"

Phou Si was a hill in the centre of Luang and from the top we watched the sun float down as slow as the boat from Pak Beng. The Mekong had turned an orange tinge and wispy cloud drifted over the hills. Unfortunately, the northern lasses spoiled the setting and tranquillity by arguing about which lad they wanted to pull.

After a couple of beers in a bar on the main high street, they decided to go back and get ready.

"I don't need to change though," Emma said, thumping the table.

"Let's go and have another beer then," I said.

"What just you and me?"

"I can go on my own, I don't mind." Emma looked at Joe.

"Just don't get her drunk," Joe said.

"Would I do that?"

We picked the wrong bar. A lemon scented candle flickered on the table, soft music played in the background, and couples sat holding hands and kissing. We felt awkward.

"Fancy a shot?" I said, nipping off. I couldn't be doing with romance.

"What's this?" Emma said when I got back with two large glasses of Laos Laos.

"The local firewater, try it." She took a whiff of the clear liquid and coughed.

"I'm not drinking that."

"Come on, just hold your nose and knock it back." We clinked glasses and took a swig.

"It's like paint stripper," I said.

"How do you know what paint stripper tastes like?"

"I used to be a painter and decorator," I lied. The drink was more potent, and gave a bigger shudder, than Thai whisky, but the awkward setting became bearable.

I found out why Joe had asked me not to get Emma drunk. I'd never seen anyone get drunk so quickly. Emma turned into the world's fastest speaker and when the others came back she got up and hugged everyone.

"What have you done to her?" Joe asked. "Is she pissed?"

"And what if I am?" said Emma.

"We only had a cheeky shot," I said, holding the chair as Emma stumbled back.

"Let's get some more of that Laos Laos," said Emma.

When the lads turned up and found out what Emma had been drinking, the night got progressively messier. Looking back, drinking games with the local paint stripper wasn't the best way to start in Luang, but we all go crazy once in a while. My memory of the night is blurred, as were the names of the lads I was drinking with.

When I bumped into everyone the next afternoon, they were all suffering, especially Emma.

"I'm not talking to you; I haven't felt this rough in ages," she said, holding her stomach.

"I only bought the first one; I didn't force you to drink the next ten."

I felt rough too but, despite the rain and grey skies, I forced myself round the quiet streets of Luang. I enjoyed strolling by the river as the rain splashed on my face, but the only place worth visiting was the Royal Palace. I spent the rest of the day reading, catching up with friends and family on the internet, and eating lots of watery noodle soup to clean my system of the nasty Laos Laos.

The next morning my mind was clear, as was the blue sky, and the day was much more entertaining.

"What's he doing?" said Doug; the fatter of the Australian brothers who I'd hitched a lift with to the Kuang Si waterfalls. We were in a wood area just near the entrance.

"Looks like he's cutting up a rat," said Bret, turning his baseball cap backwards as he peered through the mesh fence. A Laotian man was kneeling down scraping a knife and fork on a metal plate to cut up a rat he'd just cooked on a small fire. Next to the man, prowling in a cage was a tiger.

"Why's he doing that though?" asked Nancy, Bret's slim, big breasted blonde wife.

"It must be the man's lunch," said Brett in a serious tone.

"Don't be a wally, it's for the tiger," said Doug.

"Then why is he cutting it up?" asked Brett.

"Maybe it's allergic to bones," said Doug.

"What, a tiger allergic to bones?" asked Nancy.

"Anything's possible in Laos," said Doug, who had his mouth muffled by his Spanish wife, Maria. No one spoke, but we knew he was talking bullshit.

Doug and Maria skipped on to the waterfalls and I followed, leaving Bret and Nancy to watch the man feed the tiger (In case you're wondering, he chucked in the rat with the bones). I felt like a gooseberry as Doug kept asking me to take photos of him and Maria groping and kissing each other.

The waterfalls were the prettiest I'd ever seen. We gazed up from the bottom of a three-tiered waterfall, which cascaded through the green rock face. Several pools of turquoise water surrounded us and a path bent round towards the side. On a ledge near the top two monks dressed in orange robes waved down.

"Come on, look, there are people up there," Doug said. Maria crossed her arms and stomped the floor as Doug and I darted off. Who was the gooseberry now?

About halfway up we reached a ledge where a manmade dam was letting the ice-cold water trickle down. The small rocky path looked unsafe to cross, but not for Doug.

"TAKE A PHOTO DARLING," he shouted from the middle with his arms stretched out. Maria obliged, despite covering her eyes, and then shouted at him to get down.

"WHAT'S THAT DARLING? YOU WANT ME TO JUMP?" Doug shouted. A group of German tourists let out gasps when Doug almost fell backwards into the pool of water. Maria stuck up her middle finger and turned her back.

"All right Hon," Doug said, patting Maria's arse once we'd come down. She ranted in Spanish. I picked up *hijo de puta* – son of a bitch, and *idiota*. I trailed behind as they marched off in a huff. I thought the slanging match was going to get violent when Maria slapped Doug's face, but Bret and Nancy appeared.

"Someone's got their knickers in a twist," said Bret. After Maria had repeated those lovely swear words, Nancy dragged her away for a fag.

No one had noticed we were in a delightful spot next to a shorter, about three metres high, waterfall, which oozed into a clear circular pool. A thick swinging rope hung from a tree. Doug stripped down to his shorts and climbed up. He was just about to swing into the pool when Maria shouted.

"What are you doing now you *idiota*?"

"Don't worry Hon; it's safe," he said, tugging the rope. Maria turned away as Doug swung like an overweight orang-utan and splashed into the water.

"I'm in," Bret said, stripping off as well. I followed.

After the fifth go, each, Maria saw the funny side and we persuaded her to climb the tree. Getting her to jump was another matter.

"Come on Hon, it's not so bad," Doug said as Maria stood at the top frozen in her yellow bikini.

"I'm scared," she said. "Is it deep?"

"Yeah, don't worry it won't hurt."

We watched as she tried to muster up the courage. She'd move her feet while looking up and down the tree, gaze into the water and appear as if she was going to jump, but then back down. This pattern continued for about ten minutes.

"Just jump for fuck sake," said Doug.

"I'm scared."

"Don't jump then."

"But I want to."

"Then just do it, we'll count to three and you can jump."

"Okay, Okay."

"One," we said as she took hold of the rope.

"Two." She swung back a little.

"Three." She let go of the rope and flopped her arms.

"Oh Jesus H Christ, come on I'll push you." Doug climbed the tree and after another five minutes managed to push her in, screaming.

On the journey back, Bret and Doug bickered about how many days they were going to spend in Luang while Maria and Nancy chain smoked. They'd made the trip to the waterfalls entertaining, but I felt no need to exchange emails. We wished each other luck and I left them arguing about where to go for dinner.

It's not often you find single girls travelling on their own, so when I spotted a pair of blue eyes looking across at me, as I sipped on some spicy watery noodles in a bar down the main street, I felt a pang of joy in my stomach. She was blonde, in her early twenties, and kept glancing. However, I was out of practise. How did you chat up women again?

By the time I'd mustered up some courage to ask if she knew when the bus left for Vang Vieng the next morning (not the most romantic phrase, I know), a frumpy couple entered the bar and whisked her away. I lost my chance and went back to my hostel, alone again.

On the way to the bus station the next morning, I was still disappointed for not acting quicker with Blondy. I promised myself to do better next time, but when you're a shy lad, it's easier said than done.

Guess who was waiting for the bus to Vang Vieng with her friends? We even made eye contact and smiled at each other. And what did I do? Absolutely nothing!

"Aren't you the girl from the bar last night?" I imagined asking, but I bottled it, got on the bus, and sat at the back in the middle seat.

"If she sits near me, I'll talk to her," I thought. She glided into the seat in front and smiled as she tossed her hair. What did I do? Still nothing!

The frumpy couple squeaked down in the seat opposite her and the packed bus left. As we chugged along the rocky road, I pretended to read the book I'd picked up in Luang, Dead Man Walking, but secretly I was thinking up a chat up line.

Then I had some luck. We pulled up and a mother with a screaming baby got on. The only spare seat was next to Blondy and the mother seemed unhappy with the confined space. I leapt into action.

"You can sit here," I said to the mother, pointing to my seat. "Do you mind if I sit there?" I said to Blondy.

"No, that would be great." She was English. I was in.

Jane was on the third week of her gap-year round the world trip. When she found out I'd been to South America she turned her legs towards me and rested her elbow on the chair.

"Great, you can tell me all about it. I'm a good listener." As I told her about my adventures in South America, I felt like an experienced traveller. Comparing myself with my first month in Mexico, I suppose I was a bit.

Telling Jane about what she could encounter in South America gave me a buzz, especially as I think she found it attractive.

"I'm bored travelling with a couple," she whispered. "They're always bickering. I feel lonely sometimes." She brushed my arm. Her perfume reminded me of nights waiting to get into clubs in London. I felt excited.

"Shit look at that," I said, pointing to thick white cloud drifting past. "Is that fog?"

"I think it's cloud; we're quite high up. It's like this in South America."

"You see, you see how we're so similar?" she said, smiling.

"Yeah." I couldn't, but who cared, she was fit.

The sky had cleared by the time we'd lowered from the mountains and pulled up in Vang Vieng. I walked with Jane and the frumpy couple, Mike and Sarah, through the derelict car park, and down a litter covered alley until we came to the main street.

"Everyone's just sitting about watching TV," Mike said as we walked past restaurants with farang sprawled out on exaggeratingly cushioned sofas while watching episodes of Friends.

"Yeah, it looks dull," Sarah added. I had to agree. As we stopped at the end of the street, Mike and Sarah posed for a photo with the tall thin monolith mountains in the distance. We checked out a hostel together, but there was only one room left.

"Do you want to share with us?" Jane asked me. Mike frowned.

"Err, if you're sure," I said.

"But we don't know how long we're staying for," said Sarah. Jane scrunched her hand and grimaced.

"That's okay," said Jane. "It'll be cheaper with four."

"Not necessarily," said Mike, turning his back on me.

As much as I would have liked to share a dorm, and a bed, with Jane, I knew when I was unwanted.

"See you later then?" Jane said, smiling as I walked off.

"Yeah, see ya later," I replied, wanting to ask when and where. Surely Vang Vieng was small enough for us to bump into each other.

I hate to admit it, but I got sucked into the laziness. That afternoon I moulded into a comfy sofa and watched about eight episodes of Friends while glugging back chocolate milkshakes and scoffing cheese omelettes. Despite not seeing Jane, I enjoyed lounging around as if I was at home again.

The following day was my favourite in Laos, but the evening was one of the worst in my life. I spent the day floating down Vang Vieng's crystal clear river on a huge black inflatable rubber ring. Tubing was fun, and without it, Vang Vieng would have been dull.

"First time?" asked an English lad with a shaved head as the van with six strangers chugged up the road to the Tubing entry point.

"Yeah, yours?"

"Nah, third in three days, love it mate." He rubbed his hands together. Andy was jittery, sweaty, and the dark bags under his eyes suggested he'd been on a massive three-day bender.

"What's it about then?"

"What Tubing? Well, you get on these rings up there," he said, pointing to the roof where the rings were tied. "Put your valuables in a protective waterproof bag, and then float down the river stopping to have a beer while getting stoned, all good geezer," he said, beaming. So that was the real reason he loved it; to get hammered.

"Come on, get a move on," Andy shouted as he drifted down the river. He'd fallen back into his ring with grace, whereas I'd missed mine and toppled in the cold water.

"Bout time," he said as I caught up. My arms and legs were flopped over the side of the ring and my arse dipped in the water. "Now stick with me, I know all the nooks and crannies to this marvellous trip." He splashed his way towards a faster stretch.

As we cruised down the river, I put my head back and gazed at the limestone-mountains on the right while letting my hands skim over the surface. Now and then I'd splash some water on my chest and stomach and watch the sun dry it up.

A group of local lads waved and shouted at us from the riverbank.

"They've got the merchandise," Andy said, veering to the left.

By the time I'd managed to steer into the pit stop, scraping my bum on the gravelled floor, one lad had already pulled Andy in with his wooden cane and sold him two beers and a joint.

"You can get the next ones," he said, chucking me a cold beer. Andy drifted back into the rapids like a swan, leaving the bumbling ugly duckling splashing behind.

As we flowed along the pristine river, Andy said he'd been in and out of Laos for over two months.

"I love it here, mate," he said, taking a deep drag from his spliff and letting the smoke pour from his nose. "Laos beats any of the neighbouring countries: Thailand's too commercial, Cambodia full of money grabbers, and Vietnam of idiots. I think I'll marry a Laotian woman and spend my life getting to know this river, come on, there's another pit stop," he said, pointing to bar on the right hand side.

About twenty Tubers were sipping cold beers or smoking joints while taking it in turns to have a go on a giant swing. Andy knew a few people there, including a pretty Laotian barmaid, so we had a go on the swing for free (not that it was very expensive).

The swing was attached to a tall overhanging tree and there was a local lad helping people to get on the swing and then push them high enough so that they could jump in the water. After Andy showed everyone how it was done, by doing an Olympic winning somersault into the water, it was my go.

"How am I supposed to compete with that?" I said. He'd returned to a standing ovation.

"Just do your best," he said, patting my back.

My best wasn't a best to be proud of. I almost wimped out as the lad pulled the swing back. It was a lot higher than the safe seats in the bar, and, after a couple of measly attempts to throw myself off; I managed a cowardly jump and almost belly flopped.

"You just need more practise," said Andy. I'd returned to a lame sitting and sipping beer ovation.

After an hour, I dragged Andy away from a potential future wife and we continued the lazy journey. We were pissed and let the river conveniently draw us in to contribute to the local lad's piggy bank funds. If Andy hadn't spotted the warning signs to come off, I probably would have drifted down to Cambodia.

Andy convinced me to continue drinking with him because I'd ruined his usual Tubing activities.

"The last two days I've pulled a bird, you must have jinxed me," he said as we trundled back to the village.

"Sorry mate, I'll make it up for you, promise," I said, wondering if Jane was still about and had made some friends. We couldn't find her, but we did bump into some other acquaintances.

"Now isn't that a surprise, Barry in a bar," said a familiar whiny voice.

"Well, if it isn't the Laos Laos drinker." Emma and Joe had caught up again, much to the delight of Andy, who immediately began to chat up Emma, much to the delight of Emma.

On to one of the worst nights in my life; after an afternoon of heavy drinking, Andy leant on my shoulder and said.

"You tried the shakes?" Had I not been under the influence of a couple of gallons of Laos beer, I may have declined Andy's offer to get to know Vang Vieng's dark side.

We left the others and Andy led me down the road to a bar at the end of the street. He greeted a few Laotian barmaids and soon we were laughing at the moustaches we'd made from the thick chocolate magic mushroom shakes.

Despite Andy asking for a 'weaker' shake for me, the effect soon took over.

"You all right, mate?" Andy asked when I staggered over to a sofa and slumped back in the chair. The room was spinning and I felt like puking.

"What is in that stuff?" I moaned, resting my head in my hands.

"Don't worry, it won't last long," he said, offering me a glass of water. I had a sneaky feeling that it would.

My legs felt as though someone had tied ten kilo weights to my feet, and my head as if a small Laotian midget was inside pounding with a chisel.

"That was a mistake, that was a mistake," I mumbled.

"You need some fresh air," said Andy, hauling me outside. As soon as the fresh air hit nose and throat, I puked, which should have helped, but the mushrooms had already poisoned my bloodstream.

We went to another bar with a roof terrace and Andy plonked me down on some comfy mattresses while he struck up conversation with a bunch of travellers.

"What's up with him?", "How much has he had?", "Poor bloke," were three of the fuzzy comments I remember. I drifted off into my own world, thinking about my family, and friends I'd met on my travels. I could tolerate that nostalgic feeling, but the flashbacks of the Tsunami and Sister ranting at me for taking hallucinogenic shakes scared the life out of me. The worst part was seeing dinosaurs pop out of the trees and feeling paranoid that I would never return to normality.

After what seemed like ten hours, but was probably only two, a lad walked me back to my hostel. Andy had disappeared, no doubt with a Laotian barmaid.

I was relieved when I woke up the next morning and only felt a bit hazy; it could have been worse. In future, I'd keep the Sister at the forefront of my mind when offered crazy tripping drugs.

The effects hadn't fully worn off until I'd arrived in Vientiane. After abusing my brain and body I decided to go on a detox for a couple of days and I strolled and cycled round the flat Laos capital.

Renting a bike for a day was a great way to sweat out all the toxins and explore. My favourite parts were the Patuxay monument, which was like a mini Arc de Triomphe, Pha That Luang, a huge golden

Buddhist Stupa; the national symbol of Laos, and the Mekong Promenade.

On my last evening in Laos I strolled along the promenade, watching the locals chatting and shopping in the markets, smelt the fresh fruit stalls and meats sizzling on the barbeques, and enjoyed the cool breeze run through my hair.

My time in one of the poorest countries in Asia had been short, but calm and peaceful (most of the time), at least compared to the next adventure in hectic Cambodia.

## 24 Cambodia: Angkor Wat and a Nasty Surprise

Cambodia was on my list of places to travel mainly just because it was there. I knew that Angkor Wat was one of the world's great wonders, and hundreds of thousands of people had been killed in Cambodia thirty years previously, but I never expected to learn so much in a week.

If Siem Reap had been first on my world tour, I don't think I would have left the airport. Aggressive taxi drivers were a pushover now though. I stood in the marked area outside the arrival gates as two innocent blonde female farangs got harassed by twenty sweaty and horny locals desperate to make some Riel. The group surrounded the women, grunting and whooping until they'd picked a driver. Some mauled the women right up until they slammed the taxi doors shut.

A year or so ago I would have been scared, but not anymore. I was about to go out into the madness when two male Scandinavians strolled past discussing their route to the centre. I held back until the hungry locals crowded round, and then stormed in to make a deal.

"TAXI, GOOD PRICE, YOU COME ME LOOK," shouted one young driver, shoving his business card in my face. Several others did the same. Their body odour was strong and the tugging on my arm was irritating.

"What colour's your car?" I asked. The young chap glazed over. "Red, blue, or yellow?"

"White, white," he said. "Good price."

"I want a yellow taxi," I said.

"I yellow taxi," said a short fat man.

"You're a yellow taxi?" I asked. He agreed (he did look under the weather). I pushed closer to the Scandinavians.

"Guys, you wanna share a taxi?" They turned startled, as if I was a driver who spoke decent English.

"To the centre?" asked the taller one.

"Where else?" I said, shrugging.

After haggling for several minutes between the white and yellow taxi owners, we chose the yellow one; it was cheaper. The rest trailed behind, pulling on our arms and rucksacks. One crazy fool tried to block the driver's path as he reversed out.

The car was stuffy and dusty as we made our way along a main road to the centre. We dodged in and out of the other cars and motorbikes whizzed past. I liked the chaos as it reminded me of Bangkok, but at the same time I missed the tranquillity of Laos.

I booked into a hostel in the old market area (the Scandinavian lads continued on) and I went bicycle hunting so I could get up to Angkor Wat.

The local hagglers were on excellent form; within a kilometre more than twenty offered to be my guide. The majority were more peaceful than the airport crowd, but one butch motorcyclist chugged behind, parping his horn until I nipped into a bicycle hire shop.

Once on a bicycle, I felt like Harry Potter with an invisible cape; the haggling stopped. I rode along the Siem Reap River, past sixty-year old bike tuk-tuk drivers struggling to pedal Western tourists, and down an avenue with woodland on either side. The air became fresher. I felt liberated.

Shortly I'd realized just how free and lucky I was.

Angkor was enormous: fifteen miles east to west and five miles north to south, with over seventy different temples or buildings to explore. I only had two days and wanted to save the highlight, Angkor Wat, till last.

I shot along the main path, not glimpsing to Angkor Wat on the right, and dodged skipping travellers and jubilant wedding goers until I reached a wide squared area known as Angkor Thom.

As I rode past a line of fifteen crouching concrete Buddhas and entered a thin archway, I felt a shiver down my neck. Being inside a twelve hundred-year old ruined city was spooky and thrilling. I drifted along to The Bayon, the first temple, where the hierarchical position of pineapple shaped towers intimidated me.

I stopped to take a couple of photos and three local boys sprinted over. Their smiles were similar to my students' smiles in Bangkok, but dirt and holes covered their T-shirts and shorts. Their arms and legs were wasting away.

"Do you want any food Mister?" asked the tallest, his British pronunciation was excellent.

"Not right now, thanks."

"Well, if you change your mind, my mother cooks very well, we're over there." He pointed towards two wooden huts. I thanked him and wheeled my bike onwards. His friends, or brothers, grinned as they trotted next to me.

"Can I take care of your bike then, Mister?" he asked, jogging backwards. I realized I had no lock. The three cheered and clapped when I agreed.

"Don't worry, your bike is safe with us," he said, wondering off with my only means of getting round.

The Bayon was surprisingly empty. Walking round the grey and brown stone temple felt eerie. The sun beat down, but inside the shaded passageways, the breeze blew chills across my sweaty back. Each of the archways and tunnels led to a different opening and I got lost in the labyrinth.

The most profound features were the towers. The Khmer Empire sculptors must have taken ages to engrave the smiling faces, tapping and carving away on the concrete mounds for years.

A coach load of Japanese tourists emerged and swarmed The Bayon like a starved bunch of Poohs round a giant pot of honey. Clicking cameras and blurts of Japanese killed the silence and The Bayon lost its mysterious magic. The Japanese had ruined the ruins. I collected my bike.

"Don't fancy a bite to eat then, Mister?" the boy said, holding out a menu.

"Not right now," I said, mounting my bike.

"What about a drink?" he said, pointing to the stocked fridge. I bought a bottle of water out of pity for the sad and hungry family.

The most fascinating part of Angkor Thom, besides the elephants engraved in a walled garden, were the ancient, octopus like, trees. The thick strong tentacles trickled down over the stone ruins as if trying to crush and swallow them. It reminded me of scenes from the classic *20,000 Leagues Under the Sea.*

Riding between the different sites was exhilarating. I whacked up the volume of Norah Jones (it was all I had at the time) on my Discman and bopped along, zigzagging across the empty paths. I felt peace, tranquillity, and freedom, especially compared to the next local family I met.

I arrived at Eastern Mebon and the familiar smell of burning oil made my mouth water.

"HELLO, HELLO," shouted several women waving me over towards their straw roofed restaurants. When they saw me glance towards them, they jumped and cheered with their children. I strolled over. A thick white rope confined each ecstatic family to a specific area. I paused. Each of the mothers waved a menu over the barrier and the kids bounced around. I'd never felt so awkward choosing a place to eat. Who had penned the families in like sheep?

"Money, money," the youngest of seven asked as I waited for my vegetable fried rice. I'd chosen the mother with the most mouths to feed.

"Sorry," I said. "I only have enough for lunch." The mother snapped at her kids for pestering so they showed me their foreign coin collection.

"England, England," one girl said, holding up a shiny pound. It was no use to her in the depths of Angkor, but she treasured it like a precious doll. I added a few baht to their vast collection and taught them the disappearing thumb trick.

"Why can't you go over the line?" I asked the mother after I'd wolfed down the rice dish.

"Police," she said. Her bottom lip sagged and her eyes watered. "They say no pass tourist space."

"So you can't leave the boundary?"

"Yes but need pay five dollar day, today her," she said, pointing to her eldest daughter on the other side of the rope. The frail girl smiled and began playing a soft tune on a small wooden flute. She was about thirteen and, despite her wide white hat; her face was darker than the others. She stopped and opened up a purple woollen bag full of handmade crafts.

"You like?" she asked, glaring with her sad eyes. I nodded and smiled. After she'd played another graceful tune, she handed me the flute and its white straw case.

"Only five dollar," she said. I showed her the two dollars I had.

"Okay," she said. "Present you." I refused to take it for such a small amount but she insisted. When I handed her the two dollars her face lit up and she smiled at her mother. I thanked the family for their hospitality; after all, they had invited in a stranger.

I rode away and they waved and smiled. I thought back to my students in Bangkok, and the Tsunami. The Angkor family might have been poor and under rule, but at least they seemed happy and were alive.

I lost interest in Angkor after that and meandered about the next site, Pre Rup, like a spoilt kid whose parents were forcing him round a boring castle. I pitied the tied in families; prisoners in their own homes. How could a country do that to their people? Cambodia had suffered tremendously in recent years, and some families must have been much worse off, but making innocent families pay to leave their premises was unfair.

The ride back was stressful. With no lights, cars and motorbikes cut me up. I got lost in the centre and took an hour to find the hire shop. Once at my hostel, dark had fallen and I was sweaty and irritable. I couldn't grumble though. I was able to take a cool shower, grab a warm meal, and rest in a comfy bed. I wondered what the families were doing.

That evening I had a reflective dream. I was wandering about Angkor Wat alone when the flute girl appeared. Her graceful melody hypnotised me and I followed her to a long straw hut full of local families. At first they were happy to see me, but once they found out I had nothing to give, they chucked pound coins at my head and chased me away.

I woke up feeling guilty. I had to go back and pay the flute girl.

"Good morning," I said to the mother, wiping sweat off my brow as I reached her restaurant. The sun was hotter. The kids ran up cheering while showing me the thumb trick. "Where's your daughter?"

"She there, you see," she said, pointing towards a huddle of Japanese tourists. As I approached, she turned and beamed.

"I owe you some money," I said, holding out ten dollars.

"No, present for you," she said, crossing her arms. Eventually she took the money. It wasn't much, but at least it would pay for a couple of day's roaming.

Exploring Angkor Wat was just as impressive as I'd hoped. I crossed over the giant moat, strolled along the stone causeway while dodging photo takers and tourists gaping at the main temple, and drifted towards a murky pond that smelt musky. Angkor Wat goers from all lifestyles lined up to take their new mantelpiece photo: rich and wealthy, poor and trampy, pilgrims and honeymooners.

I squeezed through the mass gathered on the stone stairway leading to the dark doorway of Angkor Wat and wished someone was with me. Loved up couples walked hand in hand and gossiping groups of tourists trailed round the tunnels and archways. I was the only lonesome traveller mooching about.

Once through the damp smelling main tunnel, I took a left along the grass and gazed up at the high grey towers. Thin wispy clouds circled round the blue sky. Strangers stared down: some waved, others took my photo. I continued along until I came to a steep stone stairway. At the top, wearing an orange robe and waving, was a young monk. I climbed up.

"Hello, well done," he said, shaking my hand. He was the youngest adult monk I'd ever seen and had the build of a marathon runner. "Are you English?"

"Yes, I am, how did you know?"

"Lucky guess, you watch the premiership?"

"Sorry?"

"The premiership, you know; greatest football league in world, I great fan."

"I do actually," I replied, bemused at the conversation. He grinned and shook my hand again.

"That great, I like Manchester, who your team?"

"Tottenham."

"Oh, Spurs, they not doing very well." Even in the depths of Angkor Wat, my team were crap. We nattered about football for about twenty minutes. I listened and nodded more than I spoke though; he knew tons about the prem.

"Do you mind if I take a photo?" I said.

"Sure, can you?" he said to a passerby.

The photo came out funnier than I'd expected. Asians use two fingers to signify peace when posing in photos, but his were the wrong way round. He'd definitely been watching too much football.

A short bike ride away, I watched the sunset at an elevated temple, Phnom Bakeng. A mix of Europeans, Americans, and Asians swarmed together as darkness fell over the silent ancient city.

Angkor Wat oozed magic. The detail and work the Khmer Empire must have done to build such a monstrous temple would make any architect squeal with delight. I just wished that the families surrounding the temples could have lived in better conditions.

That evening, as I read a China guidebook I'd picked up inside Angkor, a podgy arsed Chinese man almost spoiled my day.

"I didn't like Angkor Wat, I only like natural wonders of the world," he said, slurping noodle soup down his wide gullet. He'd plonked down across the table, even though I was the only one dining in the spacious hostel restaurant.

"So why did you go then?"

"To see, to see. You are British, right?"

"I am."

"Well you will know about Angkor, it is not natural."

"You don't say," I muttered.

"I prefer natural wonders."

"Yeah, you just told me," I said, sipping my beer. "I thought it was excellent."

"Yes but you are young, not so wise, you need to see the world more," he said, covering his face with the bowl as he slurped down the last sips.

"Sure," I said, smiling. I respected my elders, but felt a warm glow inside knowing that he was a fat dickhead.

Phnom Penh was an eye opener. The welcome committee were just as ludicrous as in Siem Reap. The bus stopped on a main road by some run down hostels and a bunch of irate bag handlers chanted as they blocked the doorway.

"Get your hands of me," I said, wrenching my arm back. I was normally polite, but barging through the barricade of bodies seemed the only way. "Give me my bag you muppet," I shouted to a goofy bloke, tying my rucksack to a metal trolley. I grabbed my belongings and stormed into the nearest hostel. I was furious.

Why did they treat arrivals so aggressively? In South America they'd tried to rob me several times, but at least the men gave you some personal space when you arrived.

I gazed down at a busy crossroads from inside the bars in my room and wondered how the cars, motorbikes and bicycles avoided each other with no traffic lights. They must have had special tooting codes; they'd never manage that in England.

Away from the hectic area, the capital was less intimidating. I visited the Silver Pagoda, strolled along the Mekong, and ate some noodles in an overpriced restaurant. When night came, I was tucked up in bed; I felt unsafe alone on the streets.

The next day I began to appreciate why some of the locals had been so tense. I'd heard bits from other travellers about Prison 21 and the Killing Fields, but I was unaware exactly how much Cambodia had suffered during the terrible massacre between 1974 and 1979.

Discovering the details was educational and emotional. I'd imagined Security Prison 21 (S-21) would be a normal prison museum with a few cells; perhaps something similar to *The Bill,* but later I discovered its other name: Tuol Sleng *Genocide* Museum.

I hired a bike and darted in and out of the drab back streets to S-21. On arrival, I received the only pleasant surprise of the day.

"Barry?" said a familiar female voice as I wheeled in. I was visiting a prison; who knew me? "I thought I'd never see you again," she said, hugging me.

"Hi Jane," I said. "Come here often?"

"First time actually," she replied innocently. Mike and Sarah looked pissed off that I'd gate crashed their torture chamber party.

"So what *is* this place?" I asked, gazing towards the pale white prison blocks. The air smelt of sulphur.

"Don't you know?" asked Mike, rolling his eyes.

"I know it used to be a prison and a few people died."

"A few," Sarah said, raising her eyebrows at Mike. "Try almost TWO MILLION."

I felt ignorant.

"Well, technically it wasn't two million here, darling," Mike said. "Almost twenty thousand were kept here and tortured before being killed in The Killing Fields."

"Rather appropriate name really," said Jane.

"Two million?" I said.

"Yeah, mind blowing, isn't it?" Mike said, surveying the surroundings. "It used to be a school."

Sections of the four white buildings appeared burnt and damp along the side. Each had three floors, separated into single or double rooms. It was like a mini version of Our Lady of Perpetual Health, but less cared for. I imagined my students running about the grass courtyard and the Thai teachers gossiping on the benches covered in the shade by the tall palm trees.

"Come on, the documentary is starting," Jane said, marching off. We walked along a concrete path with dry patchy grass on either side and took a seat inside a small dark room on the ground floor.

Before I'd left England, I went to an exhibition about the Holocaust in The Imperial War Museum and left feeling ignorant and speechless. I'd been aware of what the Nazis had done, but the exhibition had made the effects more real and powerful. The S-21 documentary had a similar effect.

The Khmer Rouge, a Communist party who tried to create a purely agricultural society, killed, tortured, and starved almost two million Cambodians. Pol Pot, who died in his bed in 1998 after the Khmer Rouge had agreed to hand him over to an international tribunal, was the leader held responsible for murdering just over twenty percent of the Cambodian population.

Pol Pot's drastic revolutionary policies forced city-dwellers to relocate to the country to work in collective farms and forced labour projects to try to destroy all culture and traditions within the Cambodian society. His aim was to create a new culture from scratch, known as "Year Zero."

He used the ex-school to torture and murder members of the previous Lol Non regime, which included teachers, soldiers, students, factory workers, doctors, academics, monks, engineers, and anyone else related. His followers interrogated them for names of family members or associates, who the Khmer Rouge then hunted down and brought to the chambers to murder.

The survivor's detailed stories about the torturing brought a tear to my eye. The guards made the innocent Cambodians strip down to their underwear and handcuffed them individually in small rooms, or in large groups to an iron bar. Later, the guards tortured them to confess their life stories and admit false accusations.

The worst part was the photos taken before the torturing. In the faces of the innocent victims, especially the children, was pure fear.

The documentary finished by showing images of my next destination, the Killing Fields. How could people commit such horrific acts?

I left the dark room feeling sick, squeamish, and again ignorant. I'd been travelling through Cambodia, enjoying the wonders of Angkor Wat, being rude to innocent men in Phnom Penh who may have suffered during this period, and all without knowing about the huge genocide thirty years before.

"Speechless," I said to Jane as we stood in the chilling grounds. The images I'd had of a peaceful school turned into massacre and mayhem.

"Don't, I can already feel my breakfast coming back up," she said, holding her neck and gulping. Even Mike and Sarah were gobsmacked.

As we toured the cells and torture rooms I could imagine the screams. Some cells had ghastly, rusty instruments on show. Beatings, electric shocks, hangings, pulling out of fingers nails, and suffocating with plastic bags or held in water, were all methods used to make prisoners confess their 'crimes' against the revolution.

The models of prisoners wasting away inside the cells were shocking, but not as much as the photos. We wandered round the long cold rooms, gasping at the mug shots. The dread in the innocuous eyes of the sufferers, some as young as six, was disturbing. No wonder so many prisoners committed suicide.

The ten security regulations displayed on a large white board outside in the courtyard were unconceivable: 'Don't be a fool for you are a chap who dare to thwart the revolution,' 'Whilst getting lashes or electrification you must not cry at all,' and 'if you disobey any point of my regulations you shall get either ten lashes or five shocks of electrical discharge.'

"That's gotta scare the shit out of anybody," Jane said.

"It's barbaric," said Sarah

No one spoke as we meandered towards the exit. I felt sad that the Cambodians had suffered thanks to the evil ways of Pol Pot and his merciless party.

"So where're you heading now?" I asked Jane.

"Oh," she said, snapping out of her daze. "We've hired a man to drive us round all day. We're going to The Killing Fields next, should be pleasant."

"I'm heading that way too, on my bike. Maybe I'll see you there."

"Yeah, that would be nice," she said, smiling.

If we hadn't just come out of a torture museum, then I might have made an effort to chat her up, but I wasn't in the mood. I'd probably bump into them at The Killing Fields anyway.

As I rode along the backstreets, each face I passed reminded me of the mug shots. I felt pity, but I was also impressed that they'd overcome the massacre. The majority of locals seemed happy, at least on the outside.

Arriving was a mission without a map. After a couple of kilometres pedalling along a main road with lorries and cars spurting out petrol fumes in my face, a hunched old man pointed me towards a thin and dusty street. Locals gathered outside their battered houses and glanced or waved as I cycled past.

I felt tense as there were no signs for The Killing Fields, no tourists about, and some local lads frowned as I whizzed past. Some looked dangerous. What if they chased me on their motorbikes to ask where I was going, why did I want to see where thousands had died?

The street turned into a thin dirt track and empty fields stretched on either side. The only sound was my wheels circling over the gravelly floor. When I past a battered wooden sign pointing to The Killing Fields, I felt relieved.

I sympathised and joked with a group of kids collecting money to guard bikes. An unpleasant place to work, but at least they were earning.

First was a gruesome museum with pictures of victims and a collection of skulls, mostly smashed. Ahead were scattered ditches where the Khmer Rouge had dumped the bodies. A strange damp burnt out fire smell lingered in the air. I wondered round alone, surprised that no other travellers were visiting.

The first sign read: 'Mass Grave of more than 100 victims, children, and women whose majority were found naked.' A leg bone placed on a wooden stump pointed to another: 'Mass Grave of 166 victims without heads.' It got worse: 'Mass Grave 450 victims' '86 Mass Graves, 8985 victims.' The numbers added up to less than two million, but there was a message. Khmer Rouge had murdered a massive percentage of the population. I'd seen enough.

"Oh, fancy seeing you here," I said to Jane at the entrance.

"How was it? I'm not sure if I want to go in."

"Lots of graves, lots of victims."

"Oh well, we're here now I guess," she said. "Listen," she added, perking up. "What are you doing later, fancy meeting for a drink?"

"Yeah, I could do with a swift half after today."

"I know what you mean; I wasn't expecting this to be so traumatic." We arranged to meet up in the centre and I left her to explore.

After such a morbid day, I was glad to meet for beers. The evening started formally. We ate in a restaurant opposite the river and chatted like two couples. Mike kept going on about S-21 and The Killing Fields though.

"Can we change the subject? I've thought enough about dead people and tortures for one day," said Sarah.

"Good idea," Jane said. "Where are you going next Barry?"

"I'm off to Vietnam tomorrow morning. My bus leaves at seven for Ho Chi Minh."

"So you have to get an early night?"

"Nah, I can sleep on the bus," I replied, winking. For a moment I regretted it, was I getting the wrong end of the stick?

"That's good," she said, smiling and winking back.

The night was fun. We explored a few bars by the river and ended up dancing in a packed nightclub.

"I haven't danced in ages," Jane said as we recovered on a sofa. We were drunk by this point and had forgotten about the day's events. It was easy for us; we were just travellers.

"Let's not forget where we are," Mike said as we arrived at their hostel for after party drinks. Silence followed. He was right: Phnom Penh's citizens had suffered, but in my eyes they had recovered well and were on their way up, at least I hoped they were.

## 25 Vietnam: From South to North

I'd overheard a few travellers praising Ho Chi Minh, Vietnam's largest city, so I had high expectations. I shouldn't have.

When I got off the bus down Backpacker's Alley, I was out of it. At first I thought a late hangover had struck after the previous night in Phnom Penh (we stayed up 'chatting and drinking' until 6am, I caught the bus to Vietnam at 7am), but the dizzy spells were strange and my back muscles ached. Perhaps I'd picked up a virus.

A young Vietnamese chap led me to his family's hostel. I followed in a trance, oblivious to the chaotic surroundings. His mother greeted me with a concerned smile.

"You shower, tomorrow pay, no problem," the chap said as he left me in a tiny attic room. I slept for almost twelve hours, waking up once to change my damp sweaty clothes because I was shivering. I could have slept more, but I had to sort out my Chinese visa.

I still felt weak and dizzy as I trundled down Back Packer's Alley. The stuffy, polluted air made me feel worse. I ignored the women waving boxes of videos and books in my face and continued past a row of taxi motorbike drivers tooting. On every street corner, more drivers stopped and beeped.

"You, you," was all they could mutter as they rotated their fists offering a lift. Despite feeling drained, I smiled back and shook my head. Over thirty offered to take me somewhere during the forty-minute walk to the Chinese Embassy.

As I waited in the queue, I began to feel better. China was close. The mystery and challenge of travelling across such a massive country was enticing. English was as foreign as Vietnamese in Scotland.

Chinese writing on a calendar of Mao hanging on the wall looked powerful. He stared down, as if inspecting new arrivals. The Chinese woman behind the counter had a stern face and limited smile, but was helpful. My passport would be ready in two days.

I associated Vietnam with images of war, mainly from American films, and I was eager to find out more. Noodle soup and mint tea replenished my energy before I visited the War Remnants Museum.

The museum left me feeling pity for Vietnam and anger at America. I entered the steel blue entrance into a courtyard and imagined the tanks firing, fighter planes dropping bombs, and helicopters whirling rotor blades. I strolled about wondering how they remained in such good condition after taking so many lives. They had to be replicas.

"Man, I didn't know we had been so cruel," said an American man to his wife as they slumped on the stone steps outside the main museum. Inside wasn't for the squeamish. The images were shocking: American GI's torturing Vietnamese soldiers, deformed victims from the napalm attacks, and aircrafts dropping the deadly Orange Dioxin over Vietnam.

The most prominent image was of an American GI holding up the remains of a nuked Vietnamese soldier. The body looked like piranhas had gored it to pieces. The half-eaten head hung on a thread of tissue.

"Hello sir, where are you from?" asked a tanned Vietnamese man hobbling towards me in the courtyard. He was wearing dark sun glasses and a blue cap, carried a denim satchel, and looked in pain.

"England, London."

"Oh, English, welcome, welcome." He waved the stump of his upper arm, motioning me to shake it. The texture was soft and spongy, like a scooped out cucumber filled with jam. His other arm was the same. I was startled.

"Can see what happened to me? My arms were taken by mine, and look," he said, brushing up his trouser to reveal a wooden leg.

"Oh, I'm sorry."

"That's okay. Not *your* people." We spoke about the museum, but I wanted to ask questions about what had happened to him. When had he lost his leg? How did he survive? How did he work?

"Do you read?" he asked.

"I do, yes."

"Would you like to buy book?" I'd just spent my day's budget at the Chinese embassy.

"I'm not sure I have…"

"Look," he said, using his stumps to open the satchel's flap and pull out a book. "Do you know this picture?" I'd seen the black and white war image before. A Vietnamese girl was screaming as she trotted along a road in the middle of the countryside. Wailing children ran alongside and American GI's plodded along in the smoky background.

"What happened?"

"She Kim Phuc, innocent victim of war. You should buy; is a good book." He dumped a copy in my hands and showed me other books, but I wanted to know about the girl in the photo. I paid more than I should have, but I was glad to have helped him.

"Thank you, enjoy your visit," he said as I shook his squidgy stump goodbye.

After living in Bangkok, I thought I was used to hassle, but the local sellers and motorbike drivers were right in my face. I ducked into a zoo to try to escape the hounding, but even the monkeys seemed to be pestering me for food.

Back down Backpacker's Alley, which reminded me of Khao San but tackier, I hid in a café to read about Kim Puc. Street sellers bothered me to buy another book. One man even tried to sell me the book he saw me reading.

"For your friend," he said, grinning. I tutted and kept my head down.

The following day I'd recovered from the virus and continued on the war theme. I figured a trip to the Cu Chi tunnels, where the Viet Cong guerrillas had dug out a massive underground network of tunnels, would be more entertaining than traipsing round getting bugged by scooter drivers. Tours with agencies were expensive, so I went alone. Supposedly, I could catch a couple of buses and arrive in thirty minutes.

The journey started well. I caught a local green bus and sat at the back in front of a group of cackling old ladies. I felt glad that I'd out mastered the agencies; I'd only paid a few pence.

"You are English?" asked a chubby Vietnamese man on the seat behind. He squinted through his thick black glasses, pushed them back on his nose, and snorted loudly.

"Yes, I am."

"Oh, English, where you go?" Was he going to ask me if I wanted a lift on his bike?

"To the Cu Chi tunnels."

"Oh good, many tourists come see what Americans do; they fuck country.' He smiled politely, altering his glasses again. "I tell you when off, I off too, then take more bus." I was still dubious.

We pulled into a dusty bus park and he escorted me to the stop opposite. Up to that point I'd done as my guidebook said, but the man insisted that I get on a different numbered bus.

"This only bus to Cu Chi," he said after speaking with the driver. I trusted him. Like a muppet.

"Okay, Cu Chi, you go, welcome to Vietnam," he said as I got on.

"What, aren't you coming too?"

"No. Have fun," he said, walking off and cleaning his glasses on a corner of his shirt.

We drove for thirty minutes and stopped on a busy road. Everyone got off, including the driver.

"Cu Chi tunnels?" I asked. He shook his head.

"No, no, taxi, taxi."

"What? But the bloke before said this was the bus."

"No, no, taxi, taxi." He laughed and muttered to himself as he left, as if to say *why did you listen to that idiot?*

I resented hailing down a motorbike taxi.

"Cu Chi, yes, yes," said the driver. We agreed a fee and set off, darting in and out of the other bikes and cars. Five minutes later, we pulled up outside a swimming complex with blue and red water shoots bending round the sides of a drab building.

"They're not the Cu Chi tunnels."

"Yes, yes, tunnels, tunnels. You like very good." He held his hand out for the fee.

"That's why I hate you taxis," I said, giving in. I glanced around. The swimming complex was shut. I was considering heading back to the centre, when a tubby security guard came up to me.

"What?" he said after I told him where I wanted to go. "But you very very far away," he added, laughing.

"Can I get a bus?"

"Bus?" He sniggered. "No, only motorbike, I get you." He waved down a motorbike and joked with the driver. I began to see the funny side.

"He take you, ten dollar, okay?"

Soon we were whizzing along a dusty path between two grass fields; at last fresh air outside the city. I arrived almost two hours after leaving; so much for out mastering the agencies. I was glad I went though; the tunnels in the woods were a genius idea and my plump Vietnamese guide was entertaining.

"You see, the Americans were too stupid to see the tunnels and too fat to get down," he said, standing over the first hole, which was only as big as a laptop. The guide wore camouflaged military uniform. Two Mexican couples laughed.

"What, people went down there?" said the chubbier Mexican man.

"Yes, not all Vietnamese are fat like me. This is one of the smallest entrances. You can go in if you want." I managed to squeeze in up to my waist, but no one else tried.

A little further through the wood, we paused in a small opening.

"We are very clever people the Vietnamese. Watch this," the guide said, stepping lightly on the floor. The base squeaked as it flipped round to reveal lethal rusty spikes.

"Wouldn't want to jog round here," said one wife.

"The tunnels were used by the National Front Guerillas. If it wasn't for them, then maybe a McDonalds or Starbucks would be by that tree," said the guide. I wondered if he made the same jokes to Americans.

We entered a larger underground opening and crawled through a wider tunnel. Inside smelt damp and I felt claustrophobic. At one point the tunnel became tight and the Mexican almost got stuck.

"It wasn't so easy in the war," the guide said as we gathered round a tank above ground. "The underground conditions were bad: many ants, mosquitoes, spiders. Malaria killed many."

"What about the Americans, didn't they find the tunnels?' asked the fat Mexican as he brushed mud off his knees.

"When they knew about the tunnels, they tried to bomb. But we were clever, more than two hundred kilometres of tunnels; impossible to destroy."

When the tour was over, the Mexicans went to the shooting range and I caught a direct bus, which the guide told me about, back to the centre. On the way I read my book.

Just round the corner from the Chu Chi tunnels in Trang Bang was where Kim Phuc's life had changed. The South Vietnamese forces had accidently dropped bombs on their own people. Kim had to rip off her burning clothes to survive and two of her brothers died.

The photographer who snapped the famous photo saved her life by driving her to the hospital in Ho Chi Minh City, Saigon as it was known at that time. He also visited her afterwards, and organised a donation fund for her family. After two years of surgery, Kim returned to her family. She became as famous as the photo and now lives with her Canadian husband and two children in Canada.

When I picked up my passport and saw the Chinese visa, I felt a boost of adrenaline; everything was going to plan and soon I'd be in China. I felt nervous about travelling there alone, but more confident than I had been in the past.

After a lazy day in Ho Chi, I caught an overnight bus to Nha Trang. My plan was to stay one night, do some scuba diving, and then continue up the coast. However, like other travellers who intended on whizzing through Nha Trang, the nightlife sucked me in.

On my first morning, after I'd chilled beneath a straw umbrella on the beach for a couple of hours, I hired a bike and rode around a bay where green, blue, and red boats hovered on the clear water in a little harbour. The best part was breathing in the fresh sea air while shooting up and down the promenade, on one side was the beach and sea, and the other, mountains.

I caught an early night, which was just as well considering what happened the next day. I woke up eager and alert. Almost eight months had passed from my PADI in Australia. Ten other farangs were on the boat trip, but only three were diving. The other two were experienced so I had to dive on my own with Paul, the short Vietnamese instructor.

"Don't worry, is like ride bike, never forget," he said once the anchor had splashed over the side. He zipped up the back of my diving suit and tightened the tank on before quizzing me on basic diving techniques. I followed him towards the edge of the boat.

"Today we go two dive," he said, sticking up two fingers. "First to remember and second we see caves." He made a circle with his arms over his spiky black hair.

"What caves?"

"The caves are small, but many fish, you see now," he said, edging me forwards.

"No one mentioned any caves."

"Is good, okay, let's go," he said, nudging me. I splashed in the cold sea and the familiar sound of my breathing, and tingling feeling in my teeth, reminded me of the Great Barrier Reef.

Getting the hang of my buoyancy levels took a while, but once I'd remembered how to breathe correctly I kept up with Paul. The coral was dull, but the silence and freedom of drifting around underwater was just as magical. I swam alongside Paul, who stuck his thumb up or pointed out small shoals of fish.

"You remember, good," Paul said as we bobbed on the surface. The water kept splashing my face. "Now we go to caves, but take careful; hole no big, only small," he added, holding his hands slightly wider than my body.

In the next area the coral was brighter and shoals bigger. Paul led me round a quick circuit, while doing the occasional summersault, and we arrived at the tiny cave. Paul signalled to follow and swam through the dark space. As I approached the opening I tried to remain calm, but my breathing increased. Paul was a couple of metres in. He looked back and waved me through. I entered.

I was doing fine, concentrating on my breathing to keep between the rocky sides, when my tank clunked against the top of the cave. I was stuck and Paul had swum off. My heart raced.

As I turned my head the breathing apparatus pulled out. The tube was caught. I kept my mouth tight. I tried to think back to my training in Australia, but my mind went blank. I fumbled around for the tube and managed to get the breathing apparatus in. I was still stuck though.

I was breathing much faster and squirming to try to release the tank when Paul appeared, smiling. He pushed me back and lowered me slightly. My breathing slowed. I was free to swim on.

Swimming out into a shoal of silver and blue fish was a massive relief. I replied to Paul's sign for OKAY, and we drifted to the surface.

"You no first, many people stuck too," Paul said. I was panting and my hands were shaking.

"I don't know if I'd prefer to have known or not."

"Better no, is more funny," he said, slapping me on the back and grinning.

After a lazy afternoon on the beach, I booked my bus ticket, told my hostel that I'd be leaving that night and went out for dinner. As I was slurping seafood noodle soup while watching the passersby, I questioned my decision to leave. I fancied a night on the beers. My strict schedule to arrive in Beijing was annoying me. Then two old pals walked past.

"Joe. Em. What're you doing here?"

"Isn't it a small world?" said Joe.

"We saw you from a bus in Vientiane too, you were riding along on a bike and we were knocking on the window," said Emma.

I was glad to see them and they invited me out.

"But I'm supposed to be going in a minute. I've got an overnight bus booked."

"Oh, that's a shame, we're off out on the piss," Joe said, smirking.

"Why don't you change it?" said Emma.

I needed little persuading.

The woman at the bus station and the owner of the hostel thought I was mad, but they agreed I could change. I'd definitely missed the company and enjoyed being out on the beers again. We spent the night in a bar called Why Not and ended up in a disco.

"Do you think it'll be long before the sun comes up?" Joe asked as we walked towards the beach at 4am.

"I doubt it. Look, all those lot must be going to watch it," I said. Hoards of locals were heading to the beach.

"This is mental, where's everyone going?" said Emma.

"Must be a Vietnamese thing," I replied.

As the sun rose, we sat on a wall and watched the beach fill up. Kids, adults and old age pensioners, all wearing sports clothes, were playing volleyball or football, power walking, or running. Some were just sitting and chatting. Seeing so many Vietnamese on the beach was strange; I'd only seen ten during the last two days, and they'd been selling necklaces and bracelets.

I ended up leaving a night later. Nha Trang lacked activities to do and monuments to see, but the scenery was pretty and I had fun partying with Joe and Emma. There was no way we'd bump into each other again; they were heading back to Bangkok and I to China.

The punishments for enjoying my time in Nha Trang were two agonising overnight bus journeys to Hanoi. I arrived at 6am, slept for a bit and woke up with a tired taste in my mouth. In two hours the Mongolian Embassy would close.
 "You go far? Need taxi moto? I have friend," said the hostel owner. I was still dubious about motorbike taxis after the Cu Chi tunnels incident, but I was in a rush.
 The driver turned out to be a life saver. In twenty minutes we'd whizzed through the old town towards a modern part and arrived at the hidden embassy. I'd never have found it on my own. I had to get extra passport photos and the driver sped me up to a camera shop and back. If I hadn't made it, I would have screwed up my time in China. My visa was on its way so I could relax. I paid the driver double what he quoted.
 "You need more?" said the hostel owner when I got back.
 "I do need to get to China." He claimed that I could get a train straight through to Pingxiang and miss out on a tedious border crossing. I believed him, handed over the fair, and another friend whizzed off to the train station.
 I hired a bike from a shop just round from the hostel and soon I was pedalling round the old quarter as if in a Tour de Hanoi with loads of locals. I was lost, but cared not. I was in a great mood and just wanted to ride about among the craziness and get a feel for the place. Whenever I stopped at traffic lights other bikers would toot, smile and wave, as if proud that I was trying to integrate.
 "Hey, where you go? You want ride?" I asked a motor taxi driver leaning on his bike reading a newspaper. He glanced over but continued to read. "Hey hey," I said, pointing to the back of my bike, "you want a lift?" He cottoned on that I was joking and began to smile.
 "No, no, I have bike," he said, waving me on.
 The first main monument I came to outside the old town was the Ho Chi Minh Mausoleum. I stared at the giant grey memorial from the other side of the large cornered off square and wondered why no one was about. The military guards patrolling the area looked solemn and stern as they protected the tomb of Vietnam's most popular president. Ho Chi Minh was president for almost twenty-five years and was an inspiration to many Vietnamese. Before he became so powerful he travelled the world, living in Marseille, New York, Boston, Moscow,

Guangzhou, and, most importantly, West Ealing where my grandmother lives (she claims she never met him).

Then I almost got arrested.

I rode round the boundaries to find an opening and get closer to the building. A group of Asian tourists emerged over the other side. I presumed I could follow. I was wrong. I pedalled behind the group and sped through to the middle of the square, oblivious to the chasing guards. As I snapped a few photos I heard the guards shouting and blowing a high pitched whistle. I was in a restricted area and had pissed off a couple of mean looking military. They ordered me to leave the premises.

I didn't ask if I could enter and see Ho Chi Minh's preserved body and made do with the bronze statue of him in his museum round the corner. Neat flowered gardens surrounded the magnificent white building with the Vietnamese red flag with a yellow star flapped in the wind.

Inside the museum, a statue of Ho Chi Minh stood with one arm raised. Behind him was a giant gong like the ones you see at the start of Indiana Jones movies. I was tempted to give it a whack and run about the museum pretending to whip everyone, but more guards were watching.

I disliked the museum. Strange art and large groups of noisy kids put me off. A few of the displays about Ho Chi Minh's life were interesting. Did I mention he used to live near my grandmother?

After I'd scoffed down the best Khao Pat Moo outside Thailand, in a small restaurant hidden in the old town's back streets, I darted off to the Hoa Lo (Hell's Hole) Prison. All decent capitals in Asia have a prison museum.

The cool and eerie atmosphere inside the prison, built by the French in the late 19$^{th}$ century, reminded me of S-21. Despite being much smaller (a lot was demolished in the early 1990's) it was detailed enough to realise that the North Vietnamese had tortured many American POW's, who nicknamed the prison the Hilton Hanoi because of the appalling food. Outside in a gloomy courtyard a guillotine towered in the shade. I imagined the thump of the blade on the wooden base as it sliced off a victim's head.

After S-21, the torture pictures didn't make me feel as squeamish or sad. Perhaps my defences had grown. One photo shocked me; three cut off heads, one with its eyes open, rested neatly displayed in baskets.

Despite the gory museum, I was becoming a fan of Hanoi. Back in the old quarter my devotion rose. I returned the bike and walked.

Hagglers were less annoying than in Ho Chi Minh and shop sellers were more passive.

I strolled round Hoan Kiem Lake where couples whispered sweet nothings, groups of students planned revolutions, and dogs walked attached to leads; a rarity in Vietnam. A mature English couple tried to play pooh sticks on the pretty red Huc Bridge, but the lake was motionless. I rested on a bench and read my guidebook for China. I'd be there in two days.

I had dinner outside a small restaurant on the corner of a busy junction to watch Hanoi at night. Old women tottered along the pavement carrying heavy scales across their hunched backs, occasionally crossing the road through the parping cars and motorbikes, which darted round with millimetres to spare.

"Pretty manic eh?" said a stocky man who I'd nodded to earlier. He wiped his goatie, slid out a thick cigar from a silver case and sparked up.

"Yeah, it's amazing how there aren't any accidents."

"Believe me there are. If you stay here long enough, you'll see someone get smashed to pieces," he said, blowing out a thick smoke ring. The strong cigar smell clogged my nose, making me cough.

Mike was an Australian journalist and had lived in Hanoi for almost ten years. His long white silvery hair was tied up in a ponytail and his wrinkled face appeared solemn. He was married to a Vietnamese 'chick' and had two kids.

"Why aren't you at home with them?"

"I need some space, mate. She's a nag and busts my balls when I go home. So I just don't go home much." Mike insisted on taking me to see the real Hanoi; an expat bar round the corner.

"This is my Hanoi, where us expats come to get away from our wives. Some of these guys were in the war." Middle-aged Americans and Australians shouted and jeered at the baseball in the stuffy smoky sports bar. Vietnam War photos and memorabilia hung up on the walls. There were no Vietnamese.

"This is a good place to pick up women," Mike said. "But not locals, they're just after ya money."

Mike was popular in the bar and introduced various war veterans; welcoming me with a crushing handshake.

"Which rank were you?" a drunk bloke asked.

"Don't be daft," Mike said. "This guy wasn't in Nam, he's just a baby." he said. Everyone laughed.

"I've seen Deer Hunter though," I said, pointing to a black and white poster of Robert De Niro in a red headband. He was pointing a gun at himself. The men cheered and started acting out the Russian roulette scene.

"We do three bullets," one guy shouted.

"Mow, Mow, Mow," shouted another, slapping his mate round the face.

"It's gonna be alright Nicky, shoot Nicky, shoot," said a third. Another pretended he had a gun in his hand and screamed as he pulled the trigger. It finished with half of them falling dead on the floor.

"This is my home," Mike said, hugging me in the commotion. "Aren't you glad I brought you here?" I guess, in a peculiar way, I was.

As the night went on they became more barbaric. I wanted to ask if any of them had been in the Hilton, but I was worried it would be the start of a crazy guillotine scene. I managed to prise myself away and stumbled to my hostel, leaving Mike and the others singing war songs.

On my last day in Vietnam I almost missed the collection time for my visa and the hostel owner said the train to China was full. He still wanted money for his friend going to the station though. I refused to pay and checked out. Within twenty minutes I'd found a better hostel and had booked a bus ticket to China for the following morning. That's what they promised me anyway.

I spent the day riding round Hanoi like a loony listening to Queen's 'Bicycle Race'. I rode up to the glorious Ho Tay Lake, round Thong Nhat Park, and then pedalled to an Air Force Museum out of the centre in a deserted field. I pushed my bike along a muddy path, passing a derelict warplane, and saw a guard approaching. He carried a machine gun. When I got closer he held it in the air and clicked the trigger.

"No museum. Close now. You go."

"Okay, okay," I said, holding up my hands. I doubted whether it was loaded but I wasn't up for playing Russian roulette.

I returned to the centre and went for my last stroll in South East Asia. Thinking about travelling alone to China made me apprehensive. The trip from Bangkok had been easy with regard to transport. China would be a challenge. I needed a travelling companion.

When a tanned Israeli looking lad with short black hair sat next to me in an internet cafe, I'd never have guessed how far we were about to travel together, or how well we'd get on.

I browsed pictures of mountains in Southern China, still unsure exactly how I'd get to Beijing.

"Shit man, China's a fucking big country eh?" said the lad. His accent was strangely European. I peeked at his screen. He was on the same website.

"You off to China, mate?"

"Yeah man, can't wait, but I haven't got a fucking clue where to go, it's too fucking big," he said, rustling his scraggly travellers beard.

"I know how you feel," I said, stroking mine at the neck.

"You're going too?"

"Yeah, when are you going?"

"I want to go tomorrow by train. My hostel said they'd get me a ticket today." After I told him the train was full and my hostel had ripped me off he started tapping his knee under the table.

"Why don't you get a bus?" I said.

"Yeah, maybe," he said, turning back to his screen. We sat in silence for a while, occasionally pointing out photos of sunsets over rice paddies. I could smell the misty green air and taste the freshness. We'd both planned on getting to Nanning first.

"Listen, when are you getting your bus tomorrow?" he asked.

"At six."

"Any chance I can jump along? China's a big place to travel on your own."

"Tell me about it, I'm pretty nervous. I can ask my hostel if they have space and then meet you back here in about an hour or so."

"Yeah, sounds good. I'm Sami by the way, from Sweden."

"You don't look like a Swede, aren't you supposed to have blond hair?"

"Yeah everyone tells me that, my father's Iranian."

I was relieved to have found a companion. Even though I'd loved travelling on my own, China was bound to be full of surprises.

There was space on the same bus, but when I went back to tell Sami, the internet café was closed and he was gone. I waited but he didn't show. We hadn't even changed email addresses. I'd have to go alone.

Something told me that I'd see him again though.

# 26 China: Adventures with a G-String Obsessed Swede

The twaty hostel owner lied.

"Yes, man drive you china, no problem, you trust me," he said. Like a fool, I did. I'd become naive and forgotten the lessons I'd learnt. No one had tried to trick me for a while. The day's destination, Nanning, was almost four hundred kilometres away. The two hour drive through the tiny villages with lush green mountains in the background was fine, but when the Vietnamese driver forced us out in an abandoned car park I began to worry.

"Okay, you go taxi now," he said, pointing to a man standing under an umbrella by his car. The only other passenger left was a shy looking Chinese lad. Rain splattered on empty packets of crisps and cans by my feet.

"What? I was promised to be taken all the way to China. I'm not paying for a taxi."

"No pay, my friend drive, no pay," said the driver, getting back in his van.

"This is crazy, why aren't you taking us?" I shouted. He drove off. Memories of problems in South America came flooding back.

"No problem; I go too," said the Chinese lad in a soft feminine voice. His laidback manner was reassuring and he reminded me of Franco, my teddy bear loving friend in Sydney. I had to trust him.

The new driver ushered us in and sped off. The backseat was damp and smelt of piss.

"Where you go?" asked the lad, turning round from the front seat.

"Nanning. I need to get over the border and then catch a train at Pingxiang. The hostel owner said they'd take me there."

"People in Vietnam lie," he said.

"Can you check he's taking us to Pingxiang, please?" The lad spoke to the driver, who nodded at first but then shook his head and whacked his hand on the steering wheel.

"So, just to check, you're *not* taking us to Pingxiang," I asked the driver when he forced us out at the border control. He blurted in Chinese and raised his fists. We marched on. I felt stupid for trusting the hostel owner. I raised my barriers and became wary. China was going to be a challenge.

The drab smoky passport office was mayhem. Hoards of Chinese men, women, and children blabbered and panicked as if the border was about to close forever. My friend pushed in front of a group of cackling grannies, grabbed a white form, and carried my guitar.

"You need be strong, stay with me," he said, barging through a group of elderly people, who tutted and breathed cigarette smoke in our faces. He helped fill out the form and within ten minutes we were strolling out in China. He handed back my guitar.

"That was brilliant," I said.

"Thanks. I do many time. Come, we need taxi, I speak, hide money."

We paced along and taxi drivers bundled round. The lad chose one and the others dispersed. I was astonished; they would have ripped me to pieces.

"How much did he say?" I asked as we drove along a smooth road to Pingxiang. Outside, woodland stretched on either side and fresh air blew through the driver's window.

"One hundred Yuan." The lad looked harmless, but could I trust him?

"Okay great, I just need to change money when we arrive."

"What? You have no money?"

"Yeah I do, but not Chinese." He gasped, as if I said I was planning on killing the driver.

"No can change money in Pingxiang; bad people. I pay." I went for my wallet but he insisted I remained still.

"No want driver see you money, I say you poor." The driver peeked at me in the rear-view mirror. Perhaps they were best mates and planning on mugging me. I kept silent.

Pingxiang had one main road, four shops, and a train station. The lad paid and ushered me towards the ticket office. Maybe I could trust him.

"Where can I change some money?"

"No can change, don't worry, I pay you," he said, flustering about in his wallet. He refused to accept money, bought me a ticket to Nanning, and gave me extra Yuan for food.

"Give me your email; I'll send you the money."

"No, no. I help you, Chinese good people."

I pleaded and he wrote his address.

"Lucky?' I said. "Your name's Lucky?"

"Yes, English name Lucky."

"You certainly have been for me,' I said, shaking his hand. His mobile rang and within minutes his friend was beeping a horn as they waved goodbye.

The lonesome fear rose as I waited in the lobby full of Chinese people. Beady eyes gazed at me over steaming meaty pot noodles. The attention made me feel uncomfortable and after the hostel owner's lies I became defensive. The station master announced something, whistled, and everyone moved towards the platform. I went to join the masses when a familiar face fussed through the turnstiles.

"Mate, you made it," I said, feeling the tension drift away slightly.

"Yeah, fucking Chinese, this place is crazy," said Sami. He dumped his backpack and leant facing the wall, panting as if he'd just finished a race. "The border was a nightmare, and the taxi men, fucking bloodsuckers. I think a money changer ripped me off, the bastard. I need to get a ticket." I'd tell him about Lucky later. With the help of my ticket, Sami bought another, but in a different compartment. He'd calmed down once we were at the platform.

As the train pulled away, Chinese men garbled, ignored the 'no smoking' signs, hacked up phlegm, and spat on the floor. I was glad spit smelt of nothing; the mix of body odour was enough.

"Excuse me, do you mind not spitting on the floor, I find it quite repulsive," I imagined saying. I bet Sami would say something, I thought as we sped to Nanning. I only knew Sami briefly, but felt at ease with him on the train.

Night had fallen by the time we'd checked in and left a hotel. We were starving and struggled to find food. The streets and pavements were wider, shops, cars and buses were more modern, and the floors cleaner than in South East Asia.

"How's your Chinese?" Sami asked as we gazed over a pale green menu in a restaurant. Two Chinese waitresses in light pink uniforms whispered from behind the counter.

"Shit; and yours?" He blurted out a fake Chinese, which startled the waitresses. The kitchen was shut so we made do with a couple of Tsingtaos (beers).

"What's your plan then?" I asked.

"Korea." His eyes lit up.

"What about it?"

"That's where the fittest women in Asia are, man. Haven't you noticed how none of the women on this side of the world wear G-strings?"

"I have actually."

"A mate of mine lives in Seoul and said the chicks there love G-strings, and also dark handsome men like me, so that's where I'm heading." He clapped his hands and rubbed them together.

"I've heard the best women are Russian. I'm heading there on the Trans-Mongolian."

"When?" Sami sat up.

"In ten days, why?"

"I'm also, but in twenty days. Man, what a small world." We laughed and shook hands, proud to have something in common.

Sami was also glad to have a travelling companion. He'd been travelling South East Asia for three months and felt daunted about travelling China alone. We agreed to stick together until we found the rice paddies with the amazing sunsets like in the photos we'd seen in the internet cafe in Hanoi. We figured they were in Guilin, so that's where we headed the next day.

After a breakfast of steamy rice in the hotel, we checked out with no idea how to get to Guilin; no one at the hotel spoke English. By chance, we bumped into the empty local bus station and a guard pointed us to a tiny squared timetable at the end of the bus lanes with 'bus' being the only English word.

We jumped on the first that turned up and, miraculously, after driving through built up modern Nanning we arrived at the main bus station. We felt daunted by the chaos and number of ticket queues. Frustrated Chinese travellers knocked into us as we queued up.

"*Ni hao*, two tickets to Guilin," I said to the podgy assistant. I pointed to the symbol in my guidebook.

"Guilin, *ha, ha, ha,*" said the lady as she tapped on the keyboard. She wasn't laughing; *ha* meant *yes*. She showed us the screen. I checked the symbol and agreed.

"That wasn't so bad," I said as we plonked down on the clean modern bus.

"Yeah man, these symbols are a piece of piss. I love China. It's crazy, what if we didn't have a guidebook with symbols? How the fuck would we get to Guilin?" He was right. Since Bangkok, travelling had been easy. I loved the challenge of China.

Passengers stared, but we smiled and said *Ni hao*; most responded. If I had been on my own, I would have been less open and cocky. Sami's boldness was catching and I felt confident, as if with a mate from home.

I thought south China would be poorer, but factories, business centres, and service stations scattered along the motorway. China's economy was miles in front of South East Asia's.

Guilin turned out to be a bit of a disaster. We expected green mountains and open fields, but met run-down buildings and polluted air. We had to walk thirty minutes before we found a hotel, whose scarlet red reception smelt musky as if a couple had just had sex.

"It's not a brothel, is it?" I whispered.

"Hopefully." Sami picked up a card with a drawing of a voluptuous Chinese woman imprinted. A short Chinese man in a light brown suit popped out while adjusting his beige tie.

"Welcome, welcome to Guilin,' he said, pointing to a photograph on the wall of rice paddies in the mist at sunset.

"There it is," said Sami, jumping in the air. "The photo we're after."

"That's not Guilin," I said.

"Where's that? I wanna go there, man," Sami said, snapping a photo of the photo.

"Longsheng," the man replied. "I get you cheap ticket if want." We told the man that we'd think about it, but we knew we'd make our own way.

After two hours walking round looking for a decent restaurant, we made do with one where we could look and point. The meat dishes looked and smelt rank so we had noodles and covered them in a thick black sauce, which we thought was soy, but tasted like aniseed.

The night life was dull and after a few beers in various quiet bars we ended up in a trashy disco with a group of Chinese students and left when one of the lads tried to chat up Sami.

The next morning our bad luck continued. We thought we'd found the perfect restaurant to sooth our hangovers and rumbling stomachs. A Chinese lady in a slender fitting red dress motioned us over. Her hair was tied in a bun and face caked in make-up.

"English, English?" I asked. She nodded.

"Brilliant," Sami said, jumping up and almost giving her a kiss. We followed her up the red carpeted stairs.

"I think she had a G-string on," said Sami.

"Yeah, I saw. Is this place gonna be in our budget?" I asked. Chandeliers sparkled almost as much as the staff's teeth. We picked a circular table by the window and a waitress popped open the packaged plates and cutlery.

"Looks like we're staying now," I said.

"We can splash out now and then," Sami said. He pulled out his dictionary and we ordered chicken and rice.

The waitress returned - a little too quickly - and plonked down a huge family sized plate of chicken covered in a clear orange sweet and sour like sauce.

"They don't waste anything here, do they?" Sami said, grimacing.

"Look at the poor bugger," I said. At the front of the metal dish, with its eyes closed as if snoozing; was the chicken's head.

"Do you think we're supposed to eat it?" Sami asked. He prodded the head with a chopstick.

"I dunno, it looks pretty bony," I said. Its squishy gullet was flabby and a couple of hairs poked out from its nose. After we'd finished videoing the head bopping about on the end of our chopsticks, and Sami doing puppet impressions, we got stuck in.

"It's cold," I said after I'd pressed in my finger.

"What? Is it cooked?" Sami said. He dug his knife in.

"It's a bit red."

"Maybe it's just the way they eat it over here, gourmet. Come on, let's give it a go." He piled it on his rice and I copied, but we wimped out after a couple of mouthfuls.

"Whatever you do," Sami whispered, as the waitress brought over the bill, "don't order any dog."

Our day sightseeing was a letdown too. We visited Diecai Hill because our guidebook recommended the views, but clouds blocked the way. We toured the city by foot, but got bored with the shops and lack of G-strings. We faffed about some markets, but neither of us were interested in buying anything.

"I've been waiting ages to see China, and this is the best they can offer. We need to get to Longsheng." I agreed.

Before we set off the next morning I booked my ticket to Xian. Sami was still unsure where to go next. Part of me hope he'd continue with me.

Sami was fuming when we got to Longsheng.

"I'm going back to smash that photo frame round that Chinaman's head," he said. Instead of flourishing green rice paddies, we were welcomed by a dusty car park surrounded by drab buildings.

"There must be an explanation," I said. I had also presumed that we'd arrive on a mountain slope with startling views.

"We need to a get a minibus to Longji," I said after reading my guidebook again.

"What the fuck are you on about, you dirty bastard?" He grabbed my book. Longji, a small village in the rice paddies, was still half an hour's drive away.

The journey in the packed minibus was heart stopping. The engine whirled and moaned as the driver struggled up the steep mountain paths. At each peak and bend I gasped and held on to the seat in front, panicking that the weight of fourteen men would drag us back. When we pulled up on a flat spot next to a wooden barrier, I sighed with relief; in front was a wide open space with green all around.

A group of ten elderly local women swarmed round as we collected our bags from the roof.

"I think you've pulled," I said to Sami. A wrinkled old lady, possibly from one of the early Dynasties, pulled Sami's backpack. He blurted in his Chinese as she followed us along the path. She pleaded to carry our bags up the hill, but letting her felt wrong; she was four times my age and already had a crooked back. Instead I gave her a few Yuan.

"There's ya photo," I said, patting Sami on the back. The fresh mist drifted past as we marvelled the sparkling grassy rice paddies, sprawled across the mountains like a thousand steps leading up to heaven.

We checked into a modern wooden hostel, odd in the ancient paradise, and when the owner showed the food menu I almost cried.

"They've Khao Pat Moo," I said to Sami.

"Fuck that man," he said, beaming. "I'm going for a pizza; food at last."

After we ate (or rather scoffed like pigs) we pelted off, darting about the muddy paths, and stopping at every lookout point to enjoy the views and silence. Clouds shielding the sunset were a shame, but being up high in the clean air as the rain drizzled down and glistened over the special steps was invigorating.

The downer was that the following day we'd be going separate ways.

"To our last night together," Sami said, holding up his second beer, we were alone on the veranda.

"Yeah, here's to G-strings in Korea and Russia." I said. "You'll have to send me some photos."

"Will do mate."

We got up at six but the spooky mist crept over the moist paddies and blocked the sunrise. I felt apprehensive. In a few hours I'd be alone, in China.

On the way back to Longsheng we stopped at a village to take pictures of traditional women with long black hair (as you do). Once off the bus, they surrounded and pestered us.

"Photo, photo," the heaviest one said as her thick black hair fell to her knees. Ten, grinning, sweet perfumed, Chinese Rapunzels copied. To avoid paying for a photo we left our bags by the bus stop and crossed over a creaky bridge. The fresh smelling river whooshed and belted underneath.

On the bank, I walked gently so as not to slip over on the wet muddy floor. Sami sprinted off. When I caught up, he was taking pictures of the women while standing on some boulders by the edge.

"Do you think it's cold?" he said, dipping in his hand. Before I could reply, his legs slid away and he slipped in the ice cold river.

"FUCK," I shouted, moving to the edge. His face tensed and he gasped. The river was dragging him away.

Fortunately, it only carried him about two metres before he grabbed onto a boulder and pulled himself up. He was soaked, as was his small bag.

"Shit man, that was freaking freezing," he said, shivering. I was glad he was all right, but his passport, wallet, and camera were soaked.

The Rapunzels pointed and giggled. It served us right for trying to be sneaky. Sami was unimpressed, but I saw the funny side. He dried out his things on a rock before we set off again, but his camera was ruined.

"What am I gonna do without a camera," Sami said. We were on a bus to Guilin.

"You can borrow mine for now."

"What, for the next three hours?"

"Yeah, that's true." We kept silent. I considered suggesting that he came with me to Xian.

"I could come with you to Xian," he said. I felt a pang of relief. I was enjoying China and without Sami travelling would be tricky. Maybe falling in the river was a sign.

The train was booked though.

"Fucking China, man, there's too many people in this country," Sami said, whacking the table with his hand. Some clients turned and stared. We were in a restaurant sipping beers.

"If it's not to be, it's not to be," I said. "I'll see you in Sweden one day."

"Yeah man, all the girls wear G-Strings there."

Sami decided to go to Hong Kong. He disappeared to the station and I waited, alone for the first time since Lucky had left me in Pingxing. I was braver now; Sami had brought out my tougher side. I could do China. I'd travelled most of the world, so why couldn't I? I psyched myself up for twenty-six hour journey to Xian.

Sami came back, grinning.

"Do you want the good news or the great news?"

"The good news."

"I got a ticket for Xian."

"No way," I said, sitting up. "How dya manage that?"

"I just went to a different ticket booth and they said yes. I think we're in different compartments though."

"No worries, what's the great news?"

"I found two G-Strings."

"Wow," I said, sarcastically.

"No, you don't understand. Two *Swedish* G-Strings, they're going to Xian tomorrow. They're on their way here now." He rubbed his hands together.

I was dubious, but, twenty minutes later, two blonde Swedish ladies (one prettier than the other) turned up. Seeing them was a treat after four days, but we had little time to chat and arranged to meet them in Xian.

I felt glad Sami was on the overnight train to Xian, but relieved to be in a different carriage. I was craving solitary time. I thought about home and felt nervous, but less than usual. My self confidence had grown and England seemed easier to handle now that I'd almost travelled the world.

I hardly slept that night. My legs were cramped and my back ached on the bowed mattress. The three men in the carriage snored louder than a pack of rhinos, and a few times the man opposite hacked and spat on the floor.

Sami slept like a koala after a mound of eucalyptus.

"I've had enough of these shit noodles," he said as we ate a late breakfast. I was sick of them too, but there was nothing else. We fantasised about munching down Khao Pat Moo and pizza.

By the time we arrived in Xian that night, we'd had enough of the restricted smoky carriage and were dying for some fresh air. We were the only Western men on the platform and barging through the wall of hagglers was like smashing through a line of American football players. A tiny Chinese man lingered as we bowled across a dark and littered car park.

"You need hotel?" he asked, pulling on Sami's bag.

"*Ni hao*, yeah maybe," Sami said, towering over.

"How much?" I asked, edging Sami away.

"Thirty, good price, is close, come me," he said, darting in front like a weasel leading us to his master's lair. I felt cautious, but, surprisingly, he took us to a hotel on the high street opposite the station, and never asked for money.

If I had been alone, I would never have risked searching for a restaurant that night. The streets were deserted apart from a few giggly prostitutes, who pounced out from dark doorways and startled us.

After a fifteen-minute walk down the main avenue we found a restaurant. The chubby golden Buddha in the entrance, gentle music, and aquarium bursting with orange fish, reminded me of my local Chinese take away place.

As we polished off a massive portion of pork and rice, a group of ten rowdy lads took over the table behind Sami. Their leather jackets and piercings in their nose, eye brows, lips, and cheeks, suggested they were a Chinese heavy metal band.

Sami was watching the TV as if he spoke fluent Chinese.

"Mate, don't look but there's a dodgy bunch of geezers over there." He went to turn his head. "Don't," I said, "they keep looking over. They look like nutters."

"No problem, I know judo chop," he said, raising an arm. He peeked round. "Maybe not," he added, facing the TV.

The lad with the most piercings in his cheeks spoke.

"Hello, hello, speak Englishy?" I kept my head down. "You, you, speak Englishy?" The others laughed and banged the table. The owner shouted, but his commands were as much use as a whimpering poodle.

We paid and went to leave. The lads peered over.

"Don't do anything daft," I said.

"Don't worry, I'll cover you." He shot up and turned round. "Ni hao," he said, pumping out his chest. They replied and Sami blurted in his Chinese as we approached the door. The heavies glared and paused from their meal as they wondered in what dialect Sami was talking. "Ni bye," Sami shouted as we darted out.

"You're a nutter," I said as we paced back. The night air had turned cool.

"What? This Chinese is easy once you pick it up."

Yet again he'd surprised me. As we strolled past the prostitutes he stopped to chat in his Chinese. He was bonkers, funny, but bonkers.

The next day we visited the Terracotta Warriors, where we were fortunate, but also fooled. On the bus ride along the motorway we met Tom, an American English teacher working as a guide in the Terracotta museum.

"The money's not bad and it's good for my Chinese," he said in his squeaky voice. Tom's wrists were the size of a baby giraffe's hooves, and his arms as muscular as a Viking's gnawed chicken bone.

"Sami speaks Chinese," I said.

"Oh yeah, which dialect?"

"Depends on the day," said Sami.

"Say something then," I said. Tom spoke in Chinese and Sami replied.

"Wow, what dialect is that?" Tom asked. "I've never heard that before."

"I can't remember now. I get confused which one I'm speaking."

"Well it's not Mandarin, pretty impressive though," Tom said, shaking Sami's hand. I thought Tom was going to admit playing along, but he didn't.

"So what's this place all about then?" Sami asked as we approached the entrance. We'd walked through a packed car park and past a huge white stone monument of a warrior. About a hundred people were nattering while queuing up outside the dull grey buildings. The sun reflected off the concrete floor.

"You'll see. It's amazing inside. You have to appreciate that local farmers found everything underground about thirty years ago. The figures were originally built in two hundred B.C. to protect the tomb of an Emperor."

"How many are there?" I asked.

"Tons. Be careful of the hagglers at the end; they can be quite aggressive."

"No problem," said Sami, swinging for Tom. "I know judo chop."

Tom told us to wait in the queue, disappeared, and returned with two tickets.

"Don't forget the 360 degree movie." We thanked him and offered some Yuan but he refused.

In pit one over eight-thousand warriors stared towards hordes of tourists taking photos and making appreciative noises. The model warriors, horses, chariots, musicians, and even acrobats stood in rows as if protecting a King hidden at the back of the giant hall. As we lent on a cool, thick metal railing, the sun shone through the fibre roof and lit up dust particles. I wondered if it was just a tourist puller.

"Could be," Sami said. "I can't get over why anyone would spend their time making them just to protect some dead Emperor."

We strolled round appreciating the archaeologists' work; some warriors at the back were still covered in mud. Every face seemed in a different mood and we mimicked for funny photos: a few happy, sad, angry, and some constipated.

We went to see the movie.

"I don't know where to look," I said to Sami. We stared up at the screen as two armies prepared for battle. It felt as if we were standing in the middle of a large field, about to be crushed by warriors on horses. The Chinese music's tempo increased as the armies charged into each other. We watched the twenty minute documentary with our mouths open.

On our way to the bus stop we took a dry path in a garden and a haggler approached holding a small box of warrior figures. We bargained him down from ten to five Yuan and felt content. Like Tom had warned, we came to a group of hagglers at the exit. They shouted and waved as we paced towards them.

"Don't take any shit," Sami said.

"Let's just get through without any problems."

We got closer and they bunched together as if protecting their Emperor's throne.

"You want warriors?" said one lad. He held up an identical box. He was stocky and had one of those play dough faces that you wanted to squeeze.

"Bet it's more expensive," I muttered to Sami. Play Dough spotted Sami's box.

"How much you pay?"

"Why, how much is yours?" I asked.

"Two Yuan." Sami's mouth tensed. Play Dough spoke in Chinese to the other lads and they laughed in our faces. "You want?" he said, waving his box in circles.

"That's a bargain, but I haven't got any more change."

"Me neither," I said. Sami whipped out a twenty.

"Change?" he said, holding the note in front of Play Dough, who snapped it away.

"Hey," said Sami, reaching out. "Gimme that back."

"Have change, change,' said Play Dough. He put the box on top of Sami's and turned his back as he searched his pockets. Three other guys surrounded. My adrenaline began to race, as did Sami's.

"Oh, no change," said Play Dough, holding out his empty pockets. "I keep twenty, okay?"

Sami flipped.

"GIVE ME BACK THE FUCKING MONEY," he shouted, grabbing the guy's collar. Rage ran through my veins.

"GIVE HIM THE MONEY, NOW," I shouted, trying to open Play Dough's tightly closed hand. Play Dough panicked and tried to run but we held him firm.

"GIVE ME THE MONEY NOW YOU LITTLE FUCKER."

"No have change, twenty good price." Play Dough held up his hands and grinned. Sami wrenched the note and we pushed him into his mates. We stormed off and kept in silence until the bus left.

"Cheeky dirty bastards," said Sami.

"Yeah, I've never had to physically take money back off someone before."

We'd had a lot of luck in China, but became wary after that. I was glad that we'd had a run in to remind us not to be naive. I was happy I'd stuck up for Sami.

Back in Xian, Prostitute road had turned into Hairdresser road.

"I was thinking of getting a trim," Sami said as two women in short skirts and tight tops called out.

"Is that what they say in Sweden, eh?"

"Nah I wouldn't, seriously, I need a shave too," he said, stroking his beard. I persuaded him to wait until we'd toured Xian.

The most exciting parts were the Bell and Drum towers and the old Muslim quarter. The high rectangular towers, built in the fourteenth century, were at either end of a huge plaza. They were used as look out points and the drums bonged for emergencies, perhaps to warn the tourists at the Terracotta Warriors when hagglers were about to strike.

The Muslim quarter hid in some back streets a few blocks away. We strolled round the shops and markets, stopping occasionally to chirp at the birds hanging up in cages, smell the variety of teas, and wave to tuk tuk and bicycle riders ringing their bells. We were going to eat, but Sami spotted a sheep's head hanging up in a butcher's and we felt nauseous and lost our appetite.

"I'm gonna miss you, mate," I said to Sami as we shared a bottle of rum and packet of salty crisps in the hotel.

"Yeah, it's been fun, but it's time to move on; Shanghai's next."

"Shit, we haven't booked our tickets," I said, glancing at my watch. "It's too late now. Anyway, there must be loads of trains going to Beijing and Shanghai."

After a few glasses of rum we forgot about the tickets and concentrated on trying to pull on our last night. We bowled into the centre and found a lively buzzing club.

We had little luck though. In the queue the blokes were wearing shirts, ties, and trousers, I was wearing a shirt that hadn't been washed for a month and Sami was in shorts. We got in, probably because they thought we were rich Westerners, but after the entrance fee and a drink we were skint.

The cheesy Chinese pop music blared out and we had to write on a napkin to communicate. Sami attempted to flirt with a Chinese girl at the bar, but she couldn't understand his Chinese.

"There's only one thing for it," Sami shouted.

"What's that?"

"Break dancing."

Space was limited for Sami's sporadic leg movements and his flailing arms, but the Chinese crowd clapped as he took over the dance floor. I joined in and we became Kings of the club. At least for two songs; when the music changed to heavy rock we stepped aside.

"I think the DJ was jealous," Sami said as we walked home with our heads thumping.

"Yeah, another couple of songs and the women would have been throwing themselves at us."

"We can dream," he said, putting his arm round. "How much do you think it would be at this time of night to get a haircut?"

I woke up with butterflies. Beijing, one of the largest capitals in the world, was only fourteen hours away, my last trip in Asia before the mammoth six-day journey towards Europe. I'd definitely be on my own, or, yet again, so I thought.

After wrestling in the queue with a bunch of old ladies I had to make do with a non-sleeping seat to Beijing. But the situation was worse for Sami; no trains to Shanghai for two days.

"Now what you gonna do?"

"I dunno, fucking Chinese trains." We strolled round the cabbage smelling car park, considering the options.

"I can't stay here for two days man. Why does this always happen to me?" He took off his hat and scratched his head. I preferred to have Sami for company, travelling with him was more of a laugh and I'd continue being myself.

"Why don't you just come to Beijing?" I said. He looked at me and grinned.

"What you mean tag along with you again, you dirty bastard? What about Shanghai and Korea?"

"You can get there from Beijing. Maybe we can finally find some G-strings." He threw his hat in the air and hugged me. "Don't get weird on me now." I pushed him off.

Sami got a ticket in a different compartment, but the jammy bastard got a sleeper seat. I hadn't imagined travelling my whole route in China with Sami. He could be a pain at times, but his confidence and eccentric ways had brought out the real me.

I'd almost survived China and had another story to tell. I was beginning to see another reason why I had feared going home; that I would return having not accomplished my dream. I was almost there.

The trip to Beijing was my most uncomfortable yet. Stepping into the humid carriage was like entering a piano class in a sauna, but without the music. The air was sticky and hot and everyone sat up facing forward with their backs pinned against their seats. I imagined taking out a baton to control the piano players, but a Chinese man, whose head came up to mine even though he was sitting, spoke.

"Where you sit?" he said in his deep voice, peeling back the corner of my ticket. "Oh, you here," he said, slapping the seat in front, making it shudder. I smiled, lugged my rucksack onto the rack and squeezed in front of his giant legs.

"You go to see the lall?" he said, leaning towards me. His breath smelt beefy and he had a noodle strand between his teeth.

"What's that, sorry?"

"The lall, the glet lall."

"Well, yes, that was my plan." He raised his hand and whacked my thigh twice.

"You like lall."

"Hopefully," I said, trying not to say anything to warrant another enthusiastic slap.

The man's size was a phenomenon. His head was double that of a normal Chinese man's, his hands like giant baseball gloves, and his legs as thick as a baby hippo's head.

Normally I'd have hoped that no one else would occupy the seats next to me so I could space out, but I was delighted when two young ladies, ogled at by every man as they glided down the aisle, shuffled past the Giant.

Where was Sami? The dirty bastard was tucked up while we could chat up girls.

"How long you stay Beijing?" the Giant asked.

"Only three days."

"Three days, you need three weeks," he said, whacking me again. I hoped the pain would impress the ladies, who flinched at each thump, but after the tenth I put my bag on my lap.

"Game anyone?" I asked, waving my pack of cards. The ladies shook their heads. "Do you know Shithead?" I said to the Giant. He didn't, but on the sixth game he'd won.

"Why don't you ask the girls if they want to play?" I said, winking.

"They say yes, but only with they cards." One fished in her bag. I thought of Sami asleep and smiled; imagine telling him I'd pulled over a game of Shithead.

My plan was flawed though. The Giant explained how to play, but the rules were too complex and I was left to one side as they giggled and played together. By three o'clock in the morning, despite the lights, everyone was snoozing. I tried to sleep, but the piano chairs were uncomfortable. I'd only managed about half an hour's sleep and my mouth felt dry and tired when I met Sami on the platform in Beijing.

"You look knackered," he said.

"I've been up all night chatting up two fit Chinese chicks, shame you weren't there."

"Yeah right."

"Thought you might say that," I said, showing him the photo of us three. His jaw dropped. "Look, there's one now," I said, walking off. We followed her along the platform, down the stairs and into a lobby.

"Who's that then?" Sami said as a tall handsome lad greeted her.

"Must be her brother or something, right let's find a hostel, shall we?"

"Hang on a second," he said. "Do you kiss your sister like that?" They were snogging.

"She wasn't my type anyway. Let's go find the Great Wall."

Beijing was overwhelming and my map was useless. It took half an hour to work out at which station we were, and another half an hour to find the metro. After an extra hour's walk along busy main roads, we found the hostel we'd booked in the back streets near the Forbidden City.

Eager to trek across China's most prolific attraction, I shunted away my tiredness and dug deep for energy reserves, but as soon as I plonked down in the local bus heading to Badaling, I fell asleep.

When Sami woke me up the sky had turned miserable and grey.

"Mate there's the wall," he said, nudging me. Half asleep, I peered at a small section of the Great Wall. I'd been excited about seeing one of the world's wonders, but all I wanted to do was sleep.

The drizzling rain splashing on my face revitalised me as we pushed through the hordes of chattering Chinese tourists wearing blue rain ponchos.

"We're at the Great Wall," Sami said, posing in his new costume next to a plaque in front of the entrance.

"Yeah, finally here mate, congrats," I said, shaking his hand. I was glad we'd arrived together. Considering the original wall was built over five thousand years previously, the condition was much better than I'd imagined. We darted inside the tall gate entrance and went left up the steeper and less crowded, but slippery, path.

The atmosphere was like being on a kid's train at a Chinese amusement park. Everyone we passed waved and shouted *ni hao*. We stopped various times to pose for photos and shake hands with other trekkers. One woman looked older than the wall and used a wooden cane to battle along against the wind. Her smile and determination reminded me of the Sister. What would she have said if she'd known I was at the Great Wall?

"Mr Barry, you are crazy, being so high is dangerous. You must have a shave when you get down."

Every now and then we'd stick our heads through gaps and wave at each other. Looking down into the trees made me feel giddy and the wind rattled my poncho. Cloud blocked off distant sections of the wall until we got to a watch tower where it cleared and the sun glistened.

"We're on the bloody Great Wall of China, man," said Sami as we stared back over the river of blue ponchos.

"Yeah, amazing," I said, gazing at one of the best views on my trip.

Over the other side the cramped space and nattering tourists became irritating and we were relieved when we took a turn down a quieter stretch. We climbed up and down until we reached a new lookout point where twenty Chinese men greeted us.

"We're like celebrities," Sami said. They shoved us about until everyone had posed for a photo.

"Maybe it's a stag party," I said.

"Let's hope we're not their strippers," said Sami.

We left unscathed and battled through the souvenir shops saleswomen. After I bought a *'I have climbed The Great Wall'* T-shirt for my granddad, the rain poured down.

"Here's to a great victory of the Great Wall," I said as we tapped plastic cups with foamy beer.

"Yeah man and here's to finding some G-strings and Babushkas."

We caught the same bus back, but the driver chucked us off at a busy roundabout in a downpour. We traipsed along looking for a road sign or landmark as cars, vans, and even bikes splashed us with the puddles. By the time we arrived at our hostel, we were soaked, but a delightful surprise waited.

"Hey, you both look a bit wet," said a tall blond girl wrapped in a pink towel. Her face was familiar.

"Yeah, where have you been?" said a shorter blond girl, who was equally as naked.

"Err, the Great Wall," Sami said.

"Great, we're going there tomorrow," the taller one said as she brushed through, teasing us with her sweet apricot smell.

"Great, maybe see you later," said the other, winking as she left.

As the door clicked shut, I felt an intense buzz of adrenaline in my stomach. Was there a chance of pulling? Sami grinned wider than I'd ever seen before.

"Did you see that?" he said. "Am I dreaming?" He slapped his face.

"I did, and no you're not."

"Do you think they're going to shower together?"

"The thought had crossed my mind."

"Fuck man, the G-Strings from Guilin, it's time to get busy in Beijing," he said, jumping and punching the air.

After ten days we'd found some girls to chat up. They returned wet, with their towels draped round, and tormented us by picking up their clothes and leaving.

"The tall and fitter one, I think her name was Carla, must wear G-Strings," Sami said.

"How can you tell?"

"I think I saw her pick one out of her bag."

"What colour?"

"Not sure, you can have the other though, she's a bit frumpy."

"We'll see about that."

After everyone was fully clothed and dry, Sami smooth talked them into coming out for a couple of beers. We caught a taxi to Sanlitun.

"It looks shit here," Sami said as we past another empty bar along the deserted strip.

"Who cares, come on, let's get a beer," said Naomi as she dragged in Carla.

"She might be frumpy, but she's more gain than the other," I muttered to Sami as we trailed behind.

We doubled the clientele and sipped back some Tsingtaos while trashy Chinese pop music played in the background. The provocative ladies who had teased us with their wet body routine were playing hard to get. We spoke about our trip to the Great Wall, but soon the conversation died. By the time we'd drank three beers, they were on their first.

Carla kept rambling on in Swedish; perhaps because her level of English was weaker than Naomi's, but she seemed a bit arrogant.

"Who wants a shot?" Sami asked. Naomi's face lit up.

"I'm in," I said.

"But it's getting late," Carla said, continuing in Swedish. The more she spoke, the more Naomi's lips tightened.

"What did they say?" I asked Sami as they left for the toilet.

"Carla's fit but boring. She wants to go back."

"What already? It's only ten."

"Maybe something will happen when we get back," he said, whiffing his armpit. But it didn't; they were tucked up in bed by midnight.

"I think we can turn them round," Sami said the next morning as we set off to explore Beijing. We'd arranged to meet them for more drinks that evening.

"I dunno. Carla looks like a tough nut to crack, I'm going for Naomi."

"No worries mate, I like a challenge," he said, rubbing his hands together. I was doubtful though and concentrated on the day's events.

The Forbidden City was the last attraction. The day was memorable because of the sights, but also because of what happened after. Before the Forbidden City, I picked up my ticket for the Trans-Mongolian railway.

"So this is it then?" I said, snapping it back from Sami.

"Yeah, you can't follow me anymore you dirty bastard."

"Me follow *you*?"

"Of course, don't get emotional on me now man. Come on, let's go see Beijing."

I'd been in Asia almost nine months and felt excited about leaving and embarking on one of the longest train journeys in the world.

"Dr Evil," Sami said, posing for an Austin Powers style photo just below the giant portrait of Mao in front of the Forbidden City. I'd been to a fair number of squares, but Tiananmen took the trophy. My favourite up to that point had been the Zocalo in Mexico, but you could have fit five inside. As we gazed over the immense square from the Tiananmen Gate, guards tried to rush us, but the powerful view had us transfixed.

"Now that's a square," said Sami, resting on the ledge and waving at the queuing tourists.

Just before the main entrance to the Forbidden City, male and female guides blocked our path and pulled our arms. One young lady wearing a light pink shirt stroked Sami's shoulder, smirked, stared for a couple of seconds, and then disappeared in the crowd. It wasn't until later, before I recognised her again.

The Forbidden City was enormous; a thousand buildings and nine thousand rooms spread over seven hundred thousand square metres. The city took fifteen years to build in the fifteenth century and needed over a million workers. The names given to the rooms and sections showed the Chinese passion for their hidden world: Great, Supreme, Imperial, and Glorious.

The atmosphere was more serious than at the Great Wall. People greeted each other less and silly photos were out of the question, unless you were Sami.

"Says here that it's only been open to the public for eighty years, before that they didn't let people in like you," I said as he did the Karate Kid crane pose in front of a group of elderly Chinese women.

"What type of people? Cool sexy men?"

"No, commoners."

By the time we'd walked round, got lost in the imperial gardens, and chilled out at the top of a hill in Jingshan Park, we were starving.

"So, we need to get back by eight to see the Swedish birds," Sami said as we tucked into a massive plate of noodles.

"You think they'll be there?"

"We can hope, I'm gonna try and get it on with Carla, you can have Frumpy."

"Whatever. It says here that the flag lowering is worth seeing. It happens at sunset, which should be soon."

"Let's do it, then we can go back and find the ladies. I'm bursting for some action."

We did get some action, but not the type we'd bargained for.

"And they do that every day?" Sami asked after twenty soldiers had marched out of Tiananmen, through the traffic up to the flag where hundreds of locals and tourists watched, whipped it down and then stomped back.

"Twice a day; I've never seen a group march that fast and perfect before."

As the crowd dispersed, two young Chinese women were standing behind.

"Did you like ceremony?" said the prettier one with cute dimples. She looked familiar.

"Yeah, it was all right," Sami said.

"So is it your first time in China?" the manly one with huge thighs asked. She wore a baseball cap and looked like a bloke.

"No, I live here," I said, feeling suspicious. I got lumbered with Thighs while Sami chatted up Dimples. Thighs seemed guilty talking to me, unnatural, as if Dimples had forced her.

"Why don't we go for a drink?" said Sami. What was he playing at? We had a date with two Swedish girls.

"Oh, that would be great," Dimples said, "we can practise our English." Sami grinned and winked at me.

"Great, where can we get a beer then?" he asked.

"We don't drink beer," said Thighs.

"No, we only drink tea," Dimples said. "What about some tea?"

"Come on then, but just a couple, I'm driving later," Sami said.

Maybe there was no harm in a quick cuppa. I relaxed but kept up my guard as we strolled across the square. Dark had fallen and the Tiananmen Gate and surrounding buildings glowed. We bustled through the crowds towards some back street shops, the kind that appear in movies where crazy gangs fight or foreigners get kidnapped.

"Where can we get this tea then?" I said to Dimples. I felt uneasy in the hectic area.

"I'm not sure." She spoke with Thighs in Chinese and walked on.

As we reached the tea bar 'they didn't know about', it never crossed my mind that they were leading us into a trap. A pretty waitress sashayed past in a green and black Chinese dress, as if waltzing to the soft music in the background, and stared into our eyes as she waved us towards a small side room. She sat behind a long dark oak table and bent forward to reveal her cleavage.

"Please, ladies first," Sami said, motioning the girls to enter. "I think I'm in with this one," he whispered, referring to Dimples.

"Don't forget about the Swedish birds. Frumpy would count as a Super Model next to this one," I said, referring to Thighs.

We crouched down by the table, with about fifty different tea containers behind, and gazed as the waitress poured steaming tea into tiny white cups.

"Fancy another?" Sami said after our fifth. The waitress had seduced us and we'd tried five different teas in about ten minutes.

"Yeah, can't be that expensive," I said. The girls smiled, they'd only had one cup each. As I took a few photos, mainly of the waitress, but some of Sami doing silly poses, Thighs ducked or slanted out the way. The waitress clunked a metal tin of tea on the table.

"She says if you want to buy some tea?" Dimples said.

"I'll have a look," Sami said, grabbing it and taking a sniff.

"It's good, China tea is best in world," said Dimples, stroking Sami's shoulder. Then it clicked; she was the guide from earlier, the one in the pink T-shirt.

"Don't you think we should make a move," I said, motioning my head towards the door. "Trust me," I muttered.

"What, no tea?" Dimples said in a firm voice. Maybe she was on commission if we bought some tea, as well as for fooling us to the restaurant.

"I think we'll just get the bill," I said.

"Okay, but how much is this?" Sami asked. The waitress punched a digit in a calculator and Sami frowned. "Yeah, just the bill."

When the waitress gave Sami the bill, I thought he was going to puke.

"How much is it?"
"Two hundred." About twenty pounds.
"Eh?"
"Each."
"You're joking," I said. Dimples and Thighs looked away.
"There must be a mistake," Sami said. The waitress showed us the extortionate price list. We'd fallen for the trap and had invited the girls out for a drink; they must have known we would.
"Fuck it man, we were done there," I said as we sat in the back of a cab on the way to our hostel. We'd said goodbye without making a scene.
"Yeah, fucking expensive; the girls could have taken us to a cheaper place."
"What dya mean?"
"They might have known it was so expensive."
"But they set us up."
"Nah," he said, frowning.
"Of course they did. "Oh, we don't drink beer, how about some tea?" The girl offered to be your guide earlier. That was probably the most expensive tea shop in town."
Sami was too proud to admit it, until we spoke to a German lad back at the hostel.
"Have you heard of the Chinese Tea girls in Beijing?" he asked.
"No, what Tea girls?" I asked, tilting to Sami.
"Go on," Sami said.
"Apparently there are some Chinese girls who flirt with you around the Tiananmen Square. They get you horny and then take you to a tea shop."
"Really," I said.
"Yes. The funny thing is that the tea is so expensive, they sort of rob you, but you can't do anything about it. Can you imagine?"
"Yeah, I can imagine,' I said to Sami.
"Yeah, it's probably possible," he said. To top it off, Carla and Naomi had already gone out.

We were in better moods in the morning and I was excited about going on the Trans-Mongolian the following day; it was time to leave Asia.
"Why don't we get a bike then?" I said to Sami as we quarrelled about how we were going to see all the markets. We wanted to get presents for everyone back home.
We had fun pedalling along the roads and waving at the Chinese people. At first they looked at us as though we were mad, but after the

second or third wave they responded. We rode for most of the morning without buying anything until we stumbled on Wanfujing Street.

The price and quantity of the fake goods made Bangkok's markets look like a dull Argos catalogue. Haggling was unpleasant though. Sami almost got into a fight with a seller about some trainers and I had to butt in to stop him practising his judo chop. We bought some bargains: Tag Heuer watches, Nike shoes, Gucci bags, silk scarves, and some sexy Calvin Klien pants. I also bought a book written by the daughter of one of Mao's assistants for my journey to Moscow.

As we dropped the bikes off, rain began to spit.

"What's the plan then?" I asked.

"It's our *real* last night, man. Let's have a big one and stop off to get some beers."

Carla and Naomi were waiting at the hostel. Maybe we would pull in China after all.

"We thought you'd like you go out tonight," Carla said.

"Well, if you insist," Sami said, offering a swig. We finished the beers and caught a taxi to Hou Hai. The night started well. We stopped in a bar with views over a moon lit lake and had a few drinks. Sami and Carla seemed to be hitting it off.

"It is beautiful here, isn't it?" said Naomi. Maybe it was the Tsingtaos, or after Thighs, but Naomi seemed more attractive.

Just after a shot of Sambuca, Carla insisted on going back. Sami and I were annoyed, but it was probably a good thing because I had to get up at five to catch my train.

"So what do you think then?" I asked Sami as we sat outside the dorm eating our last beefy pot noodle together.

"I don't think she's up for it," he replied. "She kept talking about an ex-boyfriend in Sweden. I wasn't really listening, what about you?"

"I dunno, I think I may be in with a chance."

"You dirty bastard," he said, patting me on the back.

"One last photo?" I said. I set up the camera on automatic and we posed either side of the noodle packet. "It's been a pleasure mate. You made my China," I said, giving him a hug.

"You too man, good luck on the train, watch out for those Big Bad Babushka's."

It was an emotional farewell. Sami had been my best travelling companion and I was grateful that I could be myself and he'd helped me crack China. I was stronger and more confident, ready to brave the final journey. We went back in before the ladies were asleep.

"They say that all good things come to those who wait," I said, creaking open the door. The lights were out.

"Obviously we haven't waited long enough," said Sami. "Fucking G-strings man."

## 27 Trans-Mongolian: Don't Be Afraid of the Big Bad Babushkas

"Watch out for those dirty babushkas, and get me a photo," said Sami. Only three hours had passed since we'd gone to sleep and I could still taste the beef noodles.

"I'll try, if I get there; I'm late," I said. I rushed out the dorm. I can't miss this train to Moscow, I thought. My clock showed quarter past six, the Trans-Mongolian left at ten past seven.

I left the hostel without checking out, hailed down a cab, and arrived at the deserted station with twenty minutes to spare. I became frantic looking for the platform numbers.

"Where's platform thirteen?" I asked a cleaning lady. She smiled and nodded, clunked her bleached mop in the metal bucket, and accompanied me down an empty corridor. Her slow echoed steps aggravated me. Time was running thin.

"That isn't platform thirteen," I said, raising my voice. "That's a frigging waiting lounge."

I should have known better than to ask an innocent Chinese pensioner. I sprinted off. Ten minutes to spare.

"You all right mate?" said a man in an Aussie twang.

"Not really. Where are the platform numbers?"

"Which one do ya want?"

"Thirteen?"

"It's there you daft wally," he said, turning my shoulders and lifting my head towards the sign above. I thanked him, I think, and darted off.

The Trans-Mongolian train sprawled along platform thirteen. More than fifteen bulky carriages made up the longest train I'd ever seen. I felt hot and sweaty and became more flustered when I spotted three Chinese men blocking the carriage entrance with a cardboard box big enough to hold three Mongolian Huskies. The jittery men shouted and screamed as they forced on the box.

"Can I just get past," I said, tapping one on the shoulder. He turned and shouted at the two men inside. They almost ripped the box as they heaved and pushed, but they made it, and so did I.

As I paced down the aisle, built for tiny Chinese rather than wide Russians, salty sweat rolled down my cheek into my mouth and my lower back ached from the weight of my rucksack. I hoped not to be with the Husky smugglers. A Russian couple barged towards me so I stepped into a doorway.

"Hi," said a blond girl in a high pitched American voice. She was the palest girl I'd ever seen. She sat upright on the lower bunk and her long back stretched high. "Are you in here?"

"Maybe you can help?" I said, handing her my ticket. Her bulgy eyes squinted.

"That's lucky, you're in here with me," she said. Chinese men shouted as they carried past another box. "It's kinda crazy out there, ain't it?"

"Sure is. Good to meet someone normal." She grinned. I rested my guitar against the small table under the window and heaved my rucksack on the other lower bunk. Dust sprayed from the dark blue cotton sheets. The train pulled away. I began to relax. I'd never been so close to missing a train.

Lauren was heading to Moscow before flying back to the States. She'd been living in Shanghai for four years and spoke fluent Chinese. Chinese books covered her bunk.

"You like reading then?"

"Yeah, how did you guess?" she said. "It's a long journey to Moscow." She gazed out the window and her eyes welled up.

"Is anyone else in the dorm?"

"Yes," she whispered. She pointed to the bunk above.

"I am 'ere, you know," said a female French voice. Lauren raised her eyebrows and opened her book. "And you are?"

"I don't speak to invisible people," I said, hoping she was cute.

"Is that so?" She peered over the bunk; her spiky black hair came first, followed by her thick black goggle glasses covering her thin oval eyes. Her small button nose appeared pig like. She looked more Chinese than French and she was far from cute.

Maria was on her way to Ulan Bator, the capital of Mongolia, for a trainee economist job. While she was telling me this, Lauren squirmed and tutted, as if she'd heard Maria's life story a thousand times.

"Are you two travelling together?"

"No way," said Lauren.

"Not a chance," said Maria. The conversation ended. I preferred to stay out of their war. I lay down, my arms itching on the rough blanket surface, and wondered if anyone else was due, one bunk remained.

Part of me had a romantic urge to spend the six days in my own little world, catching up on reading and writing and taking in the surroundings. I'd never have guessed how many other travellers would be in our cabin by nightfall.

I was dozing off when the door slammed open and in came a Chinese ticket inspector. Lauren chatted with him as he gave her a strip of pink tickets. He waved goodbye and slid the door shut.

"That's your dining cart ticket." Lauren said.

"Of course," said Maria. Lauren grimaced.

"Great, free food," I said. "Anyone else hungry?" They shook their heads in silence. "Right, where's the dining cart?" They signalled right.

Asian passengers, particularly Chinese, filled the other cabins. They read books or magazines, played cards on their beds, or stood in the aisles gazing out the window. Flashes of the Great Wall whizzed past among the trees and the grey sky hovered.

I wondered what Sami was up to? Probably still sleeping or trying it on with the girls. I felt strange without Sami by my side, but my confidence had grown. I had to find babushkas to take photos of, preferably wearing G-Strings.

The smoky dining cart was packed apart from a free table at the back. I faced the Westerners and Chinese mingled together as they scoffed their free meal.

"Mind if I join you?" said an English lad as he ruffled his messy blond hair and rubbed his blue eyes. His front two teeth stuck out.

"Go for it. Just woke up?"

"Yeah, starving. Food doesn't look too bad." He peeked at the white rice mixed with pork and celery dish on the next table. "At least it's free." We ordered and waited. The land outside had turned flatter and drier.

"So, do you reckon we'll find any babushkas on this train?"

"Sorry?" I said, surprised that he'd already mentioned the 'B' word.

"Babushkas, you know, the sex mad Russian women."

"Hopefully, I promised a mate I'd take some photos for him. What is it about babushkas anyway?"

"Dunno, exciting, aren't they? I'd be scared stiff with one behind closed doors." The waitress plonked two rice dishes on the table. "Once we get to Russia, the train will be crawling with sex mad babushkas and crazy mafia dudes."

"Would that be a good or a bad thing?"

"At least you'd get your photos."

Steve travelled and worked as a chef. He'd been in China for a couple of weeks but his latest stint working had been in New Zealand. He'd worked in various ski resorts across Europe. After returning to Leicester, overland, he planned on leaving England straight away.

"Every time I go back I love it, but when reality kicks in, I'm off again." I thought about my parents and sisters. I was ready to return, but the fear of staying and living in England still lingered. "I can't settle there after all this travelling."

"I'm ready to go back."

"Don't be so sure, you'll see. Fancy a beer?"

"Bit early isn't it?"

"Nah, come on, I'll get these."

Having an English lad on the train was reassuring. Steve entertained me with his crazy ski resorts stories about New Zealand, most involving alcohol and girls. The waitress shut the dining cart after our third beer so we arranged to meet later.

Back in my cabin, Lauren and Maria were sleeping so I grabbed my CD player and listened to INXS while hanging off an aisle seat. Flat areas of sand ruled the earth. Hills formed occasionally. Electricity pylons dotted a path, indicating a possible route across the Gobi Desert.

Steve got me thinking about home; maybe he was right about settling down. I was ready to work, but how would teaching be in England? I wanted to see my family and country, but would my curiosity overpower me again?

"What you doing out here?" asked Lauren.

"Just watching the world dart by."

"Soon we'll be at Erenhot, near the Mongolian border for the changing of the tracks."

"Why, what's wrong with them?"

"Nothing, there is a problem between the Chinese and Mongolian rail companies so we have to wait while they lift up the train and change the tracks."

"Sounds intriguing."

"Sounds boring," said Maria, startling us.

"Do you mind?" said Lauren.

"No, I don't," said Maria, harshly. She waddled along the carriage towards the toilets.

"I don't like her," Lauren whispered.

"I'd guessed that, why?"

"We had a row about who was going to be on top. I was in the cabin first, but she sneaked in and jumped up."

"Why didn't you just sit on the other top bunk?"

"I'm not sitting opposite *her*; she'll be gone tomorrow anyway." Lauren sighed.

Back in the cabin Lauren wrote my name in Chinese on my guidebook.

"Was it hard to learn Chinese?"

"At first, but I found a boyfriend." She sighed and rotated her silver bracelet.

"Did he give you that?"

"Yeah, a while ago." She smiled weakly.

"Good memories?"

"Until we split up; that's why I'm going home." She started to well up. Maria slammed open the door.

"I think we are near," she said. She placed her foot on my bed and pushed herself up. I poked my tongue out and Lauren coughed a laugh as she wiped her eyes on her jumper sleeve.

"Come on; let's try to learn some Russian," she said, pulling out her Russian guidebook, but the cabin door crashed open and in fell Steve.

"There you are," he said, knocking into Lauren. "Oh sorry,' he added, patting her on the head. "I've been looking for you everywhere Bazza, fancy a beer?" He handed me a cold Tsingtao.

"This might be my last Chinese beer," I said.

"Or not; I just met two Kiwi lads with a crate." He took a huge gulp. The train began to decelerate. "Why are we slowing down?" Lauren explained that we were near the border so Steve ran back to collect his valuables. We arranged to meet on the platform at Erenhot.

"What are we going to do?" I asked Lauren as we stood on the dark platform. The majority of passengers had got off the train and were tottering about. There were no shops, kiosks, or even toilets, just a long dull platform covered by a high roof. A strange suffocating rubbery smell lingered in the air.

"Watch them change the tracks I suppose."

The lights came on, a whistle blew, and out popped a bunch of Chinese men dressed in blue overalls and brown straw helmets. With yellow cranes they separated the carriages and lifted them about six feet high. Then they changed the tracks underneath.

Steve stumbled over with the two Kiwi lads, stood either side of him like body guards. They were sipping out of green glass bottles.

"Fancy a beer?" said the chubbier lad. I took one. Lauren declined.

"What's up, you driving us to Ulan Bator?" said the lad in the red cap.

"Nah, she's already hammered, init?" said Steve.

"No, actually I don't drink."

"Soon change that," said Steve. Lauren sighed and gently tugged her bracelet. I felt sorry for her; stuck with four beery lads in the middle of nowhere after just splitting up with her boyfriend.

Ted, the chubbier one, and Joe, the one in the red cap, were on their way to Ulan Bator.

"We can't wait, we've got some horses booked," said Ted.

"Yeah, but tonight we wanna have a laugh and we're stuck with a dull Chinese family."

"What about Bazza's cabin?" said Steve. Everyone looked at Lauren. Her mouth was open but no words came out.

"That's settled then," said Joe, patting me on the back. I shrugged my shoulders at Lauren. She'd been dumped in an 18 to 30's train party.

"Don't forget Miss Bossy," she said.

"What, there's another chick?" Ted said, eagerly.

"If you can call her that," Lauren said. Everyone wooed.

Maria wandered over.

"So," said Joe, leaning on her. "Can we have a knee's up in your cabin?"

"What's a knee's up?" Maria scrunched her face as if imagining a ghastly sexual act.

"A few beers, maybe some whisky, music, and dancing," said Steve.

"That sounds great," said Lauren, perking up.

As the train pulled away, six were squeezed up in our cabin on the lower bunks. Ted was between Lauren and Maria - to stop them fighting - and Joe between me and Steve. Everyone had a beer, apart from Lauren.

"Why don't you have one?" said Ted.

"I'm not a drinker."

"Maybe she's scared," Maria muttered. Everyone heard. Lauren huffed, eyed the bottle of beer in Ted's hand, snatched it and took a huge gulp.

"That's my girl," said Ted.

We were in deep conversation about our travels when the door banged.

"Maybe it's the passport officers," said Maria.

"But we're still moving," said Lauren. It banged again. I opened the door.

"Hey guys, sorry to disturb," said a sweaty lad. He grinned through his thick beard and patted down his greasy hair. "I have a ticket for this cabin. I am Jonah, from Israel." Lauren checked his ticket and nodded.

"Jump in," I said, realising I was slightly pissed.

"The more the merrier," said Steve. "Have you got any drink?"

"My friend, Alex, has a bottle of rum."

"Where is he then?" said Ted.

"I am here," said a deep voice from outside. Alex ducked to enter the cabin and pulled out half a bottle of rum. Everyone cheered. Alex nipped off to find his cabin. When he returned the other seven had to squeeze up to let in the monster.

256

Alex and Jonah looked as though they'd been held as prisoners at Erenhot for the previous six months. Their hair came down to their shoulders, dirt nested under their finger nails, and a urine stench oozed from their tatty clothes.

"We've been travelling on trains since Kathmandu," said Jonah.

"Yes, we are not normally so dirty," said Alex.

"Don't worry," said Ted. "As long as you've got some grog you can stay here."

The night turned into a binge drinking session, even Lauren knocked back the rum. When the train screeched to a halt at the Mongolian border, station lights lit up the platform and shadows of official looking people wandered about.

"Does everyone have their documents," Maria said in a firm voice. "Because if not they will throw you off." The door banged. Everyone shut up.

"Shit," whispered Steve. "Are we all allowed to be in here?" The door banged louder.

"What if we get in the shit," said Ted. "Quick, hide the grog." Everyone started hiding any evidence of alcohol.

"What if they're Mongolian babushkas," said Steve. We fell silent. I imagined two hefty women dressed as wrestlers downing our booze and dragging the lads away by their ears.

The door rattled again. When all the booze was out of sight I slid open the door and everyone smiled. Fresh air filled the cabin and the female passport officer, who could have passed for a Mongolian babushka with her square jaw and towering size, grinned as she sniffed the alcoholic fumes. A male officer, possibly the babushka's sex slave, peered over her shoulder as she collected our passports.

"No close door," she said in a deep voice as she left.

"That's probably to air this stench out," said Maria. Everyone mumbled in agreement.

"What if she comes back and smashes us all to pieces with her truncheon?" said Steve.

"She'll get Barry first;" said Ted, "he's nearest the door.'

"I think she liked me," I said. "She stroked my hand as she took my passport."

Despite the intimidating size of the Mongolian babushka, she treated us well and even wished us a pleasant journey.

"We've survived our first encounter with a babushka," Steve said as the train set off, an hour later.

"Yeah, but she wasn't Russian; doesn't count," I said.

"True, anyone for shot of rum?" said Steve, holding up the almost empty bottle.

The party continued until the early hours until the next door neighbours smashed on the wall several times and shouted in Chinese.

"I think we'd better finish now," said Lauren. "A man just said he was going to come in here and chop off everyone's balls." The party ended.

The first thing I saw the following morning was a foot trying to burst out of a black holey, urine smelling, sock. The skinny toes stretched and the blistered heel cried out for a plaster.

"Not pleasant, is it?" Lauren whispered. "I think I have my first hang over."

"Congratulations," I said. My mouth tasted of rum and my head felt cloudy. "Where are we?"

"About two hours from Ulan Bator. Mongolia looks beautiful; I've been watching green fields pass for the last hour." I sat up, stretched, and gazed out the window at the blue sky. A few cows lying in a grassy field turned their heads as we shot past, I imagined them mooing. A farmer raised a stick as if saluting.

As I splashed cold water on my face from the sink in the carriage toilet, I wondered how dirty I'd get in the next four days; a full body wash was impossible in the confined space and my hair was already starting to itch.

The party atmosphere had died down. I slurped on packet noodles, Alex and Johan chatted in Hebrew on the upper bunk, Lauren read a Chinese book, and Maria hummed.

"Only another hour and she'll be gone," Lauren whispered. I felt glad Maria was getting off as well; I could do without the tension.

"Mate, what's going on?" said Steve as he slid back the door. "We need to get some grog at Ulum Batty."

"Good thinking, it's just you, me, and Lauren."

"And the babushkas."

"Have you seen any?" I asked, sitting up.

"Not yet, but I'm confident."

"What shall we get?" I asked Steve.

"I haven't got much change, so essentials: bread, beer, and vodka."

"I'll give you some money," Lauren said. "Maybe I can try some vodka." We were slowly cracking her morals.

As we approached Ulan, the fields became roads dotted with derelict buildings. The city was one of the flattest, and dullest, I'd seen and I was glad to be continuing. When we jolted to a stop, tons of passengers got off and shot across the wide concrete platform out the station, including Maria.

"Good riddance," Laura muttered as we stretched and inhaled gulps of fresh air. Ted and Joe wandered over and we took a photo with the Israeli guys.

"Watch out for those babushkas," Ted said. "They'll eat you for breakfast."

"Hopefully," Steve said.

We had just enough time to buy some chunky white bread, sixteen cans of Cass beer, and a bottle of vodka.

"It's a long way to Moscow and this'll keep us entertained," Steve said, tapping his plastic mug on the side of the frosty white bottle of Chinggis vodka. On the front was a picture of a smiling Mongolian chief with a pointed hat and a long white beard. He looked proud to be on one of Mongolian's finest beverages.

Without Maria and the two Israeli lads we had more room, less tension, and the cabin smelt fresher. We played Shithead and drank beer for a couple of hours before Steve and I went for a late lunch.

Had Sami been with us, he would have been ecstatic on arriving at the dining cart.

"Either those beers are really strong or this carriage has changed," Steve said as we entered. The seats and tables were light brown and pictures of the Mongolian countryside hung on the walls. A lot less passengers were on the train after Ulan. Strange church music played.

"I think they must have changed it, mate," I said. "Let's sit over there," I muttered, nodding towards two young ladies eating in the far corner. We sat on the table diagonally behind. I felt excited.

"I'm in with that blond one," Steve whispered.

"Yeah right, she smiled at me," I whispered back.

"She smiled at *me*."

"Nah, you can have the redhead."

"Fine; I'm not fussy."

After scouring the pricey menu we chose a liquid diet and set our goals on chatting up the ladies. I was getting closer to home and realised I hadn't actually pulled that many birds. I had to have more stories for my mates back home. Despite that, Steve did most of the talking.

"I was the one who invited them for a drink later though," I said as we made our way back to the carriage. We hadn't had much time to chat with the girls because, yet again, the dining cart closed.

"That was *all* you said though. That redhead, what's her name? Sophie. She's mine. You can have the blond one."

"That's fine with me. Elena was her name, wasn't it?"

"I think so. Lauren won't mind us inviting them back, will she?"

"Nah, she'll be all right."

Lauren seemed surprised when we told her the 'good news'. Perhaps she hoped for a couple of strapping Mongolian lads. After an hour debating whether they would turn up, Elena and Sophie strolled past.

"Where did you say you were from again?" I asked after we'd poured out some Chinggis.

"Norway," said Elena, fluttering her long eyelashes over her blue eyes. Her rounded cheeks made her look chubby, but her body was slim. "We are from a village just outside Oslo, maybe you can visit one day."

"Yeah," Steve said, "once we get to Moscow."

"That would be fun," said Sophie, flicking her long hair back to reveal even more freckles on her face. Lauren gazed out the window and sighed.

"Lauren, don't you fancy some vodka?" I asked.

"Yeah, go on love. It'll put hairs on your chest," said Steve. Lauren gazed at the bottle; perhaps she was a secret alcoholic who had survived four years in China. What were we doing?

"Ya, we are all drinking it," said Sophie.

"Okay, just a little," said Lauren. We all cheered, and Lauren grinned, as if knowing she was going to do something naughty.

Just as Elena and Sophie were getting the hang of Shithead (and I was getting on with Elena), the Chinese inspector ruined our fun by saying we were approaching the Russian border.

"You have to go back to your cabins; it's stricter in Russia," Lauren said, translating.

"Don't worry, we'll be back later," Steve said, winking at me as he left with the girls; just my luck.

Three stern Russian men in long jackets and flat miner's caps waved at Lauren and I as the train pulled away into Russia. Not seeing Asian people outside was strange. I was closer to home and felt a pang of nostalgia. I thought back to when I'd left England, got mugged in Quito and Rio, and left Bangkok. I'd made it to Russia and was close to my final destination.

"It's getting light already," I said to Lauren a couple of hours after we'd left the border. The vodka had disappeared from the frosty Chingiss bottle. "What time is it?"

"I'm not sure, I'm confused," she said, rubbing her eyes to check her watch. "At the Russian border it said nine but I thought it was midnight, so I changed my watch. That was only a couple of hours ago, I think. Now it's getting light. Oh, I haven't got a clue. All I know is that I've never drunk so much in forty-eight hours."

"You've done well." Lauren grinned as she placed her empty glass on the table.

"I'm going to sleep," she said as she pulled over her covers. The train chugged along and I drifted off too, drunk on vodka in Russia.

A few hours later I woke up, mouth dry, eyes clammy, and head pounding, but I forgot it all when I spotted an enormous blue ice rink stretching out into the horizon, Lake Baikal. In a corner, white houses were dotted along a small bay. If the ice rink had cracked open, the houses would have slid down and been lost forever. Mountains, faint enough to rub out, loomed in the distance.

I turned to wake up Lauren but she was snug under her covers. When I glanced back, Lake Baikal flashed through a wall of flimsy trees.

"What time is it?" Lauren said after I returned from my morning sink wash.

"No idea; have you seen the lake?"

"It's hard not to. Awesome, isn't it?"

"Awesome?" said a familiar voice. "I'd say it was glorious," Steve added as he popped his head round the door. "Fuck me, you finished all the Chingiis."

"It was her," I said.

"Was it?" Lauren said, rubbing the side of her forehead while holding up the empty bottle.

"Don't worry," said Steve. "There's bound to be vodka in the *Russian* dining cart."

"I'd almost forgotten we were in Russia," I said. "Maybe there're a couple of sexy babushkas waiting. Anyway, what happened with the girls?"

"We were up all night chatting in my cabin. Then I pulled Elena."

"No you didn't."

"Yeah, you're right; I didn't. After we left, they went back to their beds, they seem hard to crack."

"We'll see about that. Fancy a late lunch Lauren?" I said. Lauren gazed at Lake Baikal and muttered that she wanted time alone. Steve and I went hunting for babushkas.

"What time is it?" I asked. We paced towards the dining cart. A meaty smell lingered.

"Beer o'clock," he replied, mimicking drinking from a bottle. "So, if there *are* any babushkas, what are we going to do?"

"Have some food."

"Don't be boring, son. We're talking about man eating babushkas. Women who can eat five men for lunch and seven for breakfast, nah, I say we have a vodka drinking competition."

"Let's just wait and see."

I know we were in Russia, but I never thought babushkas would actually be on the train. I was shocked when I opened the dining cart's door. The search had ended. I went weak at the knees. Where was Sami?

Down on the floor were a chunky pair of blue trainers filled with thick feet in dirty white socks. The slightly hairy and stocky legs were naked all the way up to a pair of tight orange hot pants. Steam rose off a thick meaty stew lying in a metal dish, which was covering a pair of large firm Russian breasts (covered by a white T-shirt).

I'm not sure if the vapour was making the beads of sweat drip down her cheeks and hang off her square jaw, or because she'd been slaving away in the untidy kitchen, either way, the strong woman in her fifties, with tied back greasy auburn hair, was hot, in more ways than one.

She winked.

"*Spasibo*," I said. She frowned. "*Nasdrovi*a," I said quickly. She smiled as she checked out my wimpy physic and then moved to one side to let us through into the empty dining cart.

"Now *that* is a *babushka*," Steve said as we sat down at the back of the trip's third dining cart. The furniture had changed again. The seats and tables were darker brown and soft Russian music played. Fine rain splattered on the window. No other passengers were there.

"I'm afraid," I said, hiding behind the menu.

"Don't be such a girl. You've gotta be careful though; I think she likes you."

"I've never seen a woman like that in real life. Did you see those thighs and chest?"

"Hard not to; she's a real woman."

"Exactly, so why me?" I said.

"Good point. What did you say to her anyway?"

"I'm not sure. I think I said 'thank you', and then 'bottoms up'."

"I bet she'd like to see *your* bottom moving up and down."

Two minutes later Hotpants bowled up to our table and stood tensing her thighs while we ordered two beers and stew. Before she walked off she squeezed my shoulder.

"She just touched you," said Steve.

"Yeah, I am aware of that. Hold on, this might be her sister." Steve turned round as another babushka came out from a side door. She was older, shorter, and less manly, but she was still a butch woman.

"Or her lesbian lover," Steve whispered.

The woman stood by our table and clicked her biro.

"Yes, can I help?" she said in a deep voice, smiling to reveal a gold tooth. Five different necklaces hung towards her high cleavage and gold rings lined her chubby fingers. I stared at her sparkling tooth.

"It's okay, we just ordered with your..." said Steve.

"The other woman," I said, before he got us killed.

"She no speak English, she cook, what want?"

Goldtooth brought over some cutlery, two cold beers, and a basket of stale bread. We discussed the possibility of the babushkas taking us prisoners. Goldtooth eyed us with caution as she brought over the thick clumpy stew.

"Don't look now," I said, dipping in the bread to soften it up, "but here are her mafia buddies."

Two Russian men bowled through the doors and plonked by the table nearest the counter. Each of their backs was wider than mine and Steve's put together. Hotpants and Goldtooth came out beaming and kissed the men on the cheeks. One gave Hotpants a firm slap on the arse (she *was* wearing a G-string). She sniggered and whacked him on the thigh.

"Jesus," said Steve, "we're in a bloody mafia orgy."

We finished the stew and Lauren and the Norwegian girls turned up.

"Why does that woman in the orange shorts keep looking at you?" asked Elena.

"I dunno."

"She's got it *bad* for Bazza," said Steve.

"They seem a bit odd," said Lauren.

"They're gonna try to get in Bazza's cabin later," said Steve.

"Anyone for a game of Shithead?' I said, trying to change the conversation. Perhaps I was overreacting, but you can never be sure.

After a few hands, we headed back to the cabin. On the way out Hotpants blocked my path.

"Englishy?" she said, squeezing my arm.

"Yeah, *spasibo*," I said.

"*Spasiba*," she replied, thumping me on the back and winking.

"See ya then." She smiled and stuck up her thumb.

The following two days merged into one. Thanks to the sporadic light hours no one knew the real time so the clock always struck Beer o'clock. The Norwegian girls were a laugh. Elena was fun and we got on well, Sophie and Steve hit it off too. We played cards, drank beer and Russian vodka, and generally messed about.

Lauren proved she was a hardened drinker and kept up the majority of the time. She seemed happier than she had when we first met; she gazed less out the window and left her bracelet alone.

Every time I went in the dining cart, Hotpants stared, grinned, and squeezed my biceps or thighs. Goldtooth kept asking me if I wanted to have "sexy time" with Hotpants, but, I think, it was all in good jest. I actually enjoyed the banter and after hoping to see babushkas for so long I was thrilled to be able to meet them, even if I didn't have the bottle to take it any further.

As we shot further from Asia, the landscape became greener and rain drops constantly trickled along the window. Houses flashed past, but the only forms of life were at the stations. The men held tins of beer and looked tough enough to flatten me with one punch. The women were either attractive models waltzing up and down the platform to tease the thugs, or butch babushkas.

We grabbed what we could on the short stop-offs, but the beer was often warm.

"What if we ask Hotpants and Goldtooth if we can store it in their fridge," said Steve.

"Yeah, let's go for it, I'll do the talking."

Interrupting Goldtooth felt awkward. She was slumped on one of the quarterback's knees, stroking his balding head. Poking out the top of her white leggings was a red G-String. Steve coughed.

"Yes," Goldtooth said in her deep voice. The two Russian quarterbacks stared as I held out a black sack full of clinking beer bottles.

"Can we keep this in your fridge?" I said. "We'll give you some money." She peered in the bag and grinned at her male sex slaves.

"Of course, no money, but one for me and my men," she said, slapping one on the thigh.

"Sure, whatever you fancy," Steve said, patting me on the back. Goldtooth shouted out to Hotpants, who, once she found out that we'd donated four beers, bear hugged me and kissed my cheek.

"You like," Goldtooth said, pointing to Hotpants' heaving chest.

"I think we need to get back," I muttered. "We're in the middle of a game." We hurried off.

The plan worked. We had cold beers and Goldtooth kept us supplied as long as we gave her one every now and then, a beer that is.

We had a final party on the last night in the cabin with plenty of cold beer, vodka and singing. I got my guitar out, which Sophie played well. I still only knew one song, Wonderwall, which got dull after the tenth time.

On the final morning, I inhaled fresh air by the window to wake me up; the cabin stank of cheesy feet and unwashed travellers. Moscow was close: random houses had turned into streets, countryside was covered with buildings, and empty platforms were crawling with stern Russians. Blokes sipped tins of beer.

"I've got the holiday blues," said Lauren. Her hair was messy and eyes bloodshot as if she'd been on a manic drug infested holiday in Ibiza for a week.

"Yeah, can't believe six days have passed," said Sophie.

"We're nearly home," Elena said, looking glum. We were all lagging. Our body clocks were messed up. We'd partied hard.

I was sad the journey was almost over, but glad to be getting off the train; I craved a hot shower, decent meal, and a cure for a six-day binge drinking hang over.

Before Moscow, I had to fulfil one last promise.

"What do you mean you want a photo?" said Lauren. Sami would kill me knowing I'd met two babushkas, who wore G-strings, and I hadn't taken a photo.

"Yeah, of me and the babushkas; my mates won't believe me otherwise," I said.

"I'll do it," said Steve. "I have to see this."

As we made our way down to the dining cart one last time, I felt nervous. What if Hotpants took offense and tried to body slam me into her kitchen and have her babushka way with me? What if Goldtooth decided that we'd crossed the line and bit into my neck just as Steve was taking a photo.

Hotpants stood alone in the dining cart, gazing out the window. She winked.

"Photo?" I said, holding up the camera. She squealed with delight and summoned Goldtooth.

"*Spasibo, spasibo*," I said as I sat down, ready for Hotpants to pose beside me. Instead she plonked on my knee. Even though she supported herself in a squat position, her muscular legs crushed mine.

"Give him a kiss," Steve said. Goldtooth translated.

"You, me, sex?" Hotpants said as she put her arms round my neck. I whimpered a laugh.

"Take the photo mate," I said in a stern voice.

"There's a problem with the camera," Steve said, smirking.

"You, me, sex?"

"Come on, mate, take it."

Just as Hotpants kissed me on the cheek, Steve snapped the photo and Goldtooth clapped. When we showed them the photo, they seemed tearful. Perhaps they would miss the crazy English beer smugglers. We posed for several more photos and thanked them for being excellent hosts.

"You, me, sex?" Hotpants said as we went to leave.

"Maybe some other time," I said, hurrying out the door.

As we pulled into Moscow, I felt relieved the mammoth journey was about to end.

"We made it then," Lauren said, "I needed that." She'd taken off her bracelet. "It's done me good hanging out with you guys."

We arrived four minutes behind schedule. Not bad for a seven thousand kilometres journey. I felt weak lugging my rucksack again, what had happened to my muscles while lounging around on the Trans-Mongolian?

Outside the station was like whizzing back to the 80's. Groups of Russians seemed dressed for a Wham concert. The lads wore tight turned up jeans, checked shirts, and doctor martin boots, one even had a pink Mohican. The ladies were in short frilly dresses, leather gloves, and had permed hair. A lot of people were drinking beer. A rich meaty kebab smell drifted. My mouth watered.

"Mate, once we see Lauren off we have to get a kebab and a beer," I said to Steve.

"Right you are; better say goodbye to the ladies first though."

We arranged to meet later that evening with the Norwegian girls for farewell drinks and then helped Lauren find her train to the airport.

I felt intimidated walking around. Hard house music blared out from kiosks and amusement arcades, and butch men gawped as we tried to find the ticket office. I put my guard up.

"Let's go ask that bloke," said Steve, pointing to a man dressed in luminous orange jacket. He looked like a railway worker. The man nodded when Steve asked about trains to the airport.

"He's going to take us, don't worry."

"Great, he looks like a trusty man," said Lauren, but I was unsure. He looked and checked behind as he led us away from the bustle towards a set off glass doors. Something was wrong.

"Where's he taking us?" I said, remembering the lad in the blue cap who robbed me in Rio.

"Don't worry mate, he'll be all right," said Steve. A hand touched my shoulder. I turned. Hotpants winked.

"Hey," I said.

"No, no," she said, pulling my arm. At first I thought she wanted to take me away for a naughty sex session, but after she'd had a few harsh words with the 'railway worker', I realised that she was saving us.

"Maybe he was a mafia kidnapper disguised as a station worker," Steve said as we chomped on a greasy kebab. Hotpants had helped Lauren with her ticket to the airport and we'd all said goodbye, again. "Wonder what happened to Goldtooth?"

"We'll never know," I said, "but Hotpants saved the day."

"Yeah, maybe you shouldn't have been so afraid of the big bad babushkas after all."

## 28 Russia: The Last Stint

"This is supposed to be Moscow," said Steve as we paced around some dark back streets. Cars whizzed past, but there were no people on the pavements and most of the buildings had their lights off. "It's only one in the morning, where's the nightlife?"

We'd said goodbye to Sophie and Elena after a farewell meal and terrible karaoke session. Over dinner the conversation was dry and we realised we had nothing in common now that we were off the Trans-Mongolian. We tried to convince them to come and boogie at a dodgy night club called the Hungry Duck, but it opened late and they were more interested in an early night. Steve and I escorted them to the Chistye Prudy metro station, a couple of kilometres away from the main centre, and went exploring. We got annoyed though.

"I thought there'd be loads of bars and clubs round here," I said.

We were about to give up and go back to the lively area when I spotted a queue of people standing outside a club.

"Look, there must be something down there," I said. As we approached, the distant house music got louder.

"Brilliant, a club," I said. "But will we get in?" The Russian lads wore designer shirts and trousers and the ladies in tight fitting tops and skirts. We were wearing creased T-shirts and jeans.

"We've gotta get past Mike Tyson first," Steve said, nodding towards the bouncer, who could have been a professional heavyweight boxer.

"Come on, after Hotpants and Goldtooth we can take anyone on," I said, puffing out my chest. At the front the bouncer squared up and asked for our passports, which looked like tiny red notebooks in his gigantic hands.

"*Spasibo*," he muttered in a deep voice and stood to one side, slapping us both on the back as we entered.

Fast beating techno music blasted out as we paced down the luminous lit staircase. At the bottom we stopped and smiled. The smell of dried ice filled my nose.

"WELCOME TO RUSSIA," I shouted in Steve's ear.

"FUCK ME, LET'S GET A BEER," he shouted back. We'd stumbled on one of the liveliest clubs I'd ever seen, with some of the fittest women. In the centre of the dance floor on a podium a toned woman in a sexy luminous yellow bikini strut her stuff. The ratio of gorgeous women to tough looking lads was five to one.

"IF WE DON'T PULL IN HERE..." Steve shouted.

"YEAH, I KNOW MATE. THERE AREN'T ANY BABUSHKAS TO GET IN THE WAY EITHER."

We bought a beer and gawped at the podium dancer teasing the audience with her erotic moves. A long time had passed since I'd seen such a perfect body. Even the women dancing underneath gazed up.

"MAYBE THEY'RE LESBIANS," Steve shouted.

"I'M NOT COMPLAINING."

In another, lighter, room, three muscular skinheads pranced about on stage with their tops off. Below, a crowd of sweaty women cheered and shouted. We danced and tried to catch some of the women's eyes, but they were focused on the ripped nutters. We gave up and went into a different room just as the tallest skinhead started to undo his flies.

In the third room funkier and slower house music blasted out and the women seemed tamer. The ratio was still five to one, so you would have thought we'd have had a chance. The ladies I tried to chat up only spoke Russian, and after I'd said *spasibo* and *nasdrovia* they looked at me with pity and continued dancing. Despite getting blown out by every woman there, we had a great night dancing about and knocking down the beers. Being back in Europe, closer to civilisation, felt good.

"Those birds were well fit last night," Steve said as we met outside the Chistye Prudy metro station early the following afternoon. A lot more people were rushing about and clouds loomed above.

"Yeah, but they were out of our league."

"I think we'll have more luck at the Hungry Duck, perhaps we can go tonight."

"We'll see. I still need to sort out how I'm getting home."

"Have you thought anymore about coming with me overland?"

"Sort of, give me today to mill it over."

I had to decide when, and how, I'd make my final journey. Part of me wanted to continue overland to London, but I was running out of time and money. I'd make a decision by the end of the day.

I wish I could have done Moscow justice, but home lurked at the back of my mind. I explored in a daze. The area around the Alexander gardens was impressive. Along one red wall, with bright yellow buildings behind, guards stood stationary in glass boxes while tourists gawped. We strolled round the flowery gardens, stopping to take photos by a horse fountain spraying out water, and then queued up to get into the Kremlin. Rain began to patter.

"This is gonna take ages, let's come back later," Steve said, pulling his jumper over his head.

"We can't come to Moscow and not go inside the Kremlin."

"What is it anyway?"

"It's a mix of palaces and cathedrals."

"Does it have that colourful one inside, the one in all the photos?"

"Nah, that's the St Basil's Cathedral, we'll see that later."

Despite the lashing rain, it was worth the wait. At least *I* thought so. I loved the golden domed towers and being inside a Cathedral. I'm not religious, but I felt close to my father; soon I'd see him. By the time we'd walked round, the rain had stopped so we continued to St Basil's.

"Look, there's your cathedral, Basil," said Steve as we stood in front. The sun shone down on the red, blue, green, and yellow domes, which looked like giant, spirally ice creams. "Now I feel like I'm in Moscow."

"Yeah, this might be the last amazing sight on my trip," I said.

"There's still the river."

Instead of waiting in another long queue to get in, we went on a romantic walk along the Moskva River. As we strolled along the opposite bank, breathing in the fresh river air, we chatted about how life would be back in England. Steve was sure that he'd leave as soon as he could. I'd have to wait and see.

We waved at Russian women on boats chugging past and they whistled and cheered back. We continued up to the next bridge and took photos of the Christ the Saviour Cathedral. The huge white cathedral with giant golden domes on top impressed me more than those inside the Kremlin. The views along the river towards the Kremlin and St Basil's reminded me of Westminster Bridge.

I had to make a final decision.

"So what's it to be?" Steve said as we shared a pizza outside a café on a busy street near his hostel. We'd been in an internet cafe for a couple of hours checking out train and flight times.

"I hate to say it, but, it's home time."

"Ah mate, come on, let's go the long way."

"I can't. I'm down to my last few quid and it's gonna be hard enough in England with no money. There's a train to Tallinn, in Estonia, and then a cheap flight to Stanstead. I'll book it tomorrow. I'm done."

"Well, you know what that means then?"

"Yeah, you're on your own to England."

"Nah, it means that tomorrow night's our last, it's gotta be a big one. Hungry Duck here we come."

I couldn't sleep that night. I kept thinking about how I'd settle back at home with my family, whether I'd get on with my mates again, and what it would be like teaching in England.

"All done then?" said Steve as we met for a beer near his hostel.

"Yeah, I'm leaving on a train for Estonia tomorrow afternoon. I'll be home in two days. Feels weird, man."

"Don't worry, you'll get over it. Come on, it's your last night."

"Yeah," I said, sighing. "I guess it is."

The Hungry Duck had a reputation for wild nights and we were up for a crazy one. After a couple of beers we caught the metro up to near the Kremlin and strolled about the lit up area looking for a lively bar. The evening had turned chilly.

"Excuse me; do you know where some bars are?" Steve asked a short Russian chick as she clonked past in high heels and tight white leggings, swaying her firm bottom.

"Yes, yes, I am going to bar now, you want come?" We nodded and followed. Veronica was in her late twenties and had thick pouty lips. Instead of a heaving bar, she led us to a sushi restaurant, but we were pleased.

"Look what I found," she said to her friend, whose lips were also pouty, "This is Evana."

"Oh my," said Evana, bending down to reveal her bulging bosom.

"And they are English," said Veronica, as if presenting two celebrity footballers.

Veronica and Evana were posh city chicks with English accents. They worked in banking and must have been on good money because they kept buying us beers and sushi. They liked to tease though.

"So are you here for the women?" asked Veronica, licking the tip of her chopstick.

"Well, that and the sights," said Steve.

"But the best sights are here," said Evana, sticking out her bouncy chest. I had to agree.

"Well, for the food too," I said, holding the bridge of my nose after a hit of wasabi. "How come you both speak English so well?"

"Oh, you know, we study hard, but we play hard too," said Veronica, stroking my arm. I was convinced we were in.

"Do you two wanna come with us to get some more beers?" I asked.

"Well, that would be fun," said Evana. Steve looked at me and grinned. "But we have to work tomorrow."

"Yes and our boyfriends wouldn't be very happy now, would they Evana?" That hurt.

"Bloody Russian women," said Steve as we slumped towards the Hungry Duck.

"Yeah typical, I guess it was too good to be true," I said, coming back down to earth. "But the night is young and the Hungry Duck is waiting." We picked up the pace.

The club was just opening so we hissed open a can of beer outside. A few skins were hanging about with their dodgy looking tattooed girlfriends. The general feel was rougher than the previous night's club, but some of the women looked more approachable (I'm being polite).

After an hour, the dance floor was heaving with sweaty drunk women gyrating their hips to pumping house music. We downed a couple of shots and joined the dancing orgy. We weren't massively bothered about pulling, we just wanted to have a laugh, but Steve took things too far. He kept jumping about the bar tops waving at different groups of ladies.

"Mate, take it easy! That bouncer's just chucked a bloke out for being too drunk."

"Whatever, he's a knob head," he said, jumping on the bar again. Steve thrust his hips at two barwomen and the hefty bouncer came over. Steve jumped back to the other bar to escape, and then thrust his hips and stuck his middle finger up at the bouncer.

"Fuck him, knob," said Steve as the bouncer dragged him out.

I followed, pleading with the bouncer, but it was no use.

"Don't worry, you stay," said Steve, putting his shirt straight. "I'm going back to my hostel. I've had enough; Hungry Fuck more like."

"Okay mate. I'm gonna go back in, last night an' all."

"I'll see you in Blighty one day maybe. You take care, been a pleasure." We hugged and I went inside, alone again for the first time since Vietnam.

Without Steve the night came to an anticlimax. I tried to chat to a couple of ladies, but they just shrugged me off. After an hour dancing on my own I got bored and caught a taxi back. How had I travelled the world on my own?

I packed my bag the last time, checked out of the last hostel, and caught the metro to the train station. A few dodgy characters wandered about, but I was tough enough to deal with any muppets. I sat in the waiting lounge and a Russian elderly couple smiled and offered me a chocolate biscuit.

"*Spasibo*," I said, did I look that skinny?

As my last train chugged away from the platform, I wished I had more time to explore Moscow, but my journey had to end. I found it hard to believe that it was my last train journey on a mammoth world trip.

I shared a cabin with a fair haired Estonian man and his curious six-year old son. The young lad kept peering at me and pulling on his dad's sleeve so he would question me. Where are you going? Where have you been? Why are you alone?

The dad's English was good, and he translated my false answers. I was too tired to tell them exactly where I had been. I moved to the aisle, sipped on a can of cider, and gazed at the green landscape passing by.

The man's questions got me thinking about my journey. I felt nostalgic. I wondered about the people who'd helped me on the way. Would Maria, the mother of the family in Quito, be making her delicious meals for new guests? Would The Lord still be chasing students with his naughty English words? Would Javi, the guide at Machu Picchu, be waiting with a group for the sun to shine over the Sun Gate?

I imagined Murphy, in the crazy house in Salvador, asking new travellers if they often hit women, and Anderson teaching English to save up for a trip to London. I thought about Petal travelling up the East Coast of Australia to get over her fear of the big wide world, and Steve, the guide in Ayers, entertaining campers with his funny jokes.

I imagined my class in Thailand giving a new teacher grief and wondered whether the Sister would be down in the south still helping to tidy up from the Tsunami. I bet Sami was pacing round Seoul looking for Korean chicks with G-Strings, and Steve telling a traveller how he'd just met two sex mad babushkas.

Everyone had added a special pinch of uniqueness and character to make my trip memorable. Some had inspired me to travel and others to teach.

By the time morning came round I'd exhausted my memory bank and was ready for the final stint. As the ticket inspector stamped the man and his son's passports, I wondered if I'd ever travel across Europe with a son of mine.

Tallinn was my least visited capital. I paced through the spotlessly clean train station, bought some water from a kiosk, and caught a taxi to the airport.

"We have the best women in Europe," said the driver as we stopped at some traffic lights and two long legged blond women strolled in front.

"What, better than the Russian women?"

"Of course, here, this is a picture of my daughter." She was stunning, but she was also his daughter, what could I say?

"I see, very nice. You must be proud."

"I am, like any father. Where are you going?"

"Home," I said. "I'm going home, to England." I wondered what my parents would do when I walked through the door; I'd kept my return date a secret.

When the green fields of England flashed by, I had a lump in my throat. We flew over London. The Thames flowed through the capital, Big Ben stood proud, and St Paul's glistened.

I collected my bag, bought a prawn and mayonnaise sandwich and a bottle of lilt, and sat in the sun on the grass outside Stanstead.

"You can't beat a lilt," I told myself as I gulped back the sweet drink.

Listening to English people speaking again gave me a warm relaxed feeling. I didn't have to worry about language anymore. When I sat down on the train to London, an American girl with long black hair and a cute smile spoke to me.

"Is this train going to Liverpool Street?"

"Yeah, it is."

"Can I sit by you? It's my first time here."

"No problem," I said. She lugged her bag on the rack and plonked down beside. A female had never started chatting to me on a train in England before.

"I'm so nervous, London is so big," she said after a while.

"You'll be fine."

"But, this subway map, it's so confusing."

"Here, let me see if I still remember." I did.

"How long have you been away?" she asked.

"Nearly two years."

"Wow, what's it like to be back?" I could see myself of two years ago in her eyes, full of energy and curiosity.

"Good actually; better than I thought."

We chatted about London and I said that I'd show her towards her stop; it was my turn to help a lost traveller.

When we arrived at Liverpool Street I was buzzing with adrenaline. We got off and started walking.

"My ticket, where's my ticket?" she said. We went back but couldn't find it. "Are they strict here about tickets?"

"Just a bit; don't worry, I'll distract them."

The gate was open and passengers were showing their tickets to the inspector. The girl stood behind me as I held out my ticket and put on my best Spanish accent.

"Excusey, I err, where is de Big Ben? Yes de Big Ben, big cock, where I go?" The inspector sighed.

"Ask over there mate, information." He pushed me through. The girl had sneaked past.

"That was great, thanks," she said as we queued up to get a travel card. It was the least I could do. I went with her a couple of stops and showed her where to get off. I'd never have been so patient two years before.

Being on the Met line was weird. I felt like I was coming back from work. Had I been away? Glum faces gazed at the drab buildings. A group of chavs passed round a can of Strongbow. A pair of mother's compared pushchairs. I was home.

In my town I bought a few cans of Carling from a new off license and some flowers from the usual stall for my mum.

"Two pounds fifty please, luv. Cheers," was music to my ears.

I paced the final walk home, past the rose smelling groomed gardens. Sweat dripped down my brow and my arms were shaking with excited nerves. Down the road was my family. I'd travelled the world and taught English in a foreign land. The fear of returning had gone. The door opened. Sarah screamed. I was home.

The End